THE STORYMAKERS:
WRITING
CHILDREN'S BOOKS

83 Authors Talk About Their Work

Compiled by The Canadian Children's Book Centre

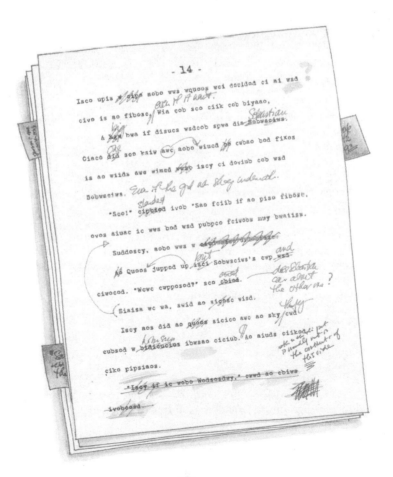

Pembroke Publishers Limited

© 2000 The Canadian Children's Book Centre

Pembroke Publishers
538 Hood Road
Markham, Ontario, Canada L3R 3K9
www.pembrokepublishers.com

Distributed in the U.S. by Stenhouse Publishers
477 Congress Street
Portland, Maine 04101
www.stenhouse.com

This project was made possible through the generous support of

The Canada Council for the Arts Writing and Publications Section.
Pembroke Publishers gratefully acknowledges the financial support
of the Government of Canada through the Book Publishing Industry
Development Program (BPIDP) for our publishing activities.

Compiler: Ian Krykorka
Editor: Gillian O'Reilly
Design and illustration: Loris Lesynski
Proofreader: Lori Burak

The Storymakers: Writing Children's Books is the second volume of the updated and revised
edition of the Centre's groundbreaking *Writing Stories, Making Pictures* (1994). A companion volume,
The Storymakers: Illustrating Children's Books (1999), looks at children's book illustrators.

Canadian Cataloguing in Publication Data
Main entry under title:
The storymakers: writing children's books; 83 authors talk about their work

Includes bibliographical references.
ISBN 1-55138-108-7

1. Authors, Canadian (English) — 20th century—- Biography. 2. Children's literature, Canadian
(English) — Bio-bibliography. I. Canadian Children's Book Centre.

PS 8081.S76 2000   C810.9'9282   C99-932849-2
PR9186.2.S76 2000

Printed and bound in Canada
9 8 7 6 5 4 3 2 1

Introduction

Once upon a time...

Welcome to *The Storymakers: Writing Children's Books* — the resource that brings you fascinating biographies of 83 Canadian authors of fiction and non-fiction whose works are considered among the best in the world. Told in the authors' own words, these biographies offer lively and illuminating insights into the worlds of these talented creators. The writers describe their creative processes, the influences on their works, their own childhoods and their advice to young creators today.

The Storymakers: Writing Children's Books has grown out of previous work by The Canadian Children's Book Centre that made available biographical and biblio-graphical information on talented authors and illustrators who create the wonderful books being published today. Such information allows readers of all ages to more fully understand and enjoy their books.

In compiling the list of authors to be included, the Centre consulted experts in the children's literature field — librarians, book-sellers and academics — and also looked at award-winning books. The resulting lists includes writers at the height of their careers as well as rising stars in the field of children's books.

Particular thanks for their assistance in developing the list go to: Ken Setterington, Trudy Carey, Dr. David Jenkinson, Karen Paul, Judy Sarick, André Gagnon, Nora Lester, Arlene Perly Rae, Muriel Morton, Virginia Davis and Phyllis Simon. Thanks are also due to researcher Ian Krykorka.

Thank you to The Canada Council for the Arts Writing and Publication Section, whose support made the publication of this book possible.

Of the 83 authors featured here, 11 are also illustrators who have created the art for all or almost all of their books. Here they talk about their writing. You'll find them and many more talented author/illustrators in the companion volume *The Storymakers: Illustrating Children's Books* where they look at the creative process from the artist's point of view.

The bibliographies accompanying each biography list the books in order of publi-cation from earliest to the present. The fleur de lis symbol (✳) indicates titles also available in French.

In these pages, you'll have the pleasure of meeting many talented, award-winning and wonderfully creative children's book authors. Discover their passions, their secrets, their sources of inspiration and their histories. Find out how they create works that fire the imagination and chal-lenge the minds of young readers today. Here are their stories... Read and enjoy!

CONTENTS

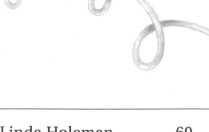

Linda Bailey
AUTHOR

Born
March 3, 1948, Winnipeg, Manitoba

School
Prince Edward Elementary School, River East High School, Winnipeg; Red River Community College, Winnipeg; University of British Columbia, Vancouver

Where I live now
Vancouver, British Columbia

My favourite books when I was young
Anne of Green Gables, Little Women, Tom Sawyer, The Little House on the Prairie, the *Freddy the Pig* series, the *Black Stallion* series. Any book with "mystery," "secret," or "clue" in its title.

My favourite book now
"Most recently, Alice Munro's *The Love of a Good Woman*. My favourite mystery writers these days are Janet Evanovich and Minette Walters."

Career
"I spent much of my twenties travelling, working as a secretary in Europe and Australia. Then I was a group travel coordinator in Vancouver before returning to university. Later, I taught adult education at a community college. Then I began to write and edit educational books for the Open Learning Agency and the British Columbia Ministry of Education and to write my own fiction for kids. Now I am a full-time writer."

Family
"I live with my husband, Bill, a geoscientist, and our two tall, basketball-playing daughters, Lia and Tess. We have a grey cat, Daphne."

The room where I create
"I work in a little office which was once part of our front porch. It has a computer, a desk, and lots of bookshelves. It looks out onto a friendly street with lots of pedestrians, including kids from the nearby school. I like to look out and feel that I am part of the world even when I'm working alone."

Spare time
"A lot of my 'spare time' is family time, driving my kids to their various activities and doing the chores that keep a family going. Besides that, I love to read. I'm a wild and happy gardener, but not a very good one. I would love to have more spare time — and more money — to travel."

When I was growing up
"My family once did a version of *Home Alone*, driving away from the house without me. (I was so immersed in a book, I didn't hear them leaving.)

"I lived on a street with very little traffic and three or four kids in every house. We played huge, endless games of good-guys-bad-guys, cowboys, cops-and-robbers, and Tarzan. We also made up plays and invited the whole neighbourhood to watch. I loved anything — book, game or play — that allowed me to have a 'pretend' adventure. I still do."

My first book (and how it happened)
"My first published book was *How Come the Best Clues Are Always in the Garbage?* I had written picture books and adult short stories, but this was the first novel I ever attempted. My daughters (then 8 and 11) were wonderful sources of ideas and feedback.

"I decided to write a mystery because I liked to *read* mysteries. I wrote about a girl named Stevie Diamond who liked to have adventures — just like me — but who was much braver and more daring than I could ever be. I spent about a year on that first book, and sent the manuscript to Kids Can Press. They liked it, and the book turned into a series. (I am now writing the sixth.)"

Where my ideas come from

"Ideas are around everyone all the time, but they're only seen by people who *look* for them. Some of the places I have found ideas include: a news item on the radio, a watch on the ankle of a friend's nine-year-old son, a glimpse of the back of President Clinton's head when he visited Vancouver, a squabble between my daughter and a neighbour boy, a walk along the beach behind a professional dogwalker, a skunk who lived underneath our back shed. I have my feelers out all the time for things that might make an interesting book."

Who and what influenced me

"Mystery and detective fiction have certainly influenced me. Some of the flavour of my favourite adult mystery writers tends to creep into my books. Humour has also influenced me. I love P.G. Wodehouse's *Jeeves* books, and I often read one before beginning a novel — just to tickle my funnybone.

"I also feel very influenced by two teachers. One was Mrs. Quesnel in Grade 5, who read *Tom Sawyer* and *Huckleberry Finn* aloud, in a glorious deep voice. The other was Mr. Visch in high school, who turned history into story-telling and half-hypnotized me with tales from the past."

How I work

"I begin a novel by daydreaming — for months, even years. I see bits and pieces in my mind — a character here, a moment of action there, a meeting, a place — and I write these down. As the time for writing the novel gets closer, I begin to daydream more deliberately, looking for connections between the ideas. Eventually, I organize my notes and ideas into a 20 to 30 page outline, which, in a general way, describes most of the events in the novel. Then I start to write. I rewrite constantly, but I work hard to keep moving and not get stalled in the rough spots. Most of the time, I stick to my outline, but I also change, add, and drop things. Once I have a complete first draft, I rewrite the whole thing a few more times. By the time I send the manuscript to the publisher, I have usually re-written most paragraphs at least 8 to 10 times."

Something nobody knew about me (until now)

"Once, in Australia, I had a close encounter with an emu — an extremely large ostrich-like bird. I was walking down a country road when the emu came from the opposite direction. It crossed the road intending (I believe) to give me a peck to see what I was. I escaped by swinging my purse and backing away for half a mile. This was the scariest *real* adventure I have ever had."

My favourite book that I've created

"My favourite one is *How Can A Frozen Detective Stay Hot on the Trail?* Part of the adventure of growing up in Winnipeg, as I did, was winter — wild blizzards and dramatic drops in temperature. Writing this book, I had a lot of fun remembering cold, snow, wind and ice and how they felt to my young self."

Tips for young creators

"Read! I don't know a single writer who wasn't a reader first. Then write the kind of story you like to read. The fact that I love reading mysteries makes them a lot easier (and a lot more fun) to write."

Linda Bailey

BIBLIOGRAPHY

Bailey, Linda. *How Come the Best Clues Are Always in the Garbage?* Toronto: Kids Can Press, 1992 Paper 1-55074-094-6. ♣

—. *How Can I Be A Detective If I Have to Baby-Sit?* Toronto: Kids Can Press, 1993 Paper 1-55074-172-1. ♣

—. *Who's Got Gertie? And How Can We Get Her Back!* Toronto: Kids Can Press, 1994 Paper 1-55074-217-5. ♣

—. *How Can A Frozen Detective Stay Hot on the Trail?* Toronto: Kids Can Press, 1996 Paper 1-55074-321-X. ♣

—. *What's A Daring Detective Like Me Doing in the Doghouse?* Toronto: Kids Can Press, 1997. Paper 1-55074-398-8.

—. *Petula, Who Wouldn't Take A Bath.* Toronto: HarperCollins, 1996 Paper 0-00-648088-8; Cloth 0-00-223903-5. Illustrations by Jackie Snider.

—. *Gordon Loggins and the Three Bears.* Toronto: Kids Can Press, 1997 1-55074-362-7. Illustrations by Tracy Walker.

—. *When Addie Was Scared.* Toronto: Kids Can Press, 1999 1-55074-431-3. Illustrations by Wendy Bailey.

—. *How Can a Brilliant Detective Shine in the Dark?* Toronto: Kids Can Press, 1999 Paper 1-55074-750-9

Awards

1993 Surrey Book of the Year for *How Come the Best Clues Are Always in the Garbage?*

1996 Arthur Ellis Crime Writers' Award for *How Can A Frozen Detective Stay Hot on the Trail?*

Selected articles about Linda Bailey

Rothstein, Ellen. "The Portrait: Linda Bailey." *The Bookmark* Dec. 1997: 146.

Michael Bedard
AUTHOR

Born
June 26, 1949, Toronto, Ontario

School
University of Toronto, B.A., Toronto, Ontario

Where I live now
"In the west end of the city in a housing co-op."

My favourite books when I was young
"Comic books. I had piles of comics."

My favourite book now
Madame Bovary by Gustave Flaubert.

Career
"Writer, though at various times I've worked in libraries and as a pressman in a printshop."

Family
Wife, Martha; four children, Isaac, Kirsten, Rebekah and Zoë.

The room where I create
Michael has a room in the basement of the house where he lives with his family.

When I was growing up
"When I was a kid I had no thought of being a writer. It was enough just being a kid. We lived in the city, constantly moving as the family grew. But even in the city there were wild places to explore, dirt lanes to wander down, lush ravines to haunt.

"I collected comics, loved to bring home loads of books from the library, and especially loved books with coloured plates in them. It was not until I was 17 that I knew I wanted to be a writer. I had just discovered poetry — the joy in the texture and taste of words. I began writing poetry myself and I haven't stopped since. I am still exploring, but the back lanes and ravines lie inward now."

My first book (and how it happened)
"My first book was called *Woodsedge*. It was a collection of original fairy tales for children. I had been writing poetry for ten years, but this was the first book I wrote specifically for children. I was employed at a small printshop at the time and I worked closely on the design, layout and printing of the book. It brought me a great deal of joy and satisfaction, and taught me just how much work goes into the making of a book."

Where my ideas come from
"The beginnings of a book for me are shrouded in a necessary mystery. If one looks too closely or examines too clinically, one runs the risk of losing the book before it has even begun. The wise course of action is simply to be as open as one is able and watch closely for what comes.

"I say 'watch' because for me a book begins with a series of images rather than ideas. I must first see it, and only later send words out after it. These images arise spontaneously in the mind, like the bubbles in a bottle of soda water. One image will spawn another and soon a fairly detailed sense of situations and setting will begin to emerge.

"All the while this is happening, I will busily write it down in a notebook, making entries that begin like, 'What if such and such were the case?' This talking to oneself may go on for months, during which time characters will begin insinuating themselves into one's consciousness, speaking in their several voices. By the end of it, a fairly good picture of what one is doing will have emerged. But it will be a picture, rather than an idea. And if the story feels right, it will have the distinctive quality of a dream."

Who and what influenced me
"Being the oldest of five children and having four children of my own has had a profound influence on me. I love the sense of awe and wonder I see in the small child and the softening influence the small child has on older siblings. To regain the

unified vision of the child is for me the aim of all art.

"The poet William Blake has also touched me profoundly. We have been close companions on this journey since I was 18 and began writing."

How I work

"I visit the room where I write every day. Normally I spend four or five hours a day there, sometimes more, sometimes less, depending upon what other demands are made upon my time. I normally begin around ten in the morning after my family is off to work and school and I have done the dishes. If I do not do the dishes the magic will not work. I go downstairs, close the door, and begin. If I do not close the door the magic will not work either. The act of writing for me is surrounded in ritual.

"The first time I write I use a pencil. I write in school notebooks and I pretend that I am not really writing so that the words will get by the guard at the gate. Later, I work at the typewriter. When I type I always play instrumental music on a small tape machine also in the room.

"When things are going well, I am conscious neither of the notebook nor the typewriter nor the music. All of that falls away and for a time I am inside the book, seeing, hearing, smelling, touching, and tasting that world and bringing back as much of it as I am able. When things are not going well, I hear the hum of the typewriter and become impatient with the music."

Something nobody knew about me (until now)

"If I hadn't been a writer, I would have liked to be a singer. I was briefly in a band just before I began writing. A good singer can still stop me in my tracks. I think

that in a way, writing is silent singing."

Tips for young creators

"Blake says: 'If the fool would persist in his folly he would become wise.' Persistence is the key. You must go on and on and on. There is really no end to learning how to shape words. Even if it seems to others like a strange and foolish waste of time, if writing is where your joy lies, pursue it with all your heart. You may not become rich, famous or powerful, but if you are true to yourself, you will become wise."

Michael Bedard

BIBLIOGRAPHY

Bedard, Michael. *Woodsedge*. Toronto: Gardenshore Press, 1979. Out of print.

—. *Pipe and Pearls*. Toronto: Gardenshore Press, 1980. Out of print.

—. *A Darker Magic*. New York: Atheneum, 1987. Toronto: Stoddart Kids, 1997 Paper 0-7737-5888-7.

—. *The Lightning Bolt*. Don Mills: Stoddart/Oxford University Press, 1989. Illustrations by Regolo Ricci. Out of print.

—. *The Tinder Box*. Don Mills: Stoddart/Oxford University Press, 1990 Cloth 0-19- 540767-9. Illustrations by Regolo Ricci.

—. *Redwork*. Toronto: Lester and Orpen Dennys, 1990 Paper 0-7737-5844-5.

—. *Emily*. Toronto: Lester Publishing, 1992 Cloth 1-895555-01-9. Illustrations by Barbara Cooney.

—. *The Nightingale*. Don Mills: Stoddart, 1991. 1994 Paper 0-7737-5699-X. Illustrations by Regolo Ricci.

—. *Painted Devil*. Toronto: Lester Publishing, 1994 Cloth 1-895555-48-5. 1996 Paper 0- 7737-5840-2.

—. *Glass Town*. Toronto: Stoddart Kids, 1997 Cloth 0-7737-2997-6. Illustrations by Laura Fernandez and Rick Jacobson.

—. *The Divide*. Toronto: Tundra Books, 1997 Cloth 0-88776-407-X. Illustrations by Emily Arnold McCully.

—. *The Clay Ladies*. Toronto: Tundra Books, 1999. Illustrations by Les Tait.

Awards

1990 Governor General's Literary Award for *Redwork*

1991 Canadian Library Association Book of the Year for Children Award for *Redwork*

1991 IODE Violet Downey Book Award for *Redwork*

1991 IODE Book Award - Municipal Chapter of Toronto for *The Nightingale*

Selected articles about Michael Bedard

Davis, Marie C. "An Interview with Michael Bedard." *Canadian Children's Literature* 82 (1996): 22-39

Findon, Joanne. "Night Vision." *Quill & Quire* April 1994: 35.

Findon, Joanne. "Darkness in the Novels of Michael Bedard." *Canadian Children's Literature* 82 (1996): 8-21.

Gertridge, Alison. *Meet Canadian Authors and Illustrators*. Richmond Hill: Scholastic Canada, 1994: 10-11.

William Bell
AUTHOR

Born
October 27, 1945, Toronto, Ontario

School
University of Toronto, B.A., M.A.; Ontario Institute for Studies in Education, M.Ed., Toronto, Ontario

Where I live now
Orillia, Ontario

Career
Writer and English teacher. Bell has taught at high schools in Orillia and Barrie, Ontario; at Harbin University of Science and Technology and the Foreign Affairs College (Beijing) in China; and at University of British Columbia.

Family
Three children, Dylan, Megan and Brendan; spouse, author Ting-xing Ye.

The room where I create
"My study: desk, computer, fax, and LOTS of books."

Spare time
Read, watch car races on TV, travel.

My first book (and how it happened)
"When I wrote my first story, I didn't even know it would be a novel. I did it for fun, writing mostly at night. After I finished writing it, I threw the manuscript into a drawer and left it there. When my daughter suggested I send it to a few publishers, I agreed. Within a year, *Crabbe* was accepted. Since then it has been published in Canada, the U.S., Holland and Denmark."

Where my ideas come from
"Sometimes the idea just pops into my head; sometimes it originates in a real event. Whatever the case, I think about the story for a long time (sometimes a year or more) before I begin to write.

"Most of my stories begin with a character rather than the plot, probably because I'm interested in relationships rather than events.

"So far, I have never gone looking for a story idea."

Writing about China and other places
Forbidden City — a story of the 1989 massacre in Tiananmen Square — is one of three novels Bell has written that are based on real events. The others are *Speak to the Earth*, which is informed by environmental protests on Vancouver Island, and *Zack*, in which the main character is inspired by the true story of an African who, in the late eighteenth century, was sold into slavery at 16 years of age and shipped to North America where he eventually gained his freedom.

Bell was able to write *Forbidden City* because of his interest in Chinese history and culture, as well as his experiences teaching English in China for two years, one of them in Beijing. He became familiar with the city by exploring it on his bicycle. His bank was on the edge of Tiananmen Square, he often visited the Beijing Hotel, and he especially loved to ride along the many hutongs that existed in Beijing at the time. This experience helped Bell imbue *Forbidden City* with an authentic flavour, including many Chinese expressions and street names.

As with *Forbidden City*, for the writing of *Speak to the Earth* and *Zack*, Bell drew upon first-hand experience of the locales: Vancouver Island for the former; southern Ontario and Mississippi for *Zack*.

How I work
"I do not work according to a set regimen. I go hard when revising and editing, and when the ideas are flowing. I take it easy when I'm stuck or between books. I submit to the story; when it's ready, it'll tell me when to start writing."

Something nobody knew about me (until now)

"Well, if I've kept it a secret for this long..."

Tips for young creators

"Write about what's important to you. Never give up. Try not to be afraid."

William Bell

SELECT BIBLIOGRAPHY

Bell, William. *Crabbe* (Gemini Series). Toronto: Stoddart, 1986 Paper 0-7736-7390-3.

—. *The Cripples' Club*, Toronto: Irwin Publishing, 1988. Rpt as *Absolutely Invincible* Toronto: Stoddart, 1991 Paper 0-7736-7411-X.

—. *Forbidden City* (Gemini Series). Toronto: Doubleday, 1990 Paper 0-385-25257-9. Toronto: Stoddart, 1991 Paper 0-7736-7391-1.

—. *Five Days of the Ghost*. Don Mills: Stoddart, 1992 Paper 0-7737-7368-7.

—. *No Signature*. Toronto: Doubleday Canada, 1992 Paper 0-385-25379-6. 1995 Paper (Seal Books) 0-7704-2706-5.

—. *Speak to the Earth*. Toronto: Doubleday Canada, 1994 Paper 0-305-25407-3. 1990 Paper (Seal Books) 0-7704-2724-3.

—. *River, My Friend*. Victoria: Orca Book Publishers, 1996 Cloth 1-55143-084-3. Illustrations by Ken Campbell.

—. *The Golden Disk*. Toronto: Doubleday Canada, 1995 Cloth 0-385-25487-3. 1997 Paper 0-385-25672-8. Illustrations by Don Kilby.

—. *Zack*. Toronto: Doubleday, 1998 Paper 0-385-25711-2.

Awards

1991 Ruth Schwartz Children's Book Award for *Forbidden City*

1992 Manitoba Young Readers' Choice Award for *Five Days of the Ghost*

1992 Ontario School Librarians Association Award for *Forbidden City*

1992 Belgium Youth Book Award for *Forbidden City*

Selected articles about William Bell

Bell, William. "It Isn't Just a Story." *Canadian Children's Literature* 84 (1996): 77-80.

Jenkinson, Dave. "Portraits: William Bell: YA Author." *Emergency Librarian* 18.2 (1990): 67-72.

For more information on William Bell, visit his Web site at: http://odcvi.scbe.on.ca

Jo Ellen Bogart
AUTHOR

Born
October 20, 1945, Houston, Texas, U.S.A.

School
Elementary schools in Houston and San Antonio; junior high in Dallas and Houston; high school in Houston, all in Texas.
University of Texas, Austin, B.A. in elementary education and psychology.

Where I live now
"I've lived in Guelph, Ontario for about 24 years. I became a dual citizen of Canada and the U.S. on May 9, 1994."

My favourite book when I was young
Star Beast by Robert Heinlein.

My favourite book now
The *Fionavar Tapestry* trilogy by Guy Gavriel Kay.

Career
"I trained as a teacher but never taught full-time. I worked as a supply teacher off and on until 1991. Now I write full-time."

Family
"Husband, Jim, is a professor of zoology at the University of Guelph; son, Adam; daughter, Jill; Australian shepherd, Sadie; Argentine desert tortoise, Tor Tor; and an African clawed frog, Astro."

The room where I create
"I took over the dining room years ago, and set up a very sturdy Mexican table with a typewriter, computer, boxes of computer disks, boxes of paper and envelopes, and eventually a telephone and answering machine. I added bookshelves, a very comfortable swivel oak chair in front of the computer and an adjustable, leather reading chair. I share the room with lots of plants. It is convenient to the kitchen so I can make tea and snitch cookies or watch meals as they cook."

Spare time
"My pets require quite a bit of care, as do my houseplants. In the summer I garden and go to a cottage. There I swim and putter with the house. My newest hobby is computer networking, where I read and take part in conversations with people all over North America about all sorts of interesting topics, including writing."

When I was growing up
"I lived in the country outside of Houston until I was eight years old and had few kids to play with. We had some neat animals like pigs and chickens and rabbits. I started school when I was almost seven and loved it. I really liked to draw when I was little, but didn't do much writing. I was always interested in words, though, and what they meant. I had two younger sisters and a brother, so life was somewhat hectic. I was often the babysitter and that wasn't so much fun. Around the age of nine, I especially remember taking long bike rides, chasing butterflies in a field by the house and swinging on a wonderful piece of play equipment at school."

My first book (and how it happened)
"The first book that was accepted was *Malcolm's Runaway Soap*. I wrote the book for a 'talk to the editor' session at a day of writers' workshops. When the idea came to me, I was taking a bath and was having trouble with the soap sticking to the bottom of the tub. In my mind, I turned the situation around and thought of the soap giving me trouble in the opposite way, by running away. I wrote the whole story in about an hour, in a little spiral notebook, while sitting in bed after my bath."

Where my ideas come from
"My ideas come from so many places it is silly. I might get an idea from something a child says or does. I might see the hint of an idea in another story, or

movie, or article in the paper. Usually something just pops out of the mess of ideas mixing together in my head when I am daydreaming.

"The spark for *Jeremiah Learns to Read* came from a real person, and came to me by way of Robert Munsch. He told me about meeting an older man who was learning to read. I thought that this was a wonderful story idea and asked Bob if he planned to use it. He said no, feel free to use it. I wrote *Jeremiah Learns to Read*, then later asked Bob again where he had been to meet the man. He said Inuvik, in the Northwest Territories. Soon after the book was published, I was invited to speak to kids in Inuvik and had the pleasure of meeting the man who inspired my book. His name is Elijah and he works at the school. We had a nice time together and he told me how he had worked hard to learn to read and is glad he did."

Who and what influenced me
"I have always enjoyed art and picture books. The combination of good story, fine words and wonderful art is such a pleasant experience that I cannot help but be transported and influenced. One book with these qualities is *The Magic Grove*, a retelling of a traditional Persian tale by the Czech couple Libuše and Josef Paleček. I also love the very simple, touching story in Maryann Kovalski's *Brenda and Edward* and the magical reunion in *Sylvester and the Magic Pebble* by William Steig. Wacky stories that make me laugh are great. Some of the things that have influenced me do not yet show in my own work."

How I work
"I often write a book on paper first, with a pencil or ballpoint pen. Eventually, the story goes on computer disk and I print a hard copy. I polish the story both on the screen and on the paper copy. I print out new versions until I feel the story is ready to show my editor. I usually make a few more minor revisions along the way as the illustrator works with the story. Barbara Reid and I worked out several changes in the book, *Gifts*, to make the text better fit her illustrations. Barb and I felt we were a good team and had a good time."

My favourite book that I've created
"I have a special feeling for *Daniel's Dog*. Perhaps it was because I was an only child until I was five, and then got three siblings in four years. I like the way *Daniel* helps himself with his own imagination and then helps his friend. *Gifts* has some special people in it too. I want to be that kind of grandmother someday."

Tips for young creators
"Pay attention to and value what is going on in your own head. Think and daydream. Wonder and ponder. Talk to people and do interesting things. Read for pleasure, and to see what is going on in other people's heads. Be curious."

Jo Ellen Bogart

BIBLIOGRAPHY

Bogart, Jo Ellen. *Dylan's Lullaby*. Toronto: Annick Press, 1988. Illustrations by Cheryl Lowrey. Out of print.

—. *Malcolm's Runaway Soap*. Richmond Hill: Scholastic Canada, 1988 Cloth 0-590-71784-7; 1990 Paper 0-590-71356-6. Illustrations by Linda Hendry. ✤

—. *Ten for Dinner*. Richmond Hill: Scholastic Canada, 1989 Cloth 0-590-73172-6. 1990 Paper 0-590-71949-1. Illustrations by Carlos Freire. ✤

—. *Daniel's Dog*. Richmond Hill: Scholastic Canada, 1990 Cloth 0-590-73344-3. 1992 Paper 0-590-73205-6. Illustrations by Janet Wilson. ✤

—. *Sarah Saw a Blue Macaw*. Richmond Hill: Scholastic Canada, 1991 Cloth 0-590-73809-7; Paper 0-590-73227-7; Big Book 0-590-74292-2. Illustrations by Sylvie Daigneault. ✤

—. *Mama's Bed*. Richmond Hill: Scholastic Canada, 1993 Cloth 0-590-74309-0. 1995 Paper 0-590-74312-0. Illustrations by Sylvie Daigneault. ✤

—. *Two Too Many*. Richmond Hill: Scholastic Canada, 1994 Cloth 0-590-74351-1. 1996 Paper 0-590-24906-1. Illustrations by Yvonne Cathcart.

—. *Gifts*. Richmond Hill: Scholastic Canada, 1994 Cloth 0-590-24177-X. 1996 Paper 0-590-24935-5. Illustrations by Barbara Reid.

—. *Jeremiah Learns to Read*. Richmond Hill: Scholastic Canada, 1997 Cloth 0-590-24927-4. Paper 0-590-51527-6. Illustrations by Laura Fernandez and Rick Jacobson.

Awards
1998 Ruth Schwartz Children's Book Award for *Jeremiah Learns to Read*

1998 Tiny Torgi Award for *Jeremiah Learns to Read*

Selected articles about Jo Ellen Bogart
Gertridge, Allison. *Meet Canadian Authors and Illustrators*. Richmond Hill: Scholastic Canada, 1994: 16-17.

"Jo Ellen Bogart." *Something About the Author: Autobiography Series*. Detroit: Gale Research, vol. 92.

Major Authors and Illustrators for Children and Young Adults. Detroit: Gale Research, 1997.

Dave Bouchard
AUTHOR

Born
September 13, 1952, Quill Lake, Saskatchewan

School
College Mathieu, Gravelbourg, Saskatchewan

Where I live now
West Vancouver, British Columbia

My favourite books when I was young
"I was a reluctant reader and read very little as a child. *Spiderman* comics were a hit with me."

My favourite book now
Charlotte's Web

Career
Principal, teacher, poet...

Family
"My wife, Vicki; a four-month-old daughter, Victoria; a 21-year-old son, Adrien; an 18-year-old son, Etienne; a 16-year-old stepson, Todd; and a 14-year-old stepdaughter, Ashleigh.

The room where I create
"A darkish study with wall-to-wall, floor-to-ceiling book-shelves; heavy, spectacular drapes and dim light."

Spare time
"Writing, reading, travelling with my wife and daughter..."

When I was growing up
"Playing with anyone — growing up on the prairie often means growing up alone! I developed my imagination through play — often playing alone!"

My first book (and how it happened)
"I wanted to get art into the hands of children. I talked with Ken Lonechild, a wonderful Cree artist, about his illustrating a book for children, in much the same style that he painted. Thus, the creation of *White Tail Don't Live in the City!*"

Where my ideas come from
"My ideas often come from beautiful art. I see myself as one who illustrates for illustrators/artists. Through my words, I come to build on what an artist is trying to do.

"Occasionally I am motivated by something else — e.g. my wife or our baby Victoria. More often than not, however, I am motivated by beautiful art. When I was introduced to the art of Gordon Miller, I created *The Journal of Etienne Mercier*.

"When Yang asked me to write a book with him, I sought an idea that suited what I loved in his painting — it had to be something with a Chinese theme — and thus *The Great Race* and then *The Dragon New Year!*"

Who and what influenced me
"The single greatest influence in my writing has been my love of art! I've also loved writing because of the flow of the English language. The poetry of Henry W. Longfellow has had an effect on my love of rhythm."

How I work
"The greatest challenge for me is to find my original idea. I sometimes have to think for years about how I can best illustrate the work of an artist. When finally I get it, the rest comes easily."

Something nobody knew about me (until now)
"The thing that is most unusual about me is that I was a non-reader until adulthood. Most writers for children were prolific readers as children. I, however, was anything but! At this point in my life, I love children's books and have yet to develop much of an interest for adult literature."

My favourite book that I've created
"I very much enjoyed creating *The Journal of Etienne Mercier* because of the language I was allowed to use. As a Francophone living in Western Canada, I often hear the accent and the cultural references that I've been allowed to incorporate in this book.

"The CD was a bonus. To read and sing a book, exactly as you would hope it to sound, is a thrill for any author!"

Tips for young creators

"Find your special area — your special talent or interest. Go there and stay there. My special talent is seeking out ideas and then using language to illustrate fine art. These books are usually referred to as crossover books. I sometimes stray away from that — and realize that this remains my primary area."

Dave Bouchard

BIBLIOGRAPHY

Bouchard, Dave. *White Tail Don't Live in the City*. Winnipeg. Blue Frog Books, 1989. Out of print.

—. *My Little Pigs*. Winnipeg. Blue Frog Books, 1991. Out of print.

—. *Koko*. Winnipeg. Blue Frog Books, 1992. Out of print.

—. *The Meaning of Respect*. Winnipeg: Pemmican Books, 1994 Paper 0-921827-37-7. Illustrations by Les Culleton.

—. *The Colours of British Columbia*. Vancouver: Raincoast Books, 1994 Paper 1-895714-52-4. Illustrations by Michael Tickner.

—. *If You're not from the Prairie*. Vancouver: Raincoast Books, 1994. 2nd Ed. Cloth 1- 895714-66-4. Illustrations by Henry Ripplinger.

—. *Voices from the Wild: an Animal Sensagoria*. Vancouver: Raincoast Books, 1996 Cloth 1-55192-040-9. Illustrations by Ron Parker.

—. *The Elders are Watching*. Vancouver: Raincoast Books, 1997 Cloth 1-55192-110-3. Illustrations by Roy Henry Vickers.

—. *The Great Race*. Vancouver: Raincoast Books, 1997 Cloth 1-55192-090-5. Illustrations by Zhong-Yan Huang.

—. *If Sarah Will Take Me*. Victoria: Orca Book Publishers, 1997 Cloth 1-55143-081-9. Illustrations by Robb Dunfield.

—. *The Dragon New Year*. Vancouver: Raincoast Books, 1998 Cloth 1-55192-200-2. Illustrations by Zhong-Yan Huang.

—. *The Journal of Etienne Mercier*. Victoria: Orca Book Publishers, 1998 Cloth (CD included) 1-55143-128-9. Illustrations by Gordon Miller.

—. *A Barnyard Bestiary*. Victoria: Orca Book Publishers, 1999 Cloth 1-55143-131-9. Illustrations by Kimball Allen.

—. *The Mermaid's Muse*. Vancouver: Raincoast Books, 1999 Cloth 1-55192-248-7. Illustrations by Zhong-Yan Huang.

Awards

1997 Lee Bennett Hopkins Poetry Award (U.S.) for *Voices from the Wild: an Animal Sensagoria*

For more information about Dave Bouchard, visit his Web site at www.davidbouchard.cjb.net

Paulette Bourgeois
AUTHOR

Born
July 20, 1951, Winnipeg, Manitoba

School
Winnipeg, Manitoba; Calgary, Alberta; Ottawa, Ontario, and Beaconsfield, Quebec.

Where I live now
Toronto, Ontario

My favourite book when I was young
The *Nancy Drew* books.

My favourite book now
"Far too many wonderful books to choose one!"

Career
Writer

Family
Children, Natalie and Gordon; dog, Dixie Lee Ragtime.

The room where I create
"A yellow office overlooking the garden."

Spare time
Quilt, ski, bike-ride.

When I was growing up
"I was born on a day so hot my mother said that you could fry eggs on the sidewalk. Back in 1951, July 20 wasn't famous for anything. Now, a lot of people know it as the day the first man stepped on the moon.

"I remember cold, cold blizzardy winter days in Winnipeg. It was so cold that we had to wear our snowsuits underneath our Halloween costumes and winter boots on Easter Sunday. I always got new white shoes for Easter and I hardly ever got to wear them.

"When I was a kid I loved Brownies (especially the badges), writing and doing my own plays, going camping with my family and just goofing around. I was never a good athlete. I took swimming lessons (but I hated diving right under the water); I played baseball (nobody wanted me in the field because I used to duck when the balls came my way); and I skated (but I used to cry when my feet froze). I even tried skiing and snorkelling. If the truth be known, I always liked curling up with a book best. I read after bedtime by sneaking a flashlight under the covers and hoping nobody would notice until the last chapter was finished."

My first book (and how it happened)
"When my daughter was born, I was often awake with her at night. One night we watched a M*A*S*H episode where Hawkeye, the main character, became claustrophobic and said, 'If I were a turtle I'd be afraid of my shell.' That was the genesis of *Franklin in the Dark*.

"Since then I have suggested books (and a couple have been rejected) and Kids Can Press has asked me to write books for them. I write fiction as well as nonfiction for a change of pace."

Where my ideas come from
"I remember the feelings I had as a child and I draw on them for story ideas. Often, something a child says or does sparks an idea. A lot of my ideas come from suggestions from my publishers."

Who and what influenced me
"I am always influenced by other authors, both writers of adult fiction and writers for children. Two teachers influenced me. One introduced me to wonderful short stories and the other said, 'I think you write well.'"

How I work
"I work two or three days a week from 8:30 until 1:00 at my desk at home. I try not to let myself leave my office until I've written something! Often I use that time to read or even think about stories.

"I used to write with a typewriter but now I have a computer. I hated my computer at first. Now, I don't think I could write without it. It makes editing so much easier and faster.

"I'm often asked how long it takes me to write a book. That's the most difficult question to answer. I write most of my books inside my head. By the time I'm ready to sit down at the computer, the book is almost finished. Many authors make copious notes while they work, but I never have. It's different with non-fiction books. I do a lot of research — in libraries, on the phone — and compile notes that I then restructure into chapters."

Something nobody knew about me (until now)

"I never expected to be a writer. What I really wanted to do was sing and act on Broadway! Too bad I can't sing...or dance!"

My favourite book that I've created

"Each new book holds the promise of being a new favourite. Grandma's Secret and The Many Hats of Mr. Minches are tied for favourite now."

Tips for young creators

"If you are stuck as you write, ask yourself the five 'W' questions. Who is my story about, what is my story about, why do my characters act the way they do, where does my story happen and when does it happen?"

Paulette Bourgeois

BIBLIOGRAPHY

Bourgeois, Paulette. The Franklin Series. Toronto: Kids Can Press. Illustrations by Brenda Clark.

Franklin in the Dark. 1986 Paper 0-921103-31-X; Cloth 0-919964-93-1. ✱

Hurry Up, Franklin. 1989 Paper 1-55074-016-4; Cloth 0-921103-68-9. ✱

Franklin Fibs. 1991 Paper 1-55074-077-6; Cloth 1-55074-038-5. ✱

Franklin is Lost. 1992 Paper 1-55074-105-5; Cloth 1-55074-053-9. ✱

Franklin is Bossy. 1993 Paper 1-55074-257-4; Cloth 1-55074-119-5. ✱

Franklin and Me: My First Record. 1994 Paper 1-55074-335-X. ✱

Franklin is Messy. 1995 Paper 0-155074-245-0; Cloth 1-55074-243-4.

Franklin's Blanket. 1995 Paper 1-55074-278-7; Cloth 1-55074-154-3.

Franklin and the Tooth Fairy. 1995 Paper 1-55074-270-1; Cloth 1-55074-280-9.

Franklin Plays the Game. 1995 Paper 1-55074-254-X.

Franklin Goes to School. 1995 Paper 1-55074-276-0 Cloth 1-55074-268-X.

Franklin's Bad Day. 1996 Paper 1-55074-293-0; Cloth 1-55074-291-4.

Franklin's School Play. 1996 Paper 1-55074-289-2; Cloth 1-55074-287-6.

Franklin Has a Sleepover. 1996 Paper 1-55074-302-3; Cloth 1-55074-300-7.

Franklin's Halloween. 1996 Paper 1-55074-285-X; Cloth 1-55074-283-3.

Franklin Goes to Day Camp. 1997 Paper 1-55074-396-1.

Fun with Franklin: Trace and Colour Book. 1997 Paper 1-55074-396-1.

Fun with Franklin: Puzzle Book. 1997 Paper 1-55074-394-59.

Franklin's New Friend. 1997 Paper 1-55074-363-5; Cloth 1-55074-361-9.

Fun with Franklin: A Learning to Read Book. 1997 Paper 1-55074-391-0.

Franklin Rides a Bike. 1997 Paper 1-55074-354-6; Cloth 1-55074-352-X.

Fun with Franklin: Activity Book. 1997 Paper 1-55074-392-9.

Finders Keepers for Franklin. 1997 Paper 1-55074-370-8; Cloth 1-55074-368-6.

Franklin and the Thunderstorm. 1998 Paper 1-55074-405-4; Cloth 1-55074-403-8.

Franklin's Christmas Gift. 1998 Cloth 1-55074-466-6.

Franklin's Valentines. 1998 Cloth 1-55074-480-1.

Franklin's Secret Club. 1998 Paper 1-55074-476-3 Cloth 1-55074-474-7.

Fun with Franklin: Math Activity Book. 1998 Paper 1-55074-452-6

Franklin's Class Trip. 1999 Paper 1-55074-472-0 Cloth 1-55074-470-4.

Franklin's Neighbourhood. 1999 Paper 1-55074-704-5 Cloth 1-55074-702-9.

—. The Amazing Apple Book. Toronto: Kids Can Press, 1987 Paper 0-921103-42-5. Illustrations by Linda Hendry. ✱

—. Big Sarah's Little Boots. Toronto: Kids Can Press, 1987 Paper 0-921103-70-0. Illustrations by Brenda Clark. ✱

—. On Your Mark, Get Set...All About the Olympics, Then and Now. Toronto: Kids Can Press, 1987. Out of print.

—. The Amazing Paper Book. Toronto: Kids Can Press, 1989 Paper 0-9211-3-82-4. Illustrations by Linda Hendry. ✱

—. Grandma's Secret. Toronto: Kids Can Press, 1989. 1991 Paper 1-55074-034-2. Illustrations by Maryann Kovalski. ✱

—. The Amazing Dirt Book. Toronto: Kids Can Press, 1990 Paper 0-921103-89-1. Illustrations by Craig Terlson. ✱

—. Too Many Chickens. Toronto: Kids Can Press, 1990 Paper 1-55074-067-9. Illustrations by Bill Slavin. ✱

—. The Amazing Potato Book. Toronto: Kids Can Press, 1991 Paper 1-55074-025-3. Illustrations by Linda Hendry. ✱

—. In My Neighbourhood Series. Toronto: Kids Can Press. Illustrations by Kim LaFave. ✱

Canadian Fire Fighters. 1991 Paper 1-55074-137-3; Cloth 1-55074-042-3.

Canadian Garbage Collectors. 1991 Paper 1-55074-138-1; Cloth 1-55074-040-7.

Canadian Police Officers. 1992 Paper 1-55074-060-1

Canadian Postal Workers. 1992 Paper 1-55074-135-7

—. The Many Hats of Mr. Minches. Toronto: Stoddart, 1994 Cloth 0-7737-28392. 1996 Paper 0-7737-5703-1. Illustrations by Kathryn Naylor.

Bourgeois, Paulette, and Martin Wolfish. Changes in You and Me: A Book About Puberty Mostly for Boys. Toronto: Somerville House, 1994. Illustrations by Louise Phillips and Kam Yu. Out of print.

—. Changes in You and Me: A Book About Puberty Mostly for Girls. Toronto: Somerville House, 1994. Illustrations by Louise Phillips and Kam Yu. Out of print.

Selected articles about Paulette Bourgeois

Mayers, Adam. "Slow Turtle on a Fast Track." The Toronto Star 4 May 1997: C1-2.

Wagner, Dale. "Introducing Paulette Bourgeois." CANSCAIP News. 14.4 (1992): 1-3.

Karleen Bradford
AUTHOR

Born
December 16, 1936, Toronto, Ontario

School
Runnymede Public School, Toronto, Ontario; Northlands, Buenos Aires, Argentina; University of Toronto, Toronto, Ontario

Where I live now
Owen Sound, Ontario

My favourite books when I was young
"*The Secret Garden* and the *Doctor Dolittle* books."

My favourite books now
"*Jacob Have I Loved; Bridge to Terabithia;* the *Earthsea* books; *A Wrinkle in Time; The Giver; Shadow in Hawthorne Bay; Warrior Scarlet;* and *Tom's Midnight Garden.*"

Career
Social worker; writer.

Family
Husband, James; children: Donald, Kathleen and Christopher. One granddaughter. One young German Shepherd, Casey, and one feisty old tabby cat named Kat.

The room where I create
"I have a home office with two big windows overlooking Georgian Bay. The walls are lined with pictures of cats and various statues of cats loll around and stare at me. My dog usually lies under my desk at, and often on, my feet.

"The bay provides a continuously changing panorama: sometimes flat and deep blue-green; sometimes flat and grey but shimmering with ripples of light, sometimes like an ocean with white-tipped waves crashing on the shore. There are ducks, geese, seagulls and the occasional heron, kingfishers, muskrats and a beaver. The view is so magnificent that sometimes I have to close the blinds in order to get any work done. I lie — often I have to close the blinds."

Spare time
"Read!"

When I was growing up
"I always liked to scribble. Plays, stories, poems. I didn't think that I'd grow up to be a writer — it didn't occur to me that 'real' people wrote books — but writing was my favourite activity next to, and along with, reading. I was an only child, and often sick with asthma, so I spent a lot of time alone, inventing my own worlds to keep me company."

My first book (and how it happened)
"I'd been writing stories for school readers and magazines, and finally thought that I could tackle a full-length book. They say that writers' first books are often autobiographical, and although the hero is a 13-year-old-boy, my first book, *Wrong Again, Robbie*, is certainly more about me than any of my others. It's about a boy who is an environmentalist and conservationist, and goes to live with a grandfather who hunts and fishes all year round. The same thing happened to me — a big-city girl who couldn't imagine why anyone would want to shoot a duck, who married into the huntingest and fishingest family you can imagine. Robbie and I both had a lot to learn."

Where my ideas come from
"I'm a snoop, an eavesdropper and a spy. I watch people all the time, listen in on conversations in restaurants, on buses, trains and airplanes. I get ideas from things that happen to me, like falling through the ice and nearly drowning or living in places where interesting things have happened. I'm always thinking, 'What if ...?' What if a boy lived on lighthouse island all his life and had to go to the mainland for high school? (*Windward Island*). Ideas are all around. You just have to learn how to see them."

Who and what influenced me
"When I was young, I would get totally lost in a good book. I was never aware of such things as my

mother calling me to dinner or telling me for the millionth time to put my light out. Books were so important to me that I couldn't imagine anything more exciting than to be able to write one. Every time I read an author who made me laugh, or cry, or feel that I had been part of something splendid or magical, I felt as if I had been given a present. I still feel that way.

"Every wonderful author has influenced me. I read a truly great book and despair that I will never write that well. Then I try, and I find that the book has become part of me and has taught me something. I've grown, and my writing has stretched because of it."

How I work

"I sit down in my room after breakfast and after I have walked the dog, and I'm usually there most of the day. I concentrate on whatever new book I'm working on in the morning because that's when I'm at my brightest. I take a short break for lunch, then either revise things or do the boring 'office' work in the afternoon. Some days I'm visiting schools or libraries, doing readings and workshops with kids, and those are fun."

Something nobody knew about me (until now)

"I really, really want to pat a tiger."

My favourite book that I've created

"It's like asking your mother which is her favourite kid! It takes from one to five years to write a book. During that time I live with the children and young people in it, and get to know them as well as I know my own. When I send the manuscript off to the publisher, I'm as sad as if I were sending my own kids away. Each book is special in its own way — just like each child."

Tips for young creators

"When people tell you to 'write about what you know,' ignore them. Instead, know what you want to write about. If you want to write about something you've never done, something you've never seen or somewhere you've never been — find out as much as you can about it. Some people call it research and make it sound boring — I call it exploring and find it exciting. You'll end up having as much fun writing your stories as your readers will have reading them. (Just make sure you've got all your facts right!)

"The next tip, of course, is: read. If a book is so good you can't stop reading until you finish it, but you don't really want to finish it because you want it to go on forever — read it again and find out how the author did that. If it's so boring you throw it down in disgust after only a chapter or two — pick it up again and find out why it was so bad — and don't make the same mistakes."

Karleen Bradford

BIBLIOGRAPHY

Bradford, Karleen. *A Year For Growing*. Richmond Hill: Scholastic-TAB Publications, 1977. Rpt. as *Wrong Again, Robbie*. Scholastic-TAB Publications, 1983 Paper 0-590- 71312-4.

—. *The Other Elizabeth*. Agincourt: Gage, 1982 Paper 0-7715-7004-X.

—. *I Wish There Were Unicorns*. Agincourt: Gage, 1983 Paper 0-7715-7005-8.

—. *The Stone In The Meadow*. Agincourt: Gage, 1984 Paper 0-7715-7014-7.

—. *The Haunting At Cliff House*. Richmond Hill: Scholastic Canada, 1985 Paper 0-590-71517-8.

—. *The Nine Days Queen*. Richmond Hill: Scholastic Canada, 1986 Paper 0-590-71617-4.

—. *Write Now!* Richmond Hill: Scholastic Canada, 1988 Paper 0-590-73175-0. ✳

—. *Windward Island*. Toronto: Kids Can Press, 1989 Paper 0-921103-75-1.

—. *There Will Be Wolves*. Toronto: HarperCollins, 1992 Paper 0-00647-391-1; Cloth 0-00223-892-6.

—. *Thirteenth Child*. Toronto: HarperCollins, 1994 Paper 0-00-647943-X; Cloth 0-00-224367-9.

—. *Animal Heroes*. Richmond Hill: Scholastic Canada, 1995 Paper 0-590-24307-1.

—. *Shadows on a Sword*. Toronto: HarperCollins, 1996 Paper 0-00-648054-3.

—. *Dragonfire*. Toronto: HarperCollins, 1997 Paper 0-00-64180-9.

—. *A Different Kind of Champion*. Richmond Hill: Scholastic Canada, 1998 Paper 0-590-50799-0.

—. *Lionheart's Scribe*. Toronto: HarperCollins, 1999 Paper 0-00-648116-7.

Awards

1979 CommCept Award for *The Other Elizabeth*

1990 Max and Greta Ebel Memorial Award for Children's Writing for *Windward Island*

1993 Canadian Library Association Young Adult Book Award for *There Will Be Wolves*

Selected articles about Karleen Bradford

Bradford, Karleen. "The Roads of Research." *Canadian Children's Literature* 83 (1996): 75-7.

CM 21.4 (1993).

Jenkinson, Dave. "Profiles: Karleen Bradford." *Resource Links* 1.4 (1996): 152-5.

Who's Who in Canadian Literature. Toronto: Reference Press, 1992.

For more information about Karleen Bradford, visit her Web site at www.makersgallery.com/bradford/

Marianne Brandis
AUTHOR

Born
October 5, 1938 in The Netherlands

School
The Netherlands, and Terrace, British Columbia. University in British Columbia, Nova Scotia, and Ontario

Where I live now
Stratford, Ontario

My favourite book when I was young
"Usually the one I was reading."

My favourite book now
"Usually the one I am reading."

Career
Writing for radio, teaching English at Ryerson Polytechnic University, writing books.

Family
"I live alone, but my brother and his two dogs are just two short blocks away."

The room where I create
"An attic with a low ceiling, dormer windows to north and south, a skylight. Desk, computer, lots of paper and pencils."

Spare time
"Walk, read, listen to music—but there isn't much spare time."

When I was growing up
"I came from Holland to Canada when I was eight-going-on-nine. Learning English as fast and as well as possible was important in my family (my parents knew English before they came), and there were always lots of books in the house. I read everything I could, no matter whether the books were meant for kids or not, and by the time I was about 15 I started to try writing something myself.

"I think it was an advantage learning English as a second language, because it made me think about language and how to use it and how it worked, and about the different ways there were of saying the same thing."

My first book (and how it happened)
"Of the first four books that I actually finished and sent to publishers, only one was good enough to be published. (Getting published isn't easy.) It was for adults and sold in both England and Canada.

"My first book for kids was *The Tinderbox*. By then I had begun writing historical fiction but had not yet had any of it published; I had also done one or two small projects with my brother Gerard Brender à Brandis, who is an artist specializing in wood engravings and hand-made books. He suggested that we do something historical together, and the result was *The Tinderbox*, which is set in Upper Canada (Ontario) in the 1830s."

Where my ideas come from
"Many of them come from the research and reading that I'm always doing, and each book I write gives me ideas for future books. I get ideas from the world around me, mainly from looking at what is there now and 'adjusting' until I can visualize how it would have looked in whatever historical period I'm recreating."

Who and what influenced me
"I've been influenced by everything I've ever read, by all the people I've met, by everything I've done and everything that has happened to me. The author Henry James said that you don't need to have an eventful life to be a good writer, you only need to be a person 'upon whom nothing is lost.'"

How I work
"I'm not a fast writer. I need quiet time and space and peace of mind.

"The planning of the story and the first, very general research start at about the same time. Once the first draft of the story is written, I can do more precise research. I write in the morning, starting at about 7:00, and do the research reading in the evening; the research seems to recharge the battery for the next morning's writing. In the afternoons I do correspondence and other paperwork which is part of being a full-time writer, as well as housework, shopping, going to the libraries for more research material, and so on.

"The book I'm working on right now is the first one I've been able to write directly onto the computer. This is important because it saves a lot of time. But I imagine that I will still do a lot of the revision on paper, with pencil and eraser."

Tips for young creators

"I think it's essential to like words, to enjoy watching how writers use them and to enjoy seeing what they can do for you — which means revising and revising, trying out this and that until you come as close as possible to getting it right. Nobody gets it right the first time, and sometimes you have the feeling that you could keep on revising forever and not be satisfied. But that's part of being a writer.

"It's essential to remember that writing is not only what you say but also how you say it. So: read, write, analyze what you read. The people who have written books and had them published are our best models."

My favourite book that I've created

"I like each of my books. Each of them, when I reread it now, brings memories of moments when, during research, I discovered some useful or delightful fact; each of them brings the memories of the work, the craftsmanship, the

painstaking weaving of the story — and of the miracle that happens when, out of nothing but black marks on white paper, and the reader's memories and dreams that those black marks awaken, a world comes to life. While writing each of them, I learned something more about myself."

Marianne Brandis

BIBLIOGRAPHY

Brandis, Marianne. *The Tinderbox*. Erin: The Porcupine's Quill, 1982 Paper 0-88984-064-4. Illustrations by Gerard Brender à Brandis.

—. *The Quarter-Pie Window*. Erin: The Porcupine's Quill, 1985 Paper 0-88984-085-7. Illustrations by Gerard Brender à Brandis.

—. *The Sign of the Scales*. Erin: The Porcupine's Quill, 1990 Paper 0-88984-103-9. Illustrations by Gerard Brender à Brandis.

—. *Fire Ship*. Erin: The Porcupine's Quill, 1992 Paper 0-88984-140-3.

—. *Rebellion: A Novel of Upper Canada*. Erin: The Porcupine's Quill, 1996 Paper 0- 88984-175-6. Illustrations by Gerard Brender à Brandis.

Awards

1986 Canadian Library Association Young Adult Canadian Book Award for *The Quarter-Pie Window*

1986 IODE Violet Downey Book Award for *The Quarter-Pie Window*

1991 Geoffrey Bilson Award for Historical Fiction for Young People for *The Sign of the Scales*

1996 Geoffrey Bilson Award for Historical Fiction for Young People for *Rebellion: A Novel of Upper Canada*

Selected reading about the author

Marianne Brandis' books are dealt with by Judith Saltman in *Modern Canadian Children's Books* (1987), published by Oxford University Press, and by Sheila Egoff and Judith Saltman in *The New Republic of Childhood* (1990), published by Oxford University Press.

Martha Brooks
AUTHOR

Born
"My sister and I were raised in a prairie valley in southwestern Manitoba on the grounds of a tuberculosis sanatorium. Our father was a thoracic surgeon, our mother a nurse. The setting, which also includes Pelican Lake, appears in fictional form in almost all of my work."

School
"I attended schools in the district, and later attended a private school in Brandon. I never attended university. Mentorship, however, was crucial to my journey as a human being and as a writer. One of the many gifted mentors who guided my art and craft was a professor who now writes for film. He has shepherded along many Winnipeg writers, poets and playwrights."

Where I live now
Winnipeg, Manitoba

My favourite book when I was young
"*The Wind in the Willows*, by Kenneth Grahame. Its lyrical and at times spiritual quality mirrored my own experiences with the numinous in the natural world. As a child I had a congenital chest condition and frequent bouts with pneumonia. The illness itself heightened my visions of light through suffering. And having my father read this book to me while I was in that strange state was an early conduit to my later life as an artist."

Career
"I work full-time as a writer and until this past year would always have one or two students whom I mentored. However for the past three years I have been using up more and more spare time and creative energy with a burgeoning career as a jazz singer. I have regular gigs around town and am lucky to be playing with some of the best jazz musicians in the city. Many years ago I trained as a coloratura soprano, but my voice is richer and deeper and smokier than it used to be and jazz was always my first love, anyway. Music and writing, I find, have a nice yin and yang balance and I'm more creative when I'm doing both. My friend, Diana Wieler — whose books I admire greatly — is doing a similar balancing act with her fine explorations into visual art. We have lots of conversations about navigating two art forms."

Family
"I've been married to the same man for over 30 years. His name is Brian and he is one of my greatest supporters and fans. We have a grown daughter named Kirsten."

The room where I create
"Brian knocked out a wall and put in a window so the skylight in the stairwell would peek into my little loft. He then painted a sky on my ceiling, did the walls an orangey yellow, put in ceiling-high sunny book shelves and designed a desk that has the effect of glass floating over trees. I hung up feathers and wild sage and can still swing open my window to touch the cedar tree that towers above the roof of our townhouse."

Spare time
"In the summer we spend as many weekends as possible at the lake where I grew up. We like to listen to jazz, and cook, and go to movies, and visit friends, and hang out with our young Airedale terrier, Drummer. She is quite nuts, well deserves her nickname "the holy terrier," and pretty much goes everywhere we go."

When I was growing up
"I was given a lot of freedom to wander into the hills and the woods above and below our house. I had time to dream and think and consider all aspects of loneliness and to watch the

drama of life and death unfold around me. People, back then, really struggled with tuberculosis and the drugs to cure it were experimental and unrefined. I made lifelong friends with a woman whose choice had been to take the drugs and possibly survive, or not take them and surely die — she had a fast-moving form of the disease. She was an artist and my first book, *A Hill for Looking*, centered around that early friendship. My friend died, slowly, of another disease just a few years ago. I still miss her. From childhood on I learned some tough lessons from her about endurance and courage and sorrow and imperfection."

Where my ideas come from

"Like all writers, many of my ideas come from what I have experienced and observed. But most writers will tell you that they are also compelled to write about characters whose lives are totally unlike their own. In 1963, Eudora Welty — a southern writer who had lived quietly in the same house all of her life — wrote a story called 'Where is the Voice Coming From?' She wrote it in one sitting on the same night Medgar Evers (a civil rights activist) was murdered in Jackson, Mississippi. She wrote it, as a work of fiction, from the point of view of the assassin. The voice is unflinchingly brutal and hateful. The actual killer was very quickly arrested, and, just as quickly, Welty's story was poised for publication in *The New Yorker*. However, Miss Welty had to go back and do some re-invention. Many of her original details had become prejudicial to the accused: they were too close to what had actually taken place. In her safe little house in Jackson, Mississippi, this writer's fiction

had accurately guessed at the truth. And this is something else most writers will tell you — writing courageously means taking risks; it means a willingness to step into the void."

How I work

"Five days a week, from 9:00 a.m. to 3:00 p.m. However, I always have whatever project I am currently working on squarely at the centre of my life. It's like a table that I have to step around in order to get on with other things. So I'll be making dinner, or walking Drummer, or travelling around in the car, or washing a floor, and I'll hear a conversation, or I'll be thinking of nothing at all and a detail I need for my book will suddenly appear. I toss it down on that imaginary table and then it's waiting for me when I get back to work."

Something nobody knew about me (until now)

"When I put eyedrops in my eyes I think of them as tears. I press a towel to my face and think about the people I most love and give them my tears. Then I pray for their safe navigation in the world."

Tips for young creators

"The French writer, Colette, said 'Look for a long time at what pleases you, and longer still at what pains you.' Every student I have mentored has this tucked away in their notes. Like all good advice, the thought is large and plainly packaged. It stays with you."

Martha Brooks

BIBLIOGRAPHY

Brooks, Martha. *A Hill for Looking*. Winnipeg: Queenston House, 1982 Paper 0-919866-78-6. Illustrations by Beverly Dancho.

—. *Paradise Café and Other Stories*. Saskatoon: Thistledown Press, 1988 Paper 0-920633-57-9.

—. *Two Moons in August*. Toronto: Groundwood Books, 1991 Cloth 0-88899-123-1. 1992 Paper 0-88899-170-3.

—. *Traveling on into the Light*. Toronto: Groundwood Books, 1994 Cloth 0-88899-220-3.

—. *Andrew's Tree*. Winnipeg: Shillingford, 1996 Paper 1-896239-12-9.

—. *Bone Dance*. Toronto: Groundwood Books, 1997 Paper 0-88899-336-6.

—. *Being with Henry*. Toronto: Groundwood Books, 1999 Paper 0-88899-377-3.

Awards

1989 Vicky Metcalf Short Story Award for "A Boy and his Dog," in *Paradise Café and Other Stories*

1989 Boston Globe Horn Book Award for "A Boy and his Dog," in *Paradise Café and Other Stories*

1996 IBBY Honour List for *Traveling on into the Light*

1998 Canadian Library Association Young Adult Canadian Book Award for *Bone Dance*

1998 Ruth Schwartz Children's Book Award for *Bone Dance*

2000 McNally Robinson Book for Young People Award for *Being with Henry*

Selected articles about Martha Brooks

Jenkinson, Dave. "Portraits: Martha Brooks." *Emergency Librarian* 22.1 (1994): 61-64.

Margaret Buffie
AUTHOR

Born
March 29, 1945, Winnipeg, Manitoba

School
Sparling Elementary; Sargeant Park Junior High; Daniel McIntyre High School; University of Manitoba, B.A., Fine Arts; all in Winnipeg, Manitoba

My favourite book when I was young
Heidi by Johanna Spyri

My favourite book now
"I don't want to leave anyone out but a few of my favourite writers are John Mortimer, Georges Simenon, Penelope Lively and Jani Howker."

Career
Writer, artist

Family
Husband, Jim Macfarlane; daughter, Christine; Scottish terrier, Logan.

The room where I create
"I now have a second floor study in the big old house we recently bought in a historic part of Winnipeg. I painted this room a cheerful cranberry red and have filled it with all of my favourite books. No ghosts yet, but I'm hoping…"

Spare time
"Read, paint, canoe, birdwatch, garden at my cabin and go for walks with my dog, Logan."

When I was growing up
"I was never comfortable in school because I was very shy. I loved to read and the one thing that I looked forward to all winter was going to our cabin in northwest Ontario with my family during the summer months. The summer I was 12 my father died. That same year, my mother sent me for painting lessons with a woman who lived across the lake from us. I have painted ever since.

"My Grade 4 teacher once told me I would probably be a writer someday. I never forgot that."

My first book (and how it happened)
"My first novel, *Who is Frances Rain?*, was written after I discovered an old pair of spectacles while digging around in a decaying garbage dump on an island near the cabin. I was looking for old bottles and was really excited to discover a pair of wire-rimmed spectacles in an old mug. When I put them on, I wondered what would happen if I could suddenly see into the past. This followed with the question, 'Can I write a book about a girl who finds a pair of spectacles in a crumbling prospector's cabin and is taken into the past by the glasses?' I thought this was a great idea for a book. I plunged right in and worked hard on it. I sent the finished novel to Kids Can Press about a year and a half after I found the spectacles and they wanted to publish it right away. Since then, it has been published in many other countries. A dream come true!"

Those fortunate enough to catch Margaret on an author tour can try out the spectacles for themselves — she always brings them along.

Where my ideas come from
"They usually begin with a place: the island at the lake, an old Victorian house, a settler's ranch in Alberta. Ideas seem to come to me when I least expect them. I see a great place and I think — yes, I'd like to write a story set here. And like magic, the characters walk into the setting, bringing along all of their problems for me to sort out."

Who and what influenced me
"I would have to say that other writers influenced me and made me want to become a writer. I read all the time as a child and I still am a voracious reader. But one person who really influenced me was my mother. As a

strong, independent, young widow, she taught her daughters that girls are just as capable of making their dreams come true as boys are. Right up until she died, she was the centre of our family and I admired her tremendously."

How I work

"I 'work' all the time, it seems. When I'm not sitting at my computer, I'm thinking about my characters and what is happening in their lives and how I can work things out for them. I usually try to get three or four hours of writing done a day and then a couple of hours of rereading and editing the day's output."

Something nobody knew about me (until now)

"Lots of kids ask me if I believe in ghosts. I usually talk around this topic because I don't want to upset anyone who might be frightened by the idea of 'real' ghosts, but secretly I think they do exist."

Tips for young creators

"Read your favourite kind of book because that is the sort of book you will probably end up writing. Study all the different writers. All the while, keep writing. Learn to spell, learn to use grammar properly, don't be sloppy. Keep a dictionary, a thesaurus, and a grammar book close by. But when you are actually writing, don't be afraid to let your imagination soar. Yes, you should write about 'what you know' in life, but there are all of those other, special worlds deep inside that are unique to you. Then when you are through writing your story, write it again. And again. Revise, edit, work hard and enjoy it all. Writing is discipline. Writing is commitment. Writing is also great fun."

Margaret Buffie

BIBLIOGRAPHY

Buffie, Margaret. *Who is Frances Rain?* Toronto: Kids Can Press, 1987 Paper 0-919964-83-4. ✢

—. *The Guardian Circle.* Toronto: Kids Can Press, 1989. Rpt. as *The Warnings.* 1994 Paper 1-55074-251-5.

—. *My Mother's Ghost.* Toronto: Kids Can Press, 1992 Paper 1-55074-091-1.

—. *The Dark Garden.* Toronto: Kids Can Press, 1995; Cloth 1-55074-288-4. 1996 Paper 1-55074-344-9.

—. *Angels Turn Their Backs.* Toronto: Kids Can Press, 1998 Paper 1-55074-417-8; Cloth 1-55074-415-1. ✢

Awards

1988 Canadian Library Association Young Adult Book Award for *Who is Frances Rain?*

1991 International Youth Library Notable New English Language YA Book List for *The Guardian Circle*

1995 McNally Robinson Book for Young People Award for *The Dark Garden*

1996 Vicky Metcalf Award for a Body of Work

Selected articles about Margaret Buffie

Gertridge, Allison. "Margaret Buffie." *Meet Canadian Authors and Illustrators.* Richmond Hill: Scholastic Canada, 1994: 22-3.

Stinson, Kathy. "Margaret Buffie." *Behind the Story.* Ed. Barbara Greenwood. Markham: Pembroke Publishers, 1995: 21-3.

Joan Clark
AUTHOR

Born
Born in Liverpool, Nova Scotia. Grew up there as well as in Sydney Mines in Cape Breton, Nova Scotia and Sussex, New Brunswick.

School
Acadia University, B.A., Wolfville, Nova Scotia; University of Alberta, Edmonton, Alberta

Where I live now
St. John's, Newfoundland

Career
Writer.

Family
Husband, Jack Clark; three children.

When I was growing up
"I was born in Nova Scotia and grew up there and in New Brunswick. I lived in Alberta for over 20 years and Ontario twice, briefly. I now spend a lot of time in a cabin in British Columbia.

"Since moving to Newfoundland, I've decided to become a humpback whale if I'm reincarnated. That way I can swim the oceans of the world singing, my mouth open to schools of fish."

Being a writer
"I've been writing fiction for 25 years; half of these full-time. I write both adult and children's literature. Although the two genres are regarded as separate, I'm reluctant to place too much emphasis on the differences. It's all too easy to get caught in the trap of making unwarranted assumptions. People who are otherwise sensible and clear-thinking will say, for instance, that those of us who write children's books work out of unhappy childhoods. Others say children's books shouldn't have abstract thoughts or long words, or much description. I don't agree with any of that. Nor do I agree that children's books are harder to write than adult books. They're not easier either. The fact is, regardless of genre, some books are harder to write than others. Every book poses its own set of problems, some of which are harder than others to solve."

Where my ideas come from
"It takes me years to finish a book. For this reason I don't worry about running out of ideas; I'll never live long enough to use them all.

"Some of my ideas want to be told through a young person's eyes and some don't; it's the point of view that decides whether I'll write a children's book or an adult book. My obsessions and preoccupations at that point in time are a major factor as well."

How I work
"I write every day, sometimes as long as eight hours, if my neck can stand it. I write everything in longhand before putting it on the computer where I endlessly revise. I find it impossible to read my work without making revisions. My copies of my published books are peppered with revisions. When I'm deep in a story, I usually forget the time, mix up appointments and become a poor listener. Fortunately my family and friends put up with this."

Joan Clark

BIBLIOGRAPHY

Clark, Joan. *Girl of the Rockies.* Toronto: Ryerson, 1968. Out of print.

—. *Thomasina and the Trout Tree.* Montreal: Tundra Books, 1971 Cloth 0-88776-018-X. Illustrations by Ingeborg Hiscox.

—. *The Hand of Robin Squires.* Toronto: Clarke Irwin & Company, 1977. Toronto: Stoddart, 1994 Paper 0-7736-74268.

—. *The Leopard and the Lily.* Lantzville, BC: Oolichan Books,

1984 Paper 0-88982-078-3. Illustrations by Velma Foster.

—. *Wild Man of the Woods*. Toronto: Penguin Books Canada, 1985 Paper 0-14-031788-0.

—. *The Moons of Madeleine.* Toronto: Penguin Books Canada, 1987 Paper 0-14-032182-9; Cloth 0-670-81284-6.

—. *The Dream Carvers.* Toronto: Penguin Books Canada, 1995 Cloth 0-670-85858-7.

Awards

1983 Alberta Publishing Award, juried by children for *The Hand of Robin Squires*

1995 Geoffrey Bilson Award for Historical Fiction for Young People for *The Dream Carvers*

1995 Mr. Christie's Book Award for *The Dream Carvers*

1998 Hibernia Book Award for *The Dream Carvers*

Selected articles about Joan Clark

Clark, Joan. "What is History?" *Canadian Children's Literature* 83 (1996): 78-81.

Aubrey Davis
AUTHOR

Born
1949, Toronto, Ontario

School
Mackenzie CI (North York, Ontario); B.A. University of Toronto, B. Ed. University of Western Ontario; M.Ed. (Adult Education and Psychology) Ontario Institute for Studies in Education (Toronto, Ontario)

Where I live now
Toronto, Ontario

My favourite books when I was young
Greek myths, Bible stories, *Tom Sawyer*, *Mad* magazine

My favourite book now
The Commanding Self by Idries Shah

Career
"Clerical and office worker; construction labourer; house painter and refurbisher; retail salesman of automotive parts; assistant technician in nuclear physics at Imperial College, London, England; garden and nursery worker; subsistence farmer; logger and forestry worker; antique restorer and salesman; professional storyteller; teacher. Currently I teach oral language to primary and developmentally disabled students."

Family
"My wife Sandra Carpenter-Davis is a storyteller, too. She also teaches parents how to use rhymes, songs and stories with babies and toddlers.

"My son Nathaniel works in a shop that constructs or finds props for major theatrical productions at home and abroad. My daughter Olwyn has completed a course in stage make-up with the Canadian Opera Company. She is now studying the technical side of theatre at Ryerson Polytechnic University in Toronto.

"We also have a 15-year-old dog named Farley and a ten-year-old cat named Cody."

The room where I create
"Often I write in my upstairs office. It has bookshelves, posters, a computer, phone, fax machine and a big window that overlooks the dead-end street where I live. But my favourite writing spot is the sunroom off the kitchen where I work early in the morning. It has one white brick wall with windows on the other three walls. It's got lots of plants, a dryer, a jar of painted Easter eggs and Cody's scratching post."

Spare time
"I like to read, hike and do tai chi. I also like canoeing, fishing and biking."

When I was growing up
"As a child I loved fishing, swimming, sailing, hot summer days, bonfires, baseball and watermelon. When I was seven, I fell off the dock into the lake. Afterwards I wandered up and down the road hoping the sun would dry my clothes before my mother found out. But the late afternoon sun was too weak. I was still soaking wet when I squeaked through the cottage door in my squishy shoes. My mother never even noticed."

My first book (and how it happened)
"I was invited to tell a Hanukkah story at Young People's Theatre in Toronto but I couldn't find a story I liked. A storytelling friend showed me a Jewish version of *Stone Soup*. I loved the story but didn't like the way it was written. So I wrote my own version and later told it to over 1500 children. They liked it so much that I sent it to a publisher. That's how *Bone Button Borscht* was born."

Where my ideas come from
"Most of my ideas have come from traditional folk tales that I've read or heard. Now that I am

beginning to write my own stories I find ideas from my own experiences, stories people tell, books, newspapers and magazines. I also get ideas from scientific research, particularly from psychology, sociology and anthropology."

Who and what influenced me

"Many people, books and experiences have influenced me. I have always loved to read. My neighbor was a writer and I had a teacher who loved my funny stories. This encouraged me to write. But later I had a teacher who hated them. So I wrote only what I had to.

"Maybe it began with the supply teacher at my high school who encouraged me to think for myself. For the first time, I began to ask myself why I thought what I thought and did what I did. The following year I joined a theatre group, volunteered with mentally handicapped children, learned to speed-read and served as president of the student council. Two years later I quit university to travel.

"On the Canary Islands I read a book called *The Sufis* by Idries Shah. This amazing book made me think in fresh new ways. It also introduced me to the idea of storytelling. I have always been interested in performance. I acted in classroom plays in public school.

"I became a storyteller. At first I told stories to my own children, then at a weekly gathering in Toronto. I told them in nursing homes, festivals, jails, on national radio and television. I created an oral language program for mentally handicapped children. They taught me how to tell and later write stories simply and dramatically.

"Who influenced me and my writing? Was it my mother, my wife, my children, my neighbour, my teachers or my students? Was it the books I read, the work I did or the places I visited? Was it luck? Was it something mysterious and hidden that guided me? I'm not really sure."

How I work

"I like to work early in the morning and during the day. Sometimes I work on the story inside my head; sometimes I write it on paper. Much of the time I write on a computer, particularly when I'm rewriting the story.

"Until recently I have rewritten traditional folk tales in my own words. First I look for a story I really like. I learn the story by letting it make pictures in my mind. Next I tell the story many times. I try to think the thoughts and feel the feelings of each and every character. This makes the story come alive. Then I write it down. I rewrite many times, changing words and ideas until it sounds just right.

"I am now beginning to write my own stories. Once I get the idea, I let grow it in my mind just as I do with folk tales. Sometimes the story does not grow enough or it grows in a way I do not like. So I put it aside and move onto another story idea. Sometimes I come back to it later on."

Something nobody knew about me (until now)

"When I was little I saw a tap dancer on television. I wanted to be a dancer, too. My mother took me to a dance class but I quit after two lessons because I had to stand in the middle of a circle of girls and play peekaboo. I was the only boy.

"When I was six, my parents took a two-week vacation and left me with a babysitter. One night, I began to worry that they might die and never come back. Suddenly I realized that everyone dies and that I would die one day, too. I cried myself to sleep."

My favourite book that I created

Bone Button Borscht

Tips for young creators

"Read and read and read. Write and write and write.

"Be yourself and think for yourself. Don't be a copycat. Read, experience and write what most interests you. But be ready to try new or different books and experiences, too. Each one of you is an individual. So if you write what really interests you, others may find it interesting, too."

Aubrey Davis

BIBLIOGRAPHY

Davis, Aubrey. *Bone Button Borscht.* Toronto: Kids Can Press, 1995 Cloth 1-55074-224-8; Paper 1-55074-326-0. Illustrations by Dušan Petričić.

—. *Sody Salleratus.* Toronto: Kids Can Press, 1996 Cloth 1-55074-281-7 Illustrations by Alan and Lea Daniel. ✤

—. *The Enormous Potato.* Toronto: Kids Can Press, 1997 Cloth 1-55074-386-4.1999 Paper 1-55074-669-3. Illustrations by Dušan Petričić. ✤

Selected articles about Aubrey Davis

Campbell, Darren. "Developing the Mind." *Slave River Journal* 27 Jan.1998: 8.

Greenwood, Barbara. "Inside Stories: New Versions of Ancient Tales." *City Parent* Sept. 1996: 13.

Jennings, Sharon. "Introducing Aubrey Davis." *CANSCAIP News* 19.2: 1-5.

Brian Doyle
AUTHOR

Born
August 12, 1935, Ottawa, Ontario

School
Glebe Collegiate; Carleton University, Bachelor of Journalism; all in Ottawa, Ontario.

Where I live now
Ottawa, Ontario

His favourite book when he was young
Batman and *Captain Marvel* comics.

Career
Teacher and writer. Brian has taught in high schools throughout the Ottawa Valley for more than 28 years.

Family
Wife, Jackie; children, Megan and Ryan.

Spare time
"My only hobby is looking at peoples' faces and trying to guess what they are thinking. It's a dangerous hobby, but it's fun."

When he was growing up
Brian is an Ottawa boy, born and bred, and his roots are in the Gatineau Hills to the north of the capital city, where his great-grandfather arrived from Ireland at the age of 11.

Brian's love for the spoken language began as he listened to his father, Hulbert, who instilled in his son a knack for story-telling. "I used to hang around with him a lot," recalls Brian. "When he wasn't working, he would take me up the Gatineau to his cabin and sit around with his pals and tell stories. They'd talk like this: 'They say that...,' 'Did ya hear about...?' That was what the conversation was, one yarn after another, nothing else, and it would go on for hours. It was an anecdotal upbringing."

Brian wanted to be a writer from the time he was ten years old, but he received little encouragement from his teachers. "I didn't do well in school until all of a sudden in Grade 10, after I got 'perfect' on a spotting test of *Julius Caesar*, I realized I had an ear for words."

My first published story
"When I was young I got a story published in a little magazine called *The Fiddlehead*. They didn't have it in any stores, but there was a copy in the public library. I went to the library and got a seat where I could see the magazine with my story in it on the rack. I waited there to see if anyone would pick it up and read it. Three weeks later a lady came in and walked over to the rack. She picked up the magazine and started flipping through it. She strolled over and sat the same table as me. She read my story and then she left. It was my mother."

My first book (and how it happened)
Brian's first novel resulted from a trip across Canada (Ottawa to Vancouver Island) that he took with his wife, Jackie, and their two children, Megan and Ryan. When the trip was over, Brian and Megan decided to create a family journal about it. He did the writing and Megan corrected the manuscript so that each incident would correspond to her memory. This journal eventually became *Hey Dad!*

Where my ideas come from
"I listened to my father tell stories at night up at the cabin with the Coleman lamp buzzing while I was in the top bunk pretending to be asleep. I'm also quite a liar. I can't help it. I'm sorry."

Who and what influenced me
His father was an important influence on Brian, the writer. Brian recalls discovering some letters and poems his father wrote to friends and being surprised when he realized "he was a really good writer."

Brian's mother was a different kind of influence. She wrote poetry: "she made me respect poets, and books. She was more elitist than my father was. He was a musician of the language, while she was an intellectual."

How I work

"I've got to write a kind of prose-poetry that has to be read aloud. I take care with my sentences: there's rhythm there because I'm writing mostly for voice. I've been given that by my father, by Dylan Thomas, by Shakespeare, by all kinds of people."

Writing for young people

Brian sees himself as a writer for young people, not adults, because he is fond of the young narrators he uses for each story. "A young narrator can have innocence, they're not childish, but they are childlike. That's a great platform to stand on, and I can stand there, where I was wise — and I was very wise, very feelingful, very tender when I was young. I think everybody lives inside himself as a kid, feels, has confidence, has fears, has victories, as a kid. I have the greatest confidence in the kid in me."

Brian Doyle

BIBLIOGRAPHY

Doyle, Brian. *Hey Dad!* Toronto: Groundwood Books, 1978. 1991 Paper 0-88899-148-7.

—. *You Can Pick Me Up At Peggy's Cove.* Toronto: Groundwood Books, 1979. 1995 Paper 0-88899-231-9.

—. *Up to Low.* Toronto: Ground-wood Books, 1982. 1996 Paper 0-88899-264-5.

—. *Angel Square.* Toronto: Ground-wood Books, 1987. 1995 Paper 0-88899-230-0.

—. *Easy Avenue.* Toronto: Ground-wood Books, 1988 Cloth 0-88899-065-0. 1996 Paper 0-88899-248-3.

—. *Covered Bridge.* Toronto: Groundwood Books, 1990 Cloth 0-88899-122-3. 1993 Paper 0-88899-190-8.

—. *Spud Sweetgrass.* Toronto: Groundwood Books, 1992 Paper 0-88899-251-3.

—. *Spud in Winter.* Toronto: Groundwood Books, 1995 Paper 0-88899-250-5.

—. *Uncle Ronald.* Toronto: Groundwood Books, 1996 Paper 0-88899-309-9.

Awards

1983 Canadian Library Association Book of the Year for Children Award for *Up to Low*

1989 Canadian Library Association Book of the Year for Children Award for *Easy Avenue*

1991 Vicky Metcalf Award for a Body of Work

1991 Mr. Christie's Book Award for *Covered Bridge*

1996 Mr. Christie's Book Award for *Uncle Ronald*

1997 Canadian Library Association Book of the Year for Children Award for *Uncle Ronald*

Selected articles about Brian Doyle

"Brian Doyle." *Something about the Author: Autobiography Series*, vol. 16: 127-141.

Budziszewski, Mary. "You Have to Think and Feel Like Your Readers" *CM* 19.2 (1991).

Dunnion, Kristyn. "Making Magic: An Interview with Brian Doyle." *Canadian Children's Literature* 76 (1994): 39-47.

Garvie, Maureen. "Up Doyle Way." *Quill and Quire* March 1995: 74-5.

Christiane Duchesne
AUTHOR

Born
August 12, 1949, Montreal, Quebec

School
1968 B.A. from Collège Jean-de Brébeuf, Montreal; 1969-70 Industrial Design, Ecole d'architecture at Université de Montréal

Where I live now
Montreal (when I'm not travelling somewhere).

My favourite books when I was young
A novel signed by Andre Maurois: *Le pays des 36,000 volontés.*

My favourite books now
"There are too many to choose one."

Career
"Editor of a magazine, teacher, illustrator, consultant in many different fields. Eighty percent of the time I am writing plays, dramas for radio, TV programs, scenarios etc."

Family
Two sons, 19 and 22 years old.

The room where I create
"A small square room on the third floor. It opens to a terrace, where a whole botanical garden grows every summer, and where several metres of snow fall between December and April."

Spare time
"Reading, writing, and listening to and playing the piano, flute and cello."

When I was growing up
"My greatest pleasure was to invent stories. I wrote a lot, I read a lot too. In fact, I can say that even when I was a child, I loved silently observing life, people, things and places. Nothing has really changed, I still get the same pleasure out of this pastime today."

My first book (and how it happened)
"*Le triste dragon*, the first 'true' book I wrote and illustrated, was published in 1975 by Editions Héritage. The strangest thing is that I did many books for children without ever considering having them published. In the case of *Le triste dragon*, somebody asked me why I never thought to get published and that's how it started."

Where my ideas come from
"It's very simple: everybody's life on earth could be the subject of a novel. It's just a matter of carefully observing; observe everything, all the time."

Who and what influenced me
"The fabulous mind of my father, who was curious, generous, and above all, patient, has most influenced my way of thinking and seeing the world. I hate borders, ideologies and established dogma. I love a free mind, and I believe flexible thought enables one to better understand people and life in general."

How I work
"I would like to be able to tell you! I write, that's it. I never work during summer time (or almost never). I write because otherwise, I risk exploding from all I have observed. I write as I have too many things to say, but hopefully, I have all my life to do so."

Something nobody knew about me (until now)
"Many people don't know I illustrated my first picture books. But what they don't know about me should perhaps stay hidden..."

My favourite book that I've created
"It's difficult to say, since I love them all, even the oldest one. However, I have a preference for *La bergère de cheveaux.*"

Tips for young creators
"Never create something precise. Above all, create for yourself, not others."

Christiane Duchesne

BIBLIOGRAPHY

Duchesne, Christiane. *The Lonely Dragon*. Trans. Rosemary Allison. Toronto: James Lorimer & Company, 1977 Paper 0-88862-168-X (French). Illustrations by the author. ♣

—. *Lazarus Laughs*. Trans. Rosemary Allison. Toronto: James Lorimer & Company, 1977. Illustrations by the author. Out of print. ♣

—. *Le loup, l'oiseau et le violoncelle*. Montreal: la courte échelle, 1978. Illustrations by the author. Out of print.

—. *Le serpent vert*. Montreal: Héritage, 1978. Illustrations by the author. Out of print.

—. *La vraie histoire du chien de Clara Vic*. Montreal: Editions Québec-Amérique, 1990.

—. *The Loonies Arrive*. Trans. Sarah Cummins. Halifax: Formac, 1992 Paper 0-88780-206-0; Cloth 0-88780-207-9. Illustrations by Marc Mongeau.

—. *Victor*. Montreal: Editions Québec-Amérique Jeunesse, 1992. Out of print.

—. *La 42e soeur de Bébert*. Montreal: Editions Québec-Amérique Jeunesse, 1993. Out of print.

—. *Loonie Summer*. Trans. Sarah Cummins. Halifax: Formac, 1994 Paper 0-88780-272-9; Cloth 0-88780-273-7.

—. *La bergère de chevaux*. Montreal: Editions Québec-Amérique Jeunesse, 1995. Out of print.

—. *Who's Afraid of the Dark?* Trans. David Homel. Richmond Hill: Scholastic Canada, 1996 Cloth 0-590-24448-5. Illustrations by Doris Barrette. ♣

Christiane is also well known for her French-English and English-French translations.

Awards

1992 Governor General's Literary Award for *Victor*

1993 Mr. Christie's Book Award for *La 42e soeur de Bébert*

1995 Mr. Christie's Book Award for *La bergère de chevaux*

1995 Prix Quebec/Wallonie-Bruxelles for *La bergère de chevaux*

Frank Edwards
AUTHOR

Born
March 9, 1952, Oshawa, Ontario

School
Dr. Robert Thornton Public School, Whitby; Anderson Collegiate Vocational Institute, Whitby; Carleton University, Ottawa, all in Ontario

Where I live now
On the outskirts of Kingston, Ontario

My favourite books when I was young
"British comic books sent by my English grandparents (*Beano, Hotspur, Dandy*, etc.). *Hardy Boys* and *Nancy Drew* series. *Black Beauty*. Eleanor Estes' *Moffats* books."

My favourite book now
"*The Shipping News* by E. Annie Proulx and mystery novels."

Career
Assistant editor, *Canadian Geographic*; associate editor, *Harrowsmith*; executive editor, *Equinox*; editor/ associate publisher, Camden House Books; co-founder/ publisher/editor, Bungalo Books.

Family
Wife, Susan, teacher; kids Kristen, Scott, Hayley; grandkid Emily.

The room where I work
"I write in the same place I work, a home office loaded with computer equipment, books and a 10-foot desk. The office is in the basement but I have a wonderful sunroom that overlooks the creek behind our house. This is where I sit when I want to edit, rewrite or just think."

Spare time
"With three kids and a business, I don't have much spare time. I volunteer at the local school working with kids just learning to read. My wife and I like to ride bikes around nearby Wolfe Island. And I am building a cottage near Frontenac Provincial Park."

When I was growing up
"I lived in a country area that was being built up very quickly with new houses. There were lots of kids living nearby but there was also lots of room to play — a local woods, a marsh that froze over every winter, orchards, acres of abandoned farmland and lots of roads and houses under construction. On weekends and summer holidays, my friends and I just roamed around on our bikes.

"As we got older, our parents let us ride into Oshawa (which had North America's largest shopping centre in the early 1960s) and we treated the stores as play areas. The elevator and escalators in Eaton's were perfect for tag and hide-and-seek.

"Later, I had a paper route to earn enough money go to the Central Canadian Exhibition at the end of the summer and spend a day with my best friend — blowing all our money at the midway."

My first book (and how it happened)
"I wrote my first kids' book in 1990 for Bungalo Books, the company that I started with John Bianchi. *Mortimer Mooner Stopped Taking a Bath* was born out of a two-hour lawn-cutting session. After repeating the main text over and over, I wrote it down and showed it to John — who fortunately insisted on a new name for the character and turned my little boy character into a pig. He turned it into a really funny book with his illustrations and it sold more than 100,000 copies in the first year."

Where my ideas come from
"I think my ideas come from the silliest part of my brain (the *medulla bizarrum*) and are based on being a dad and watching my kids and their friends. I try to take very ordinary things and turn them inside out and upside down until they are quite ridiculous."

Who and what influenced me
"Cartoonist John Bianchi has influenced my writing more than anyone. Every time I get an idea, I imagine how John would draw

it. We work together on everything. Editorially, I like being part of a team with lots of opportunity for brainstorming and John is the perfect team partner."

How I work

"John and I bat an idea around until we know what we want to accomplish. Generally, I write a very simple, straight text that is a bit ironic; it has to be understated because it's going to play straight man to John's illustrations.

"We used to share a studio and work together every day but John moved to Arizona in 1993, so now we work together 6,000 kilometres apart. We talk on the phone about four hours a week and send text and rough drawings back and forth over the Internet. We also get together about four or five times a year for three days at a time.

"Once we agree on an idea, we work on a rough text and storyboard the whole project. We brainstorm on the title and John creates a book cover. Then we create the final text and artwork. Sometimes the text is the last part to be finished because it gets changed to accommodate last minute ideas and gags.

"In recent years, I've concentrated on books for new readers, so we have to figure out how children are going to read the text and what they will learn from it before creating the story. It is a very structured process but I enjoy working within limits."

Something nobody knew about me (until now)

"I was given to the wrong mother in the hospital the week that I was born. My real mother didn't notice the switch until she heard the other mom screaming 'This is not my baby!' I have spent my whole life wondering what would have happened if no one had noticed."

My favourite book that I've created

"*Downtown Lost and Found* because I love the rhythm of the title and because it will probably be the very first book that a lot of kids learn to read all by themselves. (And I love John's picture of an elephant getting squeezed through a small door.)"

Tips for young creators

"Do lots of different stuff and pay attention to what is happening around you — even when you think it's boring. My journalist's training taught me that people are usually interested in what other people do — once you give them a chance to find out. Writing has to start with good ideas and you have to do lots of different things before you'll find your best ideas."

Frank Edwards

BIBLIOGRAPHY

Edwards, Frank. *Mortimer Mooner Stopped Taking a Bath*. Kingston: Bungalo Books, 1990 0-921285-20-5. Illustrations by John Bianchi.

—. *Melody Mooner Stayed Up All Night*. Kingston: Bungalo Books, 1991 Paper 0-921285-01-9; Cloth 0-921285-03-5. Illustrations by John Bianchi.

—. *Snow: Learning for the Fun of it*. Kingston: Bungalo Books, 1992 Paper 0-921285-09-4; Cloth 0-921285-15-9. Illustrations by John Bianchi.

—. *Grandma Mooner Lost Her Voice*. Kingston: Bungalo Books, 1992 Paper 0-921285-17-5; Cloth 0-921285-19-1. Illustrations by John Bianchi.

—. *Ottawa: A Kid's Eye View*. Kingston: Bungalo Books, 1992 Paper 0-921285-26-4; Cloth 0-921285-27-2. Photographs by J.A. Kraulis.

—. *A Dog Called Dad*. Kingston: Bungalo Books, 1994 Paper 0-921285-34-5; Cloth 0-921285-35-3. Illustrations by John Bianchi.

—. *Mortimer Mooner Makes Lunch*. Kingston: Bungalo Books, 1995 Paper 0-921285-36-1; Cloth 0-921285-37-X. Illustrations by John Bianchi.

—. *Melody Mooner Takes Lessons*. Kingston: Bungalo Books, 1996 Paper 0-921285-46-9; Cloth 0-921285-47-7. Illustrations by John Bianchi.

—. *Peek-a-boo at the Zoo*. Kingston: Bungalo Books, 1997 Paper 0-921285-52-3; Cloth 0-921285-53-1. Illustrations by John Bianchi.

—. *The Zookeeper's Sleepers*. Kingston: Bungalo Books, 1997 Paper 0-921285-54-X; Cloth 0-921285-55-8. Illustrations by John Bianchi.

—. *Downtown Lost and Found*. Kingston: Bungalo Books, 1997 Paper 0-921285-50-7; Cloth 0-921285-53-1. Illustrations by John Bianchi.

—. *Troubles with Bubbles*. Kingston: Bungalo Books, 1998 Paper 0-921285-64-7. Illustrations by John Bianchi.

—. *Is the Spaghetti Ready?* Kingston: Bungalo Books, 1998 Paper 0-921285-66-3. Illustrations by John Bianchi.

—. *New at the Zoo*. Kingston: Bungalo Books, 1998 Paper 0-921285-69-8. Illustrations by John Bianchi.

—. *Bug*. Kingston: Bungalo Books, 2000 Paper 1-894323-18-1. Illustrations by John Bianchi.

—. *Frogger*. Kingston: Bungalo Books, 2000 Paper 1-094323-20-3. Illustrations by John Bianchi.

Edwards, Frank, and Laurel Aziz. *Close up: Microscopic Photographs of Everyday Stuff*. Kingston: Bungalo Books, 1992 Paper 0-921285-24-8; Cloth 0-921285-25-6. Photographs by Alexandra Smith.

Selected articles about Frank Edwards

Holland, Elizabeth. "Hey, Bungalo Books!" *Treehouse Canadian Family*. Apr. 1998: 16.

Kastner, Susan. "Million Dollar Sale for Bungalo Books." *The Toronto Star* 11 Dec. 1994: B1.

Ross, Val. "Bungalo Boogaloo." *The Globe and Mail* 26 Feb. 1997: E1.

Sarah Ellis
AUTHOR

Born
May 19, 1952, Vancouver, British Columbia

School
Vancouver, British Columbia

Where I live now
Vancouver, British Columbia

My favourite book when I was young
"I liked *The Secret Garden* a lot. When I was a little older I really liked *I Capture the Castle* by Dodie Smith."

My favourite book now
"This changes weekly. This week it's either *Through the Dolls' House Door* by Jane Gardam or *A Pack of Lies* by Geraldine McCaughrean. My all-time favourite might be Brian Doyle's *Up to Low*."

Career
"I worked as a children's librarian for about 10 years and I'm still a librarian half the week. But for the last decade I think of myself as mostly a writer."

Family
"I live in a big old house with two adult humans and two cats."

The room where I create
"The attic. In the summer I look out over a lovely big chestnut tree. In the winter I look through the bare branches into the extremely messy yard of my across-the-street neighbour who is a junk dealer."

Spare time
"I like to read, cook, go into the basement and try to make things with bits of wood, walk, go to plays, listen to music, grow vegetables, travel and chat."

When I was growing up
"I was pretty well the same person I am now. I liked reading, picnics, comfortable clothes, school (especially school supplies), crafts, playing music and learning new things. I liked tagging along with my older brothers (especially when they got motorcycles) and I liked friends who were funny and good at make-believe, but I always felt most myself when I was alone. I didn't like arguments, peas, show-offs or going to parties where I didn't know everyone. I still like and dislike these things.

"I don't remember ever thinking about becoming a writer but the other day I met a friend whom I hadn't seen since elementary school and she said, 'Oh, I always knew you'd be a writer.'"

My first book (and how it happened)
"I wrote *The Baby Project* at the kitchen table and I didn't tell anyone what I was doing. I didn't want to be embarrassed if it didn't work. I didn't have a story when I started, just a few vague ideas, like the idea of a school project, the idea of a best friend who is the opposite of yourself (based on my friend Jane from Grade 3); and the relationship between a girl and her brother when the brother reaches dreaded adolescence (another autobiographical bit, my brother Chris still denies that he was like that). I just fooled around with these characters, much in the way you would play with dolls or action figures, and gradually a story started to happen. Then I rewrote and revised, and tinkered and then I sent to it to a publisher. And, by gum, they wanted to publish it. And now it exists in English, French, Japanese and Spanish."

Where my ideas come from
"Memories from when I was a kid; my family, friends, teachers; observing kids that I know and kids in the library; reading magazines and newspapers and listening to the radio; overhearing conversations (otherwise known as eavesdropping); stories that people tell me; dreams. And some of it is invented out of thin air."

Who and what influenced me
"I spent a lot of time in church when I was young and I think I was influenced by Bible stories

and by the language of prayers and hymns. My father was, and is, a good joke teller and I think that's why I like funny books. We were always read to when we were young, and not just picture books either, long chapter books. I think that's what turned me into a reader and into a writer. I had a couple of good English teachers in high school who introduced me to a wide variety of writing. And I'm sure I've been influenced by every single book I've read."

How I work

"I do a first draft in pencil on yellow legal paper. I write slowly and I tend to try to make it perfect as I go (not that it ever is, but I seem to need to feel that every draft is the final draft, so that I will take it seriously). I revise constantly, moving back and forth between four or five pages laid out in front of me. I don't make outlines. What it feels like is taking care of something that needs time to grow, a bit like gardening. This stage takes me about a year. Then I type this draft and if I feel more or less happy with it, I send it to the editor. Or perhaps I do another draft because I can see major problems or how the book could be better. After the editor has seen the manuscript she makes comments and suggestions and then I go through the story again with these in mind. Sometimes this happens twice. Finally someone else goes through the manuscript one last time to check for little mistakes like spelling and punctuation and then I correct those, and then my part is over."

Something nobody knew about me (until now)

"True Confession: For years I've discussed J.R.R. Tolkien's *The Lord of the Rings* with people. I've had arguments about it. I own a nice edition of it. I have this awful feeling that I've even mentioned it in lectures. But — *I have never read it*. There, it's out. I feel much better."

My favourite book that I've created

"Impossible question. I like them all for different reasons and I feel sort of loyal to them all. It is as though if I picked a favourite the others would get their feelings hurt. I know this is silly. Writers get like this."

Tips for young creators

"Keep a diary, write lists, get a penpal, become a good typist and read, read, read."

Sarah Ellis

BIBLIOGRAPHY

Ellis, Sarah. *The Baby Project.* Toronto: Groundwood Books, 1986. 1994 Paper 0-88899-222-X.

—. *Next-Door Neighbours.* Toronto: Groundwood Books, 1989 Paper 0-88899-084-7.

—. *Putting Up with Mitchell: My Vancouver Scrapbook.* Vancouver: Brighouse Press, 1990. Illustrations by Barbara Wood. Out of print.

—. *Pick-Up Sticks.* Toronto: Groundwood Books, 1991 Cloth 0-88899-146-0. 1992 Paper 0-88899-162-2.

—. *Out of the Blue.* Toronto: Groundwood Books, 1994 Cloth 0-88899-215-7.

—. *Back of Beyond.* Toronto: Groundwood Books, 1996 Paper 0-88899-269-6.

—. *The Young Writer's Companion.* Toronto: Groundwood Books, 1999 Cloth 1-88899-371-4.

—. *From Reader to Writer: Teaching Writing through Classic Children's Books.* Toronto: Groundwood Books, 2000 Cloth 0-88899-372-2.

Awards

1987 Sheila A. Egoff Children's Book Prize for *The Baby Project*

1991 Governor General's Literary Award for *Pick-Up Sticks*

1994 Mr. Christie's Book Award for *Out of the Blue*

1995 Vicky Metcalf Award for a Body of Work

1995 National Chapter of Canada IODE Violet Downey Book Award for *Out of the Blue*

1997 Sheila A. Egoff Children's Book Prize for *Back of Beyond*

Selected articles about Sarah Ellis

Jenkinson, Dave. "Profile: Sarah Ellis." *Resource Links* Feb. 1997: 103-106.

Saltman, Judith "An Appreciation of Sarah Ellis." *Canadian Children's Literature* 67 (1992): 6-18.

"Sarah Ellis." *Children's Literature Review* 42: 74-87.

Sheree Fitch
AUTHOR

Born
December 3, 1956

Schools
Hons. B.A. in English, St. Thomas University, Fredericton, New Brunswick; M.A. in English, Acadia University, Wolfville, Nova Scotia

My favourite books when I was young
"My father's stories: we called them stories with your mouth talking. *Heidi, Swiss Family Robinson*, Bible stories, a series of books called *The Best in Children's Books* that included everything from classic fairy tales and poetry to non-fiction and geography."

My favourite book now
"The one I want to write next!!!"

Career
"Stocking shelves in a convenience store; working as a sales clerk in a women's clothing store; being a civil servant; editing newsletters; scrubbing floors to pay for university; acting; teaching writing; writing and broadcasting with the CBC for one year; teaching at university and speaking at conferences. Now I write and write and read and teach."

Family
Two sons, Jordan and Dustin McCormack, now 24 and 18. Husband Gilles Plante.

The room where I create
"It overlooks a lake called Chocolate Lake where both the ducks and I swim in summer and where I skate in the winter. It's filled with books and knick-knacks that people have given me, souvenirs from travelling and mementos from school visits. There are pictures of my family, my mentor, the temple I walked to when I travelled to Bhutan a few years ago."

Spare time
"Ha!!! Well, unless you count that I walk every day for an hour and watch 'Jeopardy' every night at 7:30."

When I was growing up
"I lived in a home where language was cherished and family was everything. I wrote my first poem when I was seven, called 'Itchy Fitch,' a tongue twister about my name. I was a competitive runner and basketball player and field hockey player during my teen years."

My first book (and how it happened)
"I wrote *Toes in my Nose* for my son Jordan when I was 20. It was published when I was 30 after years of rejection. By that time, I had changed some of the poems from the original manuscript, adding ones I had written for my second son Dustin. The title poem came as a result of Jordan telling his baby brother who was sticking his feet in his mouth to 'be careful, you just might stick your toes in your nose.' I was inspired."

Where my ideas come from
"Everywhere!!! A word I fall in love with, something that happens or something somebody says, dreams, daydreams, trips — even a trip to the grocery store."

Who and what influenced me
"As a child: all the writers I read, my Grade 2 teacher Mrs. Goodwin. When I was older: the Fredericton poet, Fred Cogswell, whom I consider a mentor, and the other writers whose works I admire. I did my master's thesis on Dennis Lee's poetry so I could explore work that I considered a model of excellence in Canadian children's poetry."

How I work
"Every book is different, every poem is different. As a rule however, I usually get a burst I call the 'fever' and then reshape the text through many, many revisions. I often work on more than one piece of writing at a time. I also read like that — more than one book on the go in different rooms of my house — so maybe the way I work reflects

all of that. Plays/stories/poems are stored in different chambers of my heart and brain. I think writing is really the art of listening: listening to all those inside voices and thoughts."

Something nobody knew about me (until now)

"Most people, when they meet me, think I am very outgoing and social. The truth is, although I love being with people sometimes, I prefer long hours of solitude and am very nervous and shy when meeting people or doing something for the first time."

My favourite book that I've created

"The one I am going to do next, but...

"*If You Could Wear My Sneakers* is very special to me, because UNICEF asked me to write a book about children's rights and it's something I care about a lot."

Tips for young creators

"Read, read, read. Write, write, write. Use your five senses in your writing — and remember writing hardly ever comes out of the end of your pencil in perfect form. Revision is re-vision: looking again to see how you can make it more beautiful or funny or true or filled with nonsensical beans."

Sheree Fitch

BIBLIOGRAPHY

Fitch, Sheree. *Toes in My Nose and Other Poem*s. Toronto: Doubleday Canada, 1987. 1993 Paper 0-385-25325-7. Illustrations by Molly Lamb Bobak.

—. *Sleeping Dragons All Around.* Toronto: Doubleday Canada, 1989. 1993 Paper 0-385-25398-2. Illustrations by Michelle Nidenoff.

—. *Merry-Go-Day.* Toronto: Doubleday Canada, 1991. Illustrations by Molly Lamb Bobak. Out of print.

—. *There Were Monkeys in My Kitchen!* Toronto: Doubleday Canada, 1992. 1995 Paper 0-385-25470-9. Illustrations by Marc Mongeau.

—. *I Am Small.* Toronto: Doubleday Canada, 1994 Cloth 0 385 25455 5. 1997 Paper 0-385-25589-6. Illustrations by Kim LaFave.

—. *Mabel Murple.* Toronto: Doubleday Canada, 1995 Cloth 0-385-25634-5. 1997 Paper 0-385-25634-5. Illustrations by Maryann Kovalski.

—. *If You Could Wear My Sneakers.* Toronto: Doubleday Canada, 1997 Cloth 0-385-25597-7. 1998 Paper 0-385-25677-9. Illustrations by Darcia Labrosse.

—. *There's a Mouse in My House!* Toronto: Doubleday Canada, 1997 Paper 0-385-25706-6; Cloth 0-385-25561-6. Illustrations by Leslie Watts.

—. *The Hullabaloo Bugaboo Day.* Lawrencetown Beach: Pottersfield Press, 1998 Paper 1-895900-10-7. Illustrations by Jill Quinn.

—. *If I Were the Moon.* Toronto: Doubleday Canada, 1999 Cloth 0-385-25744-9. Illustrations by Leslie Watts.

—. *The Other Author, Arthur.* Lawrencetown Beach: Pottersfield Press, 1999 Paper 1-89590-020-4. Illustrations by Jill Quinn.

Sheree has also written many plays for children, including a theatrical adaptation of *The Hullabaloo Bugaboo Day.*

Awards

1993 Mr. Christie's Book Award for *There Were Monkeys in My Kitchen*

1995 Canadian Authors Association Mariana Dempster Award for contribution to Children's Literature

1996 Anne Connor Brimer Award for *Mabel Murple*

2000 Hackmatack Children's Choice Award (non-fiction) for *If You Could Wear My Sneakers*

2000 Vicky Metcalf Award for a Body of Work

Selected articles about Sheree Fitch

Tynes, Jeanette. "Profile, A Purple Sort of Girl." *Canadian Children's Literature* 90: 1998.

Bill Freeman

AUTHOR

Born
October 21, 1938, London, Ontario

School
McMaster University, Hamilton, Ontario; Acadia University, Wolfville, Nova Scotia

Where I live now
Toronto Island in Toronto, Ontario

Career
Writer

The room where he creates
In his study at home, where he surrounds himself with research notes, books, old photographs, cups of coffee, and "various paraphernalia."

When he was growing up
As a teenager growing up in London, Ontario, Bill hated school. "I just drifted along. I was far more interested in playing hockey and football than I was in school. The only intellectual thing I did was read adventure novels." By the time he finished Grade 13 he decided not to go on in school. "The only things that had kept me in school were athletics, and the fact that my father was a high school teacher."

Despite his parents' protests, Bill left school behind and headed west, where he worked in survey camps for a year. When he was 19 years old he travelled to Europe and spent three years doing "anything and everything," including some short-story writing. "I never had anything published or showed anyone what I'd written," he says, "because I just didn't think it was good enough."

His first book (and how it happened)
It wasn't until Bill had children of his own that he began to consider writing a children's book. He decided to write a historical adventure because he'd always been interested in historical research, and had been fascinated with adventure stories when he was growing up. His first book was *Shantymen of Cache Lake*, published in 1975.

How he works
When Bill begins to research Canada's past for a novel, he sets out to learn everything he can about the period: how people lived, their working conditions, the physical landscape, the tools they used, the homes in which they lived, and even the clothes they wore. Once he knows the details of his setting intimately, "the story seems to emerge by itself."

He used to write out the first drafts of a novel in longhand, but since he bought his first computer he works directly on the machine. Whenever possible he writes 10 to 12 hours a day. "I've learned that working intensely at a book helps me get involved emotionally in the project and in the long run helps the final product."

Throughout the rewriting process, characters may develop and the plot may change, or it may happen in reverse: new twists in the plot may require changes in the characters. "Trying to work out the action of a story while developing characters makes me feel like a juggler with many balls," Bill notes.

"Of all the tasks in writing a book," Bill admits, "I enjoy the early stages most: doing the research, dreaming up a convincing plot, developing the characters into real people, and thinking about the type of mood and setting that are appropriate. The hardest part is the actual writing."

To date there are seven books in the Bains Series but Bill plans to write another five books. "For me the project is to write a series exploring different aspects of Canadian life in the 1870s," Bill explained. "The first six books were about central and eastern Canada. *Prairie Fire!* is set on the western plains of Manitoba as the family struggles to establish a homestead. The other books will be set in the west and the far north."

Currently Bill is working with Norflicks Productions, to adapt the Bains Series into hour-long, made-for-television films. As well as writing new novels he is busy learning the skills of script writing and film production. As well as the films there will be a Web site based on the Bains Series, containing historical background on the setting of each story, music of the period, notes on the characters, games, and so on.

Recently Bill commented "the whole project of the Bains Series has suddenly taken off, and I am not sure where it is going to go next. But it is exciting and fun. I always find it interesting to learn and do new things."

Tips for young creators

"Too many people think writing is something that you're born with. It's not. Becoming a writer is just like becoming a mechanic or a doctor — it's something you learn."

Bill Freeman

BIBLIOGRAPHY

Freeman, Bill. *Shantymen of Cache Lake* (Bains Series). Toronto: James Lorimer & Co., 1975 Paper 0-88862-090-X; Cloth 0-88862-091-8.

—. *The Last Voyage of the Scotian* (Bains Series). Toronto: James Lorimer & Co., 1976 Paper 0-88862-112-4; Cloth 0-88862-113-2.

—. *Cedric and the North End Kids* (The Where We Live Series). Toronto: James Lorimer & Co., 1978 Paper 0-88862-177-9; Cloth 0-88862-187-6. Photos by Lutz Dille.

—. *First Spring on the Grand Banks.* (Bains Series) Toronto: James Lorimer & Co., 1978. Paper 0-88862-220-1; Cloth 0-88862-221-X.

—. *Trouble at Lachine Mill.* (Bains Series) Toronto: James Lorimer & Co., 1983 Paper 0-88862-672-X; Cloth 0-88862-673-8.

—. *The Harbour Thieves* (Bains Series). Toronto: James Lorimer & Co., 1984 Paper 0-88862-746-7; Cloth 0-88862-747-5.

—. *Danger on the Tracks* (Bains Series). Toronto: James Lorimer & Co., 1987 Paper 0-88862-872-2; Cloth 0-88862-833-0.

—. *Prairie Fire!* (Bains Series). Toronto: James Lorimer & Co., 1998 Paper 1-55028-608-0; Cloth 1-55028-609-9.

Awards

1975 Canada Council Children's Literature Prize for *Shantymen of Cache Lake*

1984 Vicky Metcalf Award for a Body of Work

Priscilla Galloway
AUTHOR

Born
July 22, 1930, Montreal, Quebec

Where I live now
Toronto, Ontario

My favourite book when I was young
"There were so many — Alexandre Dumas, G. A. Henty, all of L.M. Montgomery (especially *The Blue Castle*). I loved *The Odyssey*, and was a voracious reader of myth and legend. When I found an author or a series I liked, I read everything."

My favourite book now
"*The Poisonwood Bible* by Barbara Kingsolver and *No Great Mischief* by Alistair MacLeod are two superb novels I have read recently."

Career
Writer, teacher.

Family
"Children: Noël, Walt, Glenn. Grandchildren: Hugh, Leigh, Laney, Ryan, Season, Saurin. My first husband died in 1985. Howard Collum and I have been happily married since 1994; he decided not to change his name, and I decided not to change mine. My most recent pet was Melusine the cat, mighty huntress and mother of three. I don't have any pets now."

The room where I create
"I have three locations: a former main bedroom in my Toronto home, with all the paraphernalia of the information age; at my cottage, on top of a sand dune, overlooking an ocean-like expanse of Georgian Bay; and at Howard's cottage on a Group of Seven Georgian Bay Island in a one-room building, 8 feet by 12, with yellow walls and brown woodwork."

Spare time
"What do people mean by that? I do lots of things that are not 'writing,' but are part of my writing business, such as school and conference presentations, or updating my Web page. Sometimes I read, swim, kayak, scuba dive, write letters, make jam or pickles, sort family archives, or watch my grandchildren play baseball. Sometimes I knit and watch TV."

When she was growing up
The first person to recognize Priscilla's promise as a writer was her father. The summer Priscilla was in Grade 11, she was offered a part-time job. Her father matched the offer. He would pay her the same amount ($7.00 a week) if she spent her mornings writing instead. Looking back, she reflects, "the world likely lost a rotten shoe salesperson."

By the time she had finished high school, she had published stories and articles. She had also submitted poems to magazines and been devastated by her first rejection slips. However, seeing some of her work in print encouraged her in her goal of becoming a journalist. A tour of the Parliamentary Press Gallery with journalist Lotta Dempsey — an award for winning a public speaking competition — confirmed her ambition to be a writer.

Where my ideas come from
"This heading implies it's a thinking process, but it's more of a 'feeling' process. All my books grow out of ideas, events and people in the deep roots of my life. It's a kind of science fiction thing, a 'first contact' or 'Eureka!' feeling. Lots of good ideas do not lead to books. A book is a huge project; I need an idea to excite me deeply enough to make it worth all the work.

"Twice in my writing life, an idea has been instantaneous, like a sudden light in my head, and it has led to a book: a three-year-old granddaughter's reproof sparked the idea of the child and mother changing places which turned into *When You Were Little and I Was Big*. A student's question led eventually to *Too Young to Fight*. It's crucial to write the idea down without delay; I have let some dandies get away. Finding the perfect form for the book is also vital. I have worked on several good ideas where I have not yet found that form."

How she works

Priscilla works mostly at her computer, even for first drafts. When characters begin talking to each other in her head, she tries to grab her current writing notebook and scribble the dialogue. Characters often choose inconvenient times, mainly when she is drifting off to sleep. Priscilla's writing notebooks are a messy lot, bristling with post-it notes. Notes are crossed out when they've been transferred to the computer.

In tackling a book, Priscilla has bursts of frenzied activity, draft after draft, until the work feels right. Then she sets that project aside and does something else. When she comes back to her manuscript, she sees it with fresh eyes. Usually, there is another burst of frenzied activity, more revisions, more editing.

Feedback is important, but Priscilla must proceed with infinite care. "Changing a major character or event in a novel at this late stage is truly scary. Cutting something out feels like butchery. When the manuscript is right at last, though, it's like giving birth to a child: no other thrill even comes close."

My favourite book that I've created

"This is like asking parents to name their favourite child! There is only one possible answer: they are all dear to me in different ways. I love them all and have grown as a writer from each one. I am always most deeply involved with the book that I am writing now, whenever "now" may be; the people in that book live with me; their story engrosses me; and until the book is in my hands, the suspense nearly kills me.

"My most exciting book is *Too Young to Fight: Memories from our Youth during World War II*, winner of the 2000 Bologna Ragazzi Non-Fiction Award for Young Adults, the first Canadian book to have won this world-renowned prize. In this book, 11 famous authors tell what our young lives were like during World War II. In Scotland, Monica Hughes was sent away from home; in Halifax, Budge Wilson saw flames from ships attacked by German submarines; Joy Kogawa's Japanese-Canadian family were interned; Christopher Chapman's brother was killed; Claire Mackay's communist family felt much safer after Russia joined our side!

"Young people often ask where I get ideas for my books. This one was sparked by a Grade 8 student's question, 'You were our age when World War II was going on. Did the war make any difference in your life?'"

Writing children's books

"I love it when readers tell me they couldn't put my book down!"

Priscilla Galloway

SELECT BIBLIOGRAPHY

Galloway, Priscilla. *Good Times, Bad Times, Mummy and Me*. Toronto: Women's Press, 1980 Paper 0-88961-066-5. Illustrations by Lissa Calvert.

—. *When You Were Little and I Was Big* (Annick Toddler Series). Toronto: Annick Press, 1984. Illustrations by Heather Collins. Out of print.

—. *Jennifer Has Two Daddies*. Toronto: Women's Press, 1985 Paper 0-88961-095-9 Illustrations by Ana Auml.

—. *Seal is Lost*. Toronto: Annick Press, 1988. Illustrations by Karen Patkau. Out of print.

—. *Aleta and the Queen: a Tale of Ancient Greece*. Toronto: Annick Press, 1995 Paper 1-55037-462-1; Cloth 1-55037-400-1. Illustrations by Normand Cousineau. ✦

—. *Atalanta: the Fastest Runner in the World*. Toronto: Annick Press, 1995 Paper 1-55037-463-X; Cloth 1-55037-401-X. Illustrations by Normand Cousineau. ✦

—. *Truly Grim Tales*. Toronto: Stoddart Kids, 1996 Paper 0-7737-5846-1.

—. *Daedalus and the Minotaur*. Toronto: Annick Press, 1997 Paper 1-55037-458-3; Cloth 1-55037-459-1. Illustrations by Normand Cousineau.

— adapt. *Emily of New Moon* by L.M. Montgomery. Toronto: Seal Books, 1998 Paper 0-7704-2748-0; Cloth 0-385-32506-1.

—. *Snake Dreamer*. Toronto: Stoddart Kids, 1998 Cloth 0-7737-5981-6.

—. *My Hero Hercules*. Toronto: Annick Press, 1999 Paper 1-55037-568-7 Cloth 1-55037-569-5.

— , ed. *Too Young to Fight: Memories from our Youth during World War II*. Toronto: Stoddart Kids, 1999 Cloth 0-7737-31903.

Priscilla Galloway has also translated the French *Tommycat* series, written by N. Girard and P. Danheux, illustrated by Michel Bédard.

Selected articles about Priscilla Galloway

Jenkinson, Dave. "Profiles: Priscilla Galloway." *Resource Links* 2.6 (1997): 247-250.

Kirchhoff, H.J. "Priscilla Galloway." *The Globe and Mail* 2 Dec. 1995: E2.

Awards

2000 Bologna Ragazzi Award for Non-Fiction (Young Adult) for *Too Young to Fight*.

For more information about Priscilla Galloway, visit her Web site at http://webhome.idirect.com/~gallcoll

Phoebe Gilman
AUTHOR/ILLUSTRATOR

Born
April 4, 1940, New York City, New York, USA

School
Public School 86, Bronx, New York; High School of Art and Design, Manhattan, New York; Hunter College, New York; Art Students League, New York; Bezalel Academy, Jerusalem, Israel

Where I live now
Etobicoke, Ontario

Favourite books when young
Andrew Lang's fairy tales

Favourite book now
"I can't choose one. I am constantly reading. Some of my favourite authors are Jane Urquhart, Isabel Allende and Barbara Kingsolver."

Career
Author and illustrator of children's books.

Family
"I am married to Brian Bender. We have three children: Ingrid, Jason and Melissa and two grandchildren, Ariana and Emily. We have a cat, Minoo, a turtle, Dweezil, a budgie, Bernice (he's a boy but we didn't know that when we named him), and two rats, Frodo and Gimley."

The room where I create
"My studio is a room that we built over the garage of our house. It has a skylight, and a balcony that overlooks the garden."

Spare time
"I like to read, watch the water, go for walks, play with friends and family, go to the movies and go ice-skating."

When I was growing up
"My mother chose my name out of a book. She thought it was special and unusual. I didn't like it and tried to get people to give me a nickname. No one did. I guess having an unusual name helped to make me feel different. I don't mind being different now.

"If I didn't share my mother's taste in names, I did share her love of books. My favourites were fairy tales. I remember covering up the pictures with my hands. It used to bother me when the pictures didn't match the images that the author's words painted in my head. I still do that.

"I think of myself as an artist rather than a writer. It was because of my friend Gladys Hopkins, that I became an artist. When we were about to graduate from P.S. 86, she came up with the brilliant idea that we should try out for one of the special high schools in Manhattan. That way we could avoid the terrible fate of attending the all-girls high school, which was right next door to P.S. 86. That is how I happened to go to The High School of Art and Design."

My first book (and how it happened)
"It was because of my daughter, Ingrid, that I wrote my first book, *The Balloon Tree*. It was her balloon that started it all. She let go of it and up, up, up it flew until ... kablam! It popped on the branch of a tree. I wished that tree would magically sprout balloons. It didn't, but I made up a story for Ingrid about a magic tree that blossomed balloons. We liked it so much, I decided to write it down. And that's how I came to write *The Balloon Tree*. It is not how I came to be published. That took 15 years of rewriting and umpty-zillion rejection slips."

Who and what influenced me
"My mother. She loved to read and she loved to write. She believed I was special even when everybody else thought I was crazy, (when I kept rewriting *The Balloon Tree*, trying to get it published)."

How I work

"As Dr. Seuss once wrote, 'A thing my sister likes to do in evenings after supper, is sit around in her small room and use her thinker-upper.' That's what I do. I turn my thinker-upper on and it thinks up all these things. What I don't do is listen to the little voice in my head that says, 'That idea stinks.' I just keep working away, fixing and changing my picture or story until it's as good as I can make it. Sometimes that takes a month, sometimes that takes a year, sometimes that takes 15 years."

Something nobody knew about me (until now)

"I once vacuumed a chocolate chip cookie. I made it as a surprise for my husband and since I didn't want him to see it, I hid it in the oven. Unfortunately, I forgot it was there when I turned the oven on to make supper. I remembered the cookie too late to prevent the paper that covered it from melting a bit. When I tried to scrape the paper off the top of the cookie it looked messy, all those crumbs and bits of paper. So I figured if I held the vacuum hose over it, not on it, it would smooth it out. Whomp! It sucked up a big hole in the middle of my cookie. Now I had a doughnut cookie. I filled up the hole with chocolate icing and Brian never knew, but my children knew... and now you know too!"

Tips for young creators

"Get a balloon and let it go. Read. Read. Read! Write. Write. Write! To do anything well takes practice. Don't give up. Keep on trying. Don't be afraid of criticism. Learn from it."

Phoebe Gilman

BIBLIOGRAPHY

Gilman, Phoebe. *The Balloon Tree*. Richmond Hill: Scholastic Canada, 1984 Paper 0-590-71257-8; Cloth 0-590-71410-4. Illustrations by the author.

—. *Jillian Jiggs*. Richmond Hill: Scholastic Canada, 1985 Paper 0-590-74875-0; Cloth 0-590-71548-8; Big Book 0-590-71823-1. Illustrations by the author.

—. *Little Blue Ben*. Richmond Hill: Scholastic Canada, 1986 Paper 0-590-73317-6; Cloth 0-590-71692-1; Big Book 0-590-73273-0. Illustrations by the author.

—. *The Wonderful Pigs of Jillian Jiggs*. Richmond Hill: Scholastic Canada, 1988 Cloth 0-590-71868-1; Big Book 0-590-71869-X. 1990 Paper 0-590-74847-5. Illustrations by the author.

—. *Grandma and the Pirates*. Richmond Hill: Scholastic Canada, 1988. 1990 Cloth 0-590-73221-8. 1992 Paper 0-590-74840-8. Illustrations by the author.

—. *Something From Nothing*. Richmond Hill: Scholastic Canada, 1992 Paper 0-590-74557-3; Cloth 0-590-73802-X; Big Book 0-590-72827-X. Illustrations by the author.

—. *Jillian Jiggs to the Rescue*. Richmond Hill: Scholastic Canada, 1994 Paper 0-590-24178-8; Cloth 0-590-74616-2. Illustrations by the author. ✿

—. *The Gypsy Princess*. Toronto: Scholastic, Canada, 1995 Paper 0-590-12389-0; Cloth 0-590-24441-8. Illustrations by the author. ✿

—. *Pirate Pearl*. Toronto: Scholastic, Canada, 1998 Cloth 0-590-12495-1. Illustrations by the author.

—. *Jillian Jiggs and the Secret Surprise*. Toronto: Scholastic Canada, 1999 Cloth 0-590-51578-0. Illustrations by the author.

Little, Jean, and Maggie deVries. *Once Upon a Golden Apple*. Toronto: Penguin Books Canada, 1991 Paper 0-14-054164-0; Cloth 0-670-82963-3. Illustrations by Phoebe Gilman.

Awards

1993 Ruth Schwartz Children's Book Award for *Something From Nothing*

1993 Vicky Metcalf Award for a Body of Work

1993 Sydney Taylor Award for *Something From Nothing*

Selected articles about Phoebe Gilman

Gaitskell, Susan. "Phoebe Gilman." *Presenting Canscaip*. Ed. Barbara Greenwood. Markham: Pembroke Publishers, 1990: 122-127.

Greenwood, Barbara, ed. *The CANSCAIP Companion*. Markham: Pembroke Publishers, 1994.

Perly Rae, Arlene. "Phoebe Gilman (writer illustrator)." *Everybody's Favorites*. New York: Viking, 1997.

Rachna Gilmore
AUTHOR

Born
October 11, 1953, New Delhi, India

School
King's College, University of London, England, 1974; University of Prince Edward Island, 1977.

Where I live now
In Orleans, outside Ottawa

My favourite books when I was young
All the *Anne* books by L.M. Montgomery, *Little Women* by Louisa May Alcott

My favourite book now
Pride and Prejudice

Career
"I did paralegal research for a while. I had a pottery studio, before becoming a full-time writer."

Family
"Husband, Ian Gilmore; two daughters: Karen (born 1980) and Robin (born 1984); cat, Bea, often called Beazy-Wheezy. She is named after Beatrix Potter because she looks exactly like Tom Kitten, only much fatter."

The room where I create
"I have a study in my basement, lined with white desks and shelves. It is bright and extremely well lit. The walls are hung with paintings, posters, memorabilia, and bulletin boards. I work on a computer. I have a high, narrow window with a view of the sky and the branches of a flowering crabapple tree. I like to keep my study orderly and attractive so it is a happy place in which to create. What I would ideally like, though, is a study with huge windows, lots of sunshine and a view of the ocean — not likely in Ottawa."

Spare time
"I walk every day if possible. I live near the Ottawa River and there are woods nearby with many trails through them.

"I also love to garden, and my tiny backyard is surrounded by wide curving flower beds. Of course, I love to read. During the summer I try and read in my hammock in my garden — if the mosquitoes will let me."

When I was growing up
"I lived in Bombay, India, until I was 14. During those years, there was no TV in India! My favourite activity was reading. My idea of a great day was to have a stack of books, with no one to bug me, so I could read all day.

"I also enjoyed painting, drawing and writing. For a while, I even had a writing club, just as Anne did in *Anne of Green Gables*. And I loved to walk. My friends and I would wake at dawn and walk down to the sea to watch the sunrise. I loved the quiet hush of the early mornings, when everything was fresh and slightly mysterious, with a whole day ahead, full of wonderful possibilities."

My first book (and how it happened)
"My first book was *My Mother is Weird*. As I read stories to my children, I found that there were many books about kids having bad days, but none about parents having bad days. I knew there were times I wasn't in the best of moods, and how tough this was for my kids, because they couldn't send me to my room for a time-out. I like to write funny stories, so I thought I'd write about a mother who had horns and claws and pointy teeth when she was cranky. But I didn't know how to make the story work until, one day, I was in a hurry. My daughter was trying to talk to me. I said to her, 'Karen, leave me alone for now. Can't you see, I've got horns and claws and pointy teeth?' And Karen looked at me, shook her head and said, 'Ah Mom, you're weird'.

"That did it. Suddenly, I knew exactly what a kid would feel with such a mother, and I could hear the voice of a little girl saying 'My mother is so weird.

Some mornings, when she wakes up, she has horns and claws and pointy teeth...' So, even though I was in a rush, I grabbed my pencil and scribbled down the story."

Where I get my ideas from

"I get a lot of ideas from listening to my kids, and from watching life around me. Sometimes an idea starts as an image, as in *A Friend Like Zilla*. I was watching my daughters feed seagulls. I had an image of two girls, one younger and one older, who were great friends in spite of the difference in their ages.

"I also get ideas from my childhood. *Lights for Gita*, for instance, came from remembering my years in India, and how much I loved the festival of lights called Divali. Often the ideas that seize my imagination and won't let go are ideas I need to explore and understand myself."

Who and what influenced me

"Books and their characters were one of the strongest influences. When I read in *Little Women*, and the sequels, about Jo writing stories, I felt a tingle of excitement. I thought this was something I, too, could do. I scribbled stories and ideas for years but I didn't work at it seriously.

"The turning point came when I was walking on a beach with my husband, Ian. I was talking about how I must really write some more, and wondering why wasn't I doing it. Ian said something about how people often put things off because they're afraid of failing, and how it's easier to succeed in your daydreams than in real life. That really hit home."

How I work

"When such an idea hits me, I play around in my head, exploring, until I have the rough shape of the story. But I don't start to write until I also know the main character's feelings, and I have a sense of her/his voice. I try to write my first draft quickly, without worrying about spelling or grammar, so I keep the excitement and feeling of the story. Once that is done, I relax and rewrite, and rewrite, and rewrite. Often, the story or novel ends up being very different from the one I started out with. But I need all those stages to help me get to the final draft. I have a wonderful writing group with whom I meet regularly. We read our work out loud and give each other feedback on what works and what doesn't."

My favourite book that I've created

"That's like asking me which one of my kids is my favourite. If I have a favourite, it has to be the one I'm working on at the time, because I have to be interested in it to keep writing it. Once it's gone to the printers, I let go of it. After it's published I just feel a happy, distant sense of satisfaction if kids like the book and it does well."

Tips for young creators

"Trust yourself! If you like an idea, that's all that matters. Never mind if anyone else likes it or not. And just keep writing. You can read books about writing, talk about writing, go to workshops about writing — but in the end, the only way to really learn is by writing. Every writer works differently and you have to find the way that works best for you."

Rachna Gilmore

BIBLIOGRAPHY

Gilmore, Rachna. *My Mother is Weird.* Charlottetown: Ragweed Press, 1988 Paper 0-920304-83-4. Illustrations by Brenda Jones. ✤

—. *Wheniwasalittlegirl.* Toronto: Second Story Press, 1989 Paper 0-929005-01-5. Illustrations by Sally Davies.

—. *Jane's Loud Mouth.* Charlottetown: Ragweed Press, 1990. Illustrations by Kimberly Hart. Out of print.

—. *Aunt Fred Is a Witch.* Toronto: Second Story Press, 1991 Paper 0-929005-23-6. Illustrations by Chum McLeod. ✤

—. *Lights for Gita.* Toronto: Second Story Press, 1994 Paper 0-929005-61-9; Cloth 0-929005-63-5. Illustrations by Alice Priestly.

—. *A Friend Like Zilla.* Toronto: Second Story Press, 1995 Paper 0-929005-71-6. Illustrations by Alice Priestly.

—. *Roses for Gita.* Toronto: Second Story Press, 1996 Paper 0-929005-85-6; Cloth 0-929005-86-4. Illustrations by Alice Priestly

—. *Wild Rilla.* Toronto: Second Story Press, 1997 Paper 0-929005-92-9; Cloth 0-929005-94-5. Illustrations by Yvonne Cathcart.

—. *A Gift for Gita.* Toronto: Second Story Press, 1998 Paper 1-896764-10-X; Cloth 1-896764-12-6. Illustrations by Alice Priestly.

—. *Fangs and Me.* Markham: Fitzhenry and Whiteside, 1999 Paper 1-55041-512-3. Illustrations by Gordon Sauvé.

—. *A Screaming Kind of Day.* Markham: Fitzhenry and Whiteside, 1999 Cloth 1-55041-514-X. Illustrations by Gordon Sauvé.

—. *Ellen's Terrible TV Troubles.* Toronto: Fitzhenry and Whiteside, 1999 Paper 1-55041-527-1; Cloth 1-55041-525-5.

—. *Mina's Spring of Colours.* Toronto: Fitzhenry and Whiteside, 2000 Paper 1-55041-534-4.

Awards

1999 Governor General's Literary Award for *A Screaming Kind of Day*

Martyn Godfrey
AUTHOR

Martyn Godfrey died on March 10, 2000 in St. Albert, Alberta as this book was in its final stages. This is the entry he had submitted.

Born
April 17, 1949, Birmingham, England

School
"A number of schools in the Toronto area."

My favourite book when I was young
The Amazing Spiderman #6

My favourite book now
Guppy Love by Frank O'Keeffe.

Career
"I write books for young people."

Family
"I'm divorced. I have a son, Marcus, and a daughter, Selby."

The room where I create
"I write in my office."

Spare time
"Read comic books, jog and grow older."

When I was growing up
"I moved to Canada when I was eight. The plane kept popping hydraulic lines. We made emergency landings in Iceland, Greenland and Newfoundland. I loved it, but I couldn't figure out why my mother was pulling at the armrests as if that would keep the plane airborne.

"Williamson Road Elementary in Toronto was my introduction to the Ontario education system. I got beat up the first day. 'You talk funny,' this large kid with an interesting haircut grunted at me before he pounded my nose. I began to work on losing my British accent.

"I flunked Grade 3 and I hated writing because I couldn't spell. I couldn't understand why the teacher was so worried about it. But a year of writing spelling corrections 25 times paid off. By Grade 5, I was actually enjoying school, especially creative writing. It felt good to tell things in an interesting way."

Becoming a writer
"I created my first real character in Grade 7. His name was Benny Bernhart Bortorowski and he was a thinly-disguised Martyn Godfrey. With every creative writing assignment, I'd wonder how I could work B.B.B. into 'descriptive paragraphs of a winter's morning.' Finally, my teacher complained, 'Drop this guy, Godfrey.' I couldn't. Benny was part of me."

My first book (and how it happened)
"I always enjoyed writing and playing with words, but I didn't view it as a possible occupation. I wouldn't have become an author if I hadn't become a teacher and had a 12-year-old student named Tom Baker.

"Tom hated school — even gym. But he was a science-fiction fan and one January morning, he asked 'You got any space books for me to read?' A thorough search of the school library offered nothing. That same day when I assigned the weekly creative writing story, Tom declared, 'Hey, Mr. G., how come we're always writing stories and you never write a story? I think that if I'm writing a story for you, then you should write a space story for me.' 'Okay,' I said, and Tom returned my smile.

"By recess, I'd finished a page and a half of foolscap about a boy called Tom who went to school on another planet. I didn't get finished and Tom suggested the same deal for the next week. 'You bet,' I agreed. After all, Tom was showing an interest in something that went on in school. We did it for a third week. My finished story was seven pages long and Tom 'filed' it in his desk.

"A few days later, I was handing out book club forms. Tom sauntered up to my desk. 'I got an idea,' he grinned. 'Why don't you send your story to the book club guys and have them make a book out of it?' Seven pages is hardly a book, but my teacher brain saw this as a way to get Tom to do more work. We sent those seven pages to Scholastic along with a letter that Tom and I had carefully drafted. Scholastic asked me to turn the story into a book. It's called *The Day the Sky Exploded*."

Something nobody knew about me (until now)

"I'm an undercover cop."

Tips for young creators

"There was an eclipse of the sun at the very moment I was born in Birmingham, England on April 17, 1949... That's not true. The birth stuff is real. The eclipse, I made up. It sounds better that way, more interesting. Writers have to grab their readers in the first few sentences. The last thing I write in a novel is the first paragraph.

"Wherever you live in Canada, fishing village, big city, prairie farm, northern settlement, everyone is doing something that would interest a reader somewhere. Why don't you think about putting it on paper?"

Martyn Godfrey

BIBLIOGRAPHY

Godfrey, Martyn. *The Vandarian Incident*. Richmond Hill: Scholastic Canada, 1982. Rpt. as *The Day the Sky Exploded* 1991 Paper 0-590-74089-X.

—. *Alien War Games*. Richmond Hill: Scholastic Canada, 1984. Rev. Ed. 1996 Paper 0-590-71224-1.

—. *The Beast* (Series Canada 4). Don Mills: Maxwell Macmillan Canada, 1984 Paper 0-02-947160-5.

—. *Spin Out* (Series Canada 4). Don Mills: Maxwell Macmillan Canada, 1984 Paper 0-02-947170-2.

—. *Fire! Fire!* (Series Canada 5). Don Mills: Maxwell Macmillan Canada, 1985 Paper 0-02-947300-4.

—. *Here She Is, Ms. Teeny-Wonderful!* Richmond Hill: Scholastic Canada, 1984. 1991 Paper 0-590-74251-5.

—. *Ice Hawk* (Series Canada 5). Don Mills: Maxwell Macmillan Canada, 1985 Paper 0-02-947310-1.

—. *Plan B Is Total Panic* (Time of Our Lives Series). Toronto: James Lorimer & Co., 1986 Paper 0-88862-850-1; Cloth 0-88862-851-X.

—. *The Last War* (Series 2000). Don Mills: Maxwell Macmillan Canada, 1986 Paper 0-02-947380-2.

—. *Baseball Crazy*. Toronto: James Lorimer & Co., 1987. Rev. Ed. 1996 Paper 1-55028-512-2; Cloth 1-55028-513-0.

—. *It Isn't Easy Being Ms. Teeny-Wonderful*. Richmond Hill: Scholastic Canada, 1987. 1991 Paper 0-590-74252-3.

—. *It Seemed Like A Good Idea At The Time*. Edmonton: Tree Frog Press, 1987 Paper 0-88967-060-9.

—. *More Than Weird* (Series 2000). Don Mills: Maxwell Macmillan Canada, 1987 Paper 0-02-953499-2.

—. *Rebel Yell* (Series Canada 6). Don Mills: Maxwell Macmillan Canada, 1987. Out of print.

—. *Wild Night* (Series Canada 6). Don Mills: Maxwell Macmillan Canada, 1987 Paper 0-02-947420-5.

—. *Break Out* (Series Canada 7). Don Mills: Maxwell Macmillan Canada, 1988 Paper 0-02-953543-3.

—. *Mystery in the Frozen Lands* (Adventures in Canadian History). Toronto: James Lorimer & Co., 1988 Paper 1-55028-137-2; Cloth 1-55028-144-5.

—. *Send In Ms. Teeny-Wonderful*. Richmond Hill: Scholastic Canada, 1988. 1991 Paper 0-590-74253-1.

—. *In the Time of the Monsters* (Series 2000). Don Mills: Maxwell Macmillan Canada, 1989 Paper 0-02-953549-2.

—. *Why Just Me?* Toronto: McClelland & Stewart, 1989 Paper 0-7710-3367-2. Richmond Hill: Scholastic Canada, 1996 Paper 0-590-24919-3.

—. *Can You Teach Me to Pick My Nose?* New York: Avon Books, 1990. Out of print.

—. *I Spent My Summer Kidnapped Into Space*. New York: Scholastic, 1990. Out of print.

—. *Monsters in the School*. Richmond Hill: Scholastic Canada, 1991 Paper 0-590-74046-6.

—. *Don't Worry About Me, I'm Just Crazy* (Gemini Series). Don Mills: Stoddart, 1992. Paper 0-7736-7364-4.

—. *Is It Okay If This Monster Stays for Lunch?* Don Mills: Stoddart/Oxford University Press, 1992. 1997 Paper 0-7737-5893-3. Illustrations by Susan Wilkinson.

—. *The Great Science Fair Disaster*. New York: Scholastic, 1992. Out of print.

—. *Wally Stutzgummer, Super Bad Dude* (Carol & Wally Series 4). Richmond Hill: Scholastic Canada, 1992 Paper 0-590-74033-4.

—. *Please Remove Your Elbow From My Ear*. New York: Avon Books, 1993 Paper 0-380-76580-2.

—. *Meet You in the Sewer* (J.A.W.S. Mob Series). Richmond Hill: Scholastic Canada, 1993 Paper 0-590-73082-7.

—. *Just Call Me Boom Boom* (J.A.W.S. Mob Series). Richmond Hill: Scholastic Canada, 1994. Out of print.

—. *Mall Rats* (Flash Fiction Series). Edmonton: Oz New Media, 1994 Paper 1-896295-00-2.

—. *The Things* (Flash Fiction Series). Edmonton: Oz New Media, 1994 Paper 1-896295-02-9.

—. *The Hunt for Buried Treasure*. New York: Avon Books, 1996 Paper 0-380-77502-6.

—. *The Mystery of Hole's Castle*. New York: Avon Books, 1996 Paper 0-380-77501-8.

—. *The Desperate Escape*. New York: Avon Books, 1997 Paper 0-380-77504-2.

Godfrey, Martyn, and Frank O'Keeffe. *There's a Cow in My Swimming Pool*. Richmond Hill: Scholastic Canada, 1991 Paper 0-590-74045-8.

Awards

1985 Vicky Metcalf Short Story Award for "Here She Is, Ms. Teeny-Wonderful!" in *Crackers Magazine*

1987 University of Lethbridge Children's Book Award for *Here She is Ms. Teeny Wonderful!*

1989 Geoffrey Bilson Award for Historical Fiction for Young People for *Mystery in the Frozen Lands*

1993 Manitoba Young Reader's Choice Award for *Can You Teach Me to Pick My Nose?*

Linda Granfield
AUTHOR

Born
November 22, 1950, Boston Massachusetts, U.S.A.

School
"Schools in Melrose, Massachusetts. I have a B.A., an M.A. and almost a doctorate. (The doctorate is how I came to be in Canada.)"

Where I live now
"In a Toronto suburb; a brick bungalow, with loads of trees and loads of leaves to rake every fall."

My favourite book when I was young
Little Women, and the *Snipp, Snapp, Snurr* books by Maj Lindman; also biographies for children.

Career
"I have worked in libraries and milk stores, taught university classes, sold books, been a 'window display artist' and am now doing what I love best, researching, writing."

Family
Husband, Cal Smiley; two children, Devon and Brian.

The room where I create
"An unfinished area of the basement that my family called 'the pit' has been replaced by a lovely, bright room. There is a big desk for the computer, huge filing cabinets for all the research 'stuff' I collect, walls of bookcases filled with reference books, pictures of my family, an old rocking chair, and the old green stool that we used for our family circus when I was a kid."

Spare time
"Read books not related to my work, fiddle with the garden, visit art and historical museums, have picnics with my family, do needlework and art, watch good TV, go to plays, visit the ocean in the summer."

When I was growing up
"I was tall with skinny legs and ate two or three sandwiches every day for lunch. I have five brothers and sisters (I'm the oldest) and we lived 20 minutes from the Atlantic Ocean. I hated math, sports, oatmeal and dry cereals (still do!). I loved school and reading — summertime meant oodles of time to read. I thought I might be a ballerina, an airline attendant, a teacher, and/or a writer. I wrote for a school newspaper in Grade 5 and just kept on writing. And I thought I was Annie Oakley for a while (around age four).

"At 16, I was interviewing people for school and community papers. One visiting English boy I wrote about in high school is still my penpal."

My first book (and how it happened)
"I was writing for *Quill & Quire* (a newspaper about books) and went to a convention. Someone from Kids Can Press asked me when I was going to stop writing about Canadian kids' books and write one myself. The result of that conversation was *All About Niagara Falls* which was published in 1988."

Where my ideas come from
"Many of my ideas come from research I'm doing for another book. For example, when I was collecting material for *In Flanders Fields*, I found a story about 'Silent Night' being sung in the trenches during World War I. More research into that subject resulted in the book *Silent Night*. And the rodeo clown research I did for *Cowboy* led me to learn more about the circus — voila, *Circus!* I enjoyed doing the work on World War I, so I continued with World War II — now there's *High Flight*, about a young Spitfire pilot."

Who and what influenced me
"Any book I've read — any good teacher I had, someone who urged me to express myself. (Even in non-fiction, an author gets to show her own personality.) My childhood in history-rich Boston definitely shaped what I do.

When you live where history happened and people tell stories about it, history is never boring."

How I work

"Every day I work in some aspect of the book business: school visits, conferences, answering mail, writing speeches. I spend from one to four years researching a book: I collect material at libraries, museums, old junk stores, antique shops, and I also interview quite a few people when preparing a book.

"Once all the research is done (it usually fills about 1,000 pages), it's time to follow an outline and write the first draft. (That's the most difficult part for me — that first draft!) I write many drafts for each book. I enjoy working with the editor, making each draft better than the last. After the book goes to the printer, I go back to one of my other topics — I usually work at three or four at a time."

Something nobody knew about me (until now)

"When I was a baby, I won a beautiful baby contest."

My favourite book that I've created

"I'm always excited about a new project, gradually I have bad days when I get 'sick of it' and then get excited again when I see the finished product. By then, I'm all excited about another project. (There's never enough time!)"

Tips for young creators

"Read everything — cereal boxes, classics, comics, travel books, maps, candy wrappers. It all helps create your writing style. Don't lock yourself into one area; if you've run into a problem with your poem, write a short story. Keep a journal. Don't rush to 'grow up.' Most writers say their best ideas come from their childhoods."

Linda Granfield

BIBLIOGRAPHY

Granfield, Linda. *All About Niagara Falls*. Toronto: Kids Can Press, 1988 Paper 0-921103-39-5. Illustrations by Sandi Hemsworth and Pat Cupples.

—. *Canada Votes: How We Elect Our Government*. Toronto: Kids Can Press, 1990. Rev. Ed. 1997 Paper 1-55074-250-7. Illustrations by Craig Terlson.

—. *Cowboy: A Kid's Album*. Toronto: Groundwood Books, 1993 Cloth 1-55054-230-3.

—. *Extra! Extra!: The Who, What, Where, When and Why of Newspapers*. Toronto: Kids Can Press, 1993 Paper 1-55074-122-5. Illustrations by Bill Slavin.

—. *1987, the Year I Was Born*. Toronto: Kids Can Press, 1994 Paper 1-55074-144-6. Illustrations by Bill Slavin.

—. *1988, the Year I Was Born*. Toronto: Kids Can Press, 1995 Paper 1-55074-192-6. Illustrations by Bill Slavin.

—. *In Flanders Fields: The Story of the Poem by John McCrae*. Toronto: Lester Publishing, 1995. Toronto: Stoddart, 1996 Paper 0-7737-5925-5; Cloth 0-7737-2991-7. Illustrations by Janet Wilson.

—. *1984, the Year I Was Born*. Toronto: Kids Can Press, 1996 Paper 1-55074-309-0. Illustrations by Bill Slavin.

—. *Amazing Grace: The Story of the Hymn*. Toronto: Tundra Books, 1997 Cloth 0-88776-389-8. Illustrations by Janet Wilson.

—. *Postcards Talk*. Markham: Pembroke Publishers, 1997 Paper 1-55138-033-1; Cloth 1-55138-032-3. Illustrations by Mark Thurman.

—. *Silent Night: The Song from Heaven*. Toronto: Tundra Books, 1997 Cloth 0-88776-395-2. Illustrations by Nelly and Ernst Hofer.

—. *Circus*. Toronto: Groundwood Books, 1997 Cloth 0-88899-292-0.

—. *The Legend of the Panda*. Toronto: Tundra Books, 1998 Cloth 0-88776-421-5. Illustrations by Song Nan Zhang.

—. *High Flight: A Story of World War II*. Toronto: Tundra Books, 1999 Cloth 0-88776-469-X. Illustrations by Michael Martchenko.

—. *Pier 21: Gateway of Hope*. Toronto: Tundra Books, 2000 Paper 0-88776-517-3.

Granfield, Linda, and Andrea Wayne von Königslöw. *The Make-Your-Own-Button Book*. Toronto: Somerville House, 1993 Paper (with button kit) 0-921051-89-1. Illustrations by Andrea Wayne von Königslöw.

Granfield, Linda, and Pat Hancock. *Brain Quest Canada* (game). Toronto: Thomas Allen & Son, 1998 0-7611-1279-0.

Awards

1994 Information Book Award for *Cowboy: A Kid's Album*

1995 IODE Book Award — Muncipal Chapter of Toronto for *In Flanders Fields: The Story of the Poem by John McCrae*

1996 Information Book Award for *In Flanders Fields: The Story of the Poem by John McCrae*

Selected articles about Linda Granfield

"Linda Granfield." *Something about the Author: Autobiography Series*. Detroit: Gale Research, vol. 96: 112-115.

Wishinsky, Frieda. "Breathing History: Frieda Wishinsky Talks with Linda Granfield." *Books in Canada* 26.1: 1997.

Barbara Greenwood
AUTHOR

Born
September 14, Toronto, Ontario

School
Davisville Public School;
Armour Heights Public School;
Lawrence Park Collegiate;
Toronto Teachers College;
University of Toronto; all in
Toronto, Ontario

Where I live now
Toronto, Ontario

Career
Writer, teacher.

Family
Husband and four grown-up
children.

The room where I create
"My first book, *A Question of
Loyalty*, was written at the
dining room table. Now I have
an office of my own."

Spare time
"I enjoy singing in choirs."

When I was growing up
"I remember my Grade 2 teacher
reading the class a book called
Smiling Hill Farm. I've never
been able to find the book in any
library and I'm sure it wasn't
wonderful literature, but to this
day I can call up the images of its
pioneer family climbing into a
covered wagon and the slow
journey through the woods of
Indiana to their special place —
the hill on which to build first a
log cabin and finally a brick
house. I entered fully into that
special place and it coloured my
daydreams for years. The books I
chose to read were all set in the
past. In Grades 3 and 4 I followed
the Oregon Trail, was captured
by Indians, rode with the cattle
ranchers and built railroads.

"One place I never found
myself on these story-trips was
in Canada's past, and by the time
I was in my teens I wanted to
know why. I knew interesting
events had taken place here.
Almost everyday I passed the
post office on the site of
Montgomery's Tavern where
William Lyon Mackenzie and his
rebels gathered before their
brave but fruitless march down
Yonge Street to try to wrest their
rights from the Family Compact
in 1837. The story fascinated me
and that earlier Yonge Street of
mud and wild emotion lay fallow
in my imagination for many
years before I tried to make it
live for others as it lived in me."

My first book (and how it happened)
"When I decided to write, it
seemed natural that I should set
my stories in the Canadian past.
During high school I began my
first novel, a sort of '*Gone with
the Wind North*' set during the
Mackenzie Rebellion. Unfortunately, this manuscript was
lost long ago during one of my
moves.

"Years later when I decided to
make another attempt at
writing, I wondered if it even
made sense to write historical
fiction for children. My experience as a teacher and a
mother told me that children
read any story that catches their
imagination.

"Stories are about characters
in conflict. The Mackenzie
Rebellion offers many such
situations. My first book, *A
Question of Loyalty*, centres on a
family who find a wounded rebel
in the barn and then have to
choose between a safe action
and a dangerous but humani-
tarian one."

Where my ideas come from
"I always visit the area where
each book is set because I need
to establish the 'lay of the land;'
and the feel of the times.
Novelists build 'place' by sensory
detail. What did the setting feel
like, smell like, taste like, sound
like?

"Years ago, as the mother of
four children aged five to 15, I
needed an oasis of peace and
quiet in a life of bustle and noise.
Because of my interest in
Canada's pioneers, I found that
oasis at our local museum,
Gibson House. As a volunteer

guide I spent an afternoon a week dressed in an 1850s costume sitting in the front parlour doing embroidery, churning butter in the kitchen, helping with the baking and learning to spin. I took in the feel of that house, those olden times, through my ears, eyes and fingers. That experience was invaluable in creating the Wallbridge home, in *A Question of Loyalty*."

Who and what influenced me
"When I was a teenager, my reading was wide-ranging — biographies, fiction and plays. Writing, however, was not encouraged in school until Grade 11, when a wonderful English teacher who insisted on creative writing in the curriculum, urged me to write. I was also inspired by authors like the American writer Elswyth Thane, who wrote a series of fascinating historical novels. A book from my high school days, Geoffrey Trease's *Cue for Treason*, showed me how to make the reader feel comfortable with the past."

How I work
"I usually research for three or four months, filling my mind with images and the atmosphere of the time and place. As I hunt for real-life incidents to give authenticity to the story, I ask myself, 'Who could be doing this?' and the characters start to form themselves.

"Sometimes bits and pieces of people I know become part of my characters. Gottlieb Hahn from *Spy in the Shadows*, for example, started with my father, a master craftsman who designed and made fine jewellery. Just like Gottlieb, the bell-maker, my father expected his children to do their best all the time. Helped by such recollections, I find that my characters begin to take on their own personalities.

"Important as research is, I believe the novelist's skill in recreating the past comes not so much from collecting information as stripping it away so that background details enhance rather than smother the story. The essence of every story, after all, is the people and the conflicts with which they have to wrestle."

Barbara Greenwood

BIBLIOGRAPHY
Greenwood, Barbara. *A Question of Loyalty*. Richmond Hill: Scholastic Canada, 1984 Paper 0-590- 71450-3.

—. *Jeanne Sauvé*. Markham: Fitzhenry & Whiteside, 1989 Paper 0-88902-854-0.

— *Challenge of the Klondike: Rachel Hanna – Frontier Nurse* (Heritage Series). Toronto: Grolier, 1990 Cloth 0-7172-2572-0.

—. *Spy in the Shadows*. Toronto: Kids Can Press, 1990 Paper 1-55074-018-0.

— ed. *Presenting Children's Authors, Illustrators and Performers*. Markham: Pembroke Publishers, 1990 Paper 0-921217-45-5.

—. *A Pioneer Story: The Daily Life of a Canadian Family in 1840*. Toronto: Kids Can Press, 1994 Paper 1-55074-128-4; Cloth 1-55074-237-X. Illustrations by Heather Collins.

—. *Speak Up! Speak Out! Every Kid's Guide to Planning, Preparing and Presenting a Speech*. Markham: Pembroke Publishers, 1994 Paper 1-55138-030-7. Illustrations by Graham Pilsworth.

— ed. *Behind the Story*. Markham: Pembroke Publishers, 1995 Paper 1-55138-058-7.

—. *Pioneer Crafts*. Toronto: Kids Can Press, 1997 Paper 1-55074-359-7. Illustrations by Heather Collins.

—. *The Kids Book of Canada*. Toronto: Kids Can Press, 1997 Cloth 1-55074-315-5. Illustrations by Jock MacRae.

—. *The Last Safe House: A Story of the Underground Railroad*. Toronto: Kids Can Press, 1998 Paper 1-55074-507-7; Cloth 1-55074-509-3. Illustrations by Heather Collins.

—. *A Pioneer Thanksgiving: A Story of Harvest Celebrations in 1841*. Toronto: Kids Can Press, 1999 Paper 1-55074-574-3 Cloth 1-55074-744-4. Illustrations by Heather Collins.

Greenwood, Barbara, and Hancock, Pat. *The Other Side of the Story*. Richmond Hill: Scholastic Canada, 1990 Paper 0-590-73643-4.

Greenwood, Barbara, and Audrey McKim. *Her Special Vision: A Biography of Jean Little* (Contemporary Canadian Biographies Series). Concord: Irwin, 1987 Paper 0-7725-1664-2.

Awards
1982 Vicky Metcalf Short Story Award for "A Major Resolution" in *Contexts 1*

1992 White Ravens Selection of the International Youth Library, Munich for *Spy in the Shadows*

1994 Mr. Christie's Book Award for *A Pioneer Story: The Daily Life of a Canadian Family in 1840*

1995 Ruth Schwartz Children's Book Award for *A Pioneer Story: The Daily Life of a Canadian Family in 1840*

1996 Information Award for *A Pioneer Story: The Daily Life of a Canadian Family in 1840*

Selected articles about Barbara Greenwood
Goodall, Lian. "Profile: the Historical Fiction of Barbara Greenwood." *Canadian Children's Literature* 83 (1996): 69-73.

Granfield, Linda. "Barbara Greenwood." *Behind the Story*. Markham: Pembroke Publishing, 1995: 43-45.

"Profile: Barbara Greenwood." *CANSCAIP News* 13.2 (1991).

Pat Hancock
AUTHOR

Born
Hamilton, Ontario

School
St. Ann's Elementary, Cathedral Girls' High, Hamilton Teachers' College, B.A. from McMaster University, Hamilton, Ontario

My favourite books when I was young
"*Heidi, Tom Sawyer, Huckleberry Finn*; all of L. M. Montgomery's and Louisa May Alcott's books, plus any historical fiction I could find."

My favourite book now
"*To Kill A Mockingbird* is still one of my favourite books, but there are too many to name here."

Career
Playground leader, waitress, high school science and English teacher, occasional teacher for elementary school's gifted program, writer, editor.

Family
"I married Ron Hancock (from New Zealand) in 1970; we have three children, Katharine, Jennifer, Michael."

The room where I create
"I wish I could say I have a room of my own, but I end up doing almost all of my writing on the dining room table (makes for a very messy dining room sometimes when I'm knee-deep in research). I use a laptop computer."

Spare time
"What spare time?!?! Reading, watching films, playing bridge, visiting with friends."

When I was growing up
"I was the eldest (two sisters, one brother) child of hard-working parents and we didn't have much money. I hated when Stelco went on strike – my dad worked there – or when my mom was really sick – before medicare — because then we really had to pinch pennies.

"I absolutely loved school and learning new things in every subject except music, because I couldn't sing (I still can't) and the teachers used to make you sing and I was really embarrassed. In Grade 7 and 8, I had a bit of trouble fitting in, because I had skipped two grades, but high school was great, maybe in part because it was an all-girls' school. But the boys' school was just a block away, and we had lots of co-ed clubs and activities."

My first book (and how it happened)
"I'd been doing articles for a Scholastic magazine for teachers (*Classroom*) and Scholastic's annual *Get Organized: Student Planner* for a couple of years when I was asked to do a series of sticker books for them. So my first book was *Unicorns*, the first in the *Sticker Fun* series. It's just been reissued after being out of print for the last four or five years, with a wonderful new cover and some new information too."

Where my ideas come from
"From reading, from asking myself 'What if...?' and from watching, talking with and listening to people whenever I get a chance to do so."

Who and what influenced me
"Everything I read.

"A very special high school English teacher, Mrs. Evelyn Mullen, who constantly challenged me to do my best. Demanding, but always fair; she led by her example – she was very hard-working, and was always prepared. I was very lucky to have her in Grades 11, 12, and 13.

"The founding author members of CANSCAIP, especially Madeline Freeman, from whom I took a course called 'Stretch What You Know and Write for Children' in 1976-77 (that got me started), and Claire Mackay, who has always been so supportive, especially when I'm feeling overwhelmed by all the research I'm doing for a non-fiction book."

How I work

"If I'm writing a short story, I spend weeks playing around with an idea (usually for a plot) in my head. All that time, I'm looking for a way to start the story. Even if I have a really good sense of what will happen and even how the story will end, I can't begin writing until I have a good beginning.

"When I'm writing non-fiction, the first thing I do is begin reading. I dig out my own books (there are over a thousand in this house), and I head off to the library to get more. Then I start reading and making notes. I do that by hand, jotting things down as I read. Somewhere along the way, I usually come up with one really interesting fact that gives me an idea for how to start the book. Here again, I can't start writing until I have my 'beginning.' That's because how I start the book will help me shape the rest of it, and connect everything so that it feels as if one thing leads nicely to the next, all the way through.

"Many times along the way, I have to stop writing and check some facts or do a little more research. Then, when I'm finally done, I read through the book a few times, tightening it up and changing how I've worded something so that it's easier to understand or so that it sounds better. I often read what I've written out loud, especially to my writing group (of children's authors — we've been meeting once a month for 20 years). When I do that, I can tell if I like the 'rhythm' of the words and sentences. Then, I make any more final changes, and breathe a huge sigh of relief."

Something nobody knew about me (until now)

"I can't swim. I have no idea why I can't swim. I'm not afraid of water; in fact, I love it. And I took more swimming lessons than anybody else around, from when I was a kid all the way through to university. But I just can't do anything more than dog paddle for a few seconds before I start to sink. Thank goodness I can hold my breath for a long time."

My favourite book that I've created

"*The Kids Book of Canadian Prime Ministers* is special. The illustrator, John Mantha, and the people at Kids Can Press, helped me make that a book that I think will spark younger readers' interest in Canadian history, a subject I always love to learn more about."

Tips for young creators

"When trying to come up with story ideas, ask yourself, 'What if...?' Ask it about ordinary, every-day people, places, and things around you. Let your mind go where your imagination takes you in these 'what if' situations until some character or event catches your fancy. Then start writing. Jot down great ideas as soon as you get them, whether writing fiction or non-fiction. Read your work out loud — to yourself or a friend or family member — so that your ears as well as your eyes can help you make it better. Read, read, read!!!"

Pat Hancock

BIBLIOGRAPHY

Hancock, Pat. Scholastic *Sticker Fun* Series. Richmond Hill: Scholastic Canada. Illustrations by Mark Thurman.
   Unicorns 1988 0-590-71891-6.
   Weird Animals 1988 0-590-71893-2.
   Dinosaurs 1989 0-590-73167-X.
   Monsters 1989 0-590-73169-6.
   Prehistoric Animals 1991 0-590-74028-8.
   Creatures of the Night 1992 0-590-74085-7.
   Poisonous Creatures 1993 0-590-74087-3.

—. *Strange and Eerie Stories*. New York: Scholastic, 1994 0-590-20258-8. Illustrations by Allan and Deborah Drew-Brook-Cormack.

—. *1985, the Year I Was Born*. Kids Can Press, 1996 1-55074-308-2. Illustrations by Bill Slavin.

—. *1986, the Year I Was Born*. Toronto: Kids Can Press, 1997 1-55074-323-6. Illustrations by Bill Slavin.

—. *One-A-Day Facts and Fun*. Richmond Hill: Scholastic Canada 1997 Cloth 0-590-16454-6.

—. *The Kids Book of Canadian Prime Ministers*. Toronto: Kids Can Press, 1998 Cloth 1-55074-473-9. Illustrations by John Mantha.

—. *Unicorns*. 2nd Ed. Richmond Hill: Scholastic Canada 1998 Paper 0-590-03854-0. Illustrations by Yuksel Hassan

—. *Knights in Rusty Armour*. Richmond Hill: Scholastic Canada, 1998 Paper 0-590-50800-8.

—. *The Penguin Book of Canadian Biography for Young Readers: Early Canada*. Toronto: Penguin Books Canada 1999 Cloth 0-670-88600-9.

— et al. *The Pathfinder's Adventure Kit: How to Find Your Way Anywhere!* Toronto: Somerville House Publishing, 1993 Paper 0-921051-79-4. Illustrations by William Kimber.

Hancock, Pat, and Linda Granfield. *Brain Quest Canada* (game). Toronto: Thomas Allen & Son, 1998.

Hancock, Pat, and Barbara Greenwood. *The Other Side of the Story*. Richmond Hill: Scholastic Canada, 1990 Paper 0-590-73643-4.

Hancock, Pat, and Allan Gould. *Ghosts and Other Scary Stories*. Richmond Hill: Scholastic Canada, 1993 0-590-47162-7.

Pat Hancock has also written the *Classroom Teacher's Diary* and the *Scholastic Canada Student Organizer/Diary* annually since 1986.

James Heneghan
AUTHOR

Born
1930, Liverpool, England

School
St. Oswald's, St. Elizabeth's, De La Salle; Simon Fraser University, Burnaby, British Columbia

Where I live now
Vancouver, British Columbia

My favourite books when I was young
The *Saint* books (by Leslie Charteris); the *William* books (by Richmal Crompton) and all sci-fi books.

Career
"Liverpool 'copper' — policeman — two years; fingerprint specialist with Vancouver police, working in crime lab, 12 years; high school teacher in Burnaby, 20 years."

Family
"Two boys and two girls, who are now all grown up. They moved away to make their own homes. I am thinking that I might replace them with four goldfish. Or I could get a cat. Or a dog."

Spare time
"Reading, climbing the Grouse Grind (Vancouver's Grouse Mountain), drinking tea."

When I was growing up
"My brother (one year younger) and I — if we had any money — would skip out of school, buy ice cream (Walls brand), and ride on a train to the Pier Head and watch the ferry boats coming and going. Whenever we were in disgrace and were sent to our room (shared) we sometimes escaped out the window onto a lower roof (the back kitchen), and survived by stealing carrots from vegetable gardens of unsuspecting neighbours. The carrots were rubbed on shirt sleeves and eaten raw.

"It is obvious to me now that those *Saint* and *William* books were a bad influence and should have been taken away from us. This is not even mentioning the many "Saint" signs we drew or painted on neighbours' gates and doors and walls. Our parents were very happy to see us leave home."

My first book (and how it happened)
"*Puffin Rock*, Book Society of Canada, 1980, was written by myself and fellow teacher Bruce McBay (taking turns to write chapters), and was based on kids in the school where we taught (many of them looked and behaved like puffins)."

Where my ideas come from
"Newspaper stories, pictures on TV/magazines, reading materials."

Who and what influenced me
"Dunno, unless it was the idea of belonging more closely to the world of books. I've been influenced by each and every writer, and all the books I ever read."

How I work
"I drink lots of tea and hope things will work out okay.

"How long does it take to write a book? If my wife doesn't give me too many jobs to do (shopping and vacuuming and taking her stuff to the cleaners) a book takes about a year."

Something nobody knew about me (until now)
"I was the tallest kid in my elementary school. I was so tall (and skinny) that other kids who were being bullied used to come and ask me to protect them. I did the best I could, acting tough, but underneath I was really a wimp."

My favourite book that I've created
"*Promises to Come* (Kits House, 1998) has a girl protagonist. 'Write about what you know,' say the experts. Well, I've never been a girl, so I'm happy things worked out okay."

Tips for young creators
"For writers? Read! Read whatever you want. But read! Read

anything: computer and car manuals, comics, books, plays, cereal cartons. Limit your TV watching to an hour a day or less (or five to seven hours a week to be used anytime during the week). Choose your reading carefully. Except for school and homework, read only stuff you enjoy reading. Try to get in the habit of reading every day. Keep it up and soon you will have bulging muscles on your brain and you will be itching to write your own stuff."

James Heneghan

BIBLIOGRAPHY

Heneghan, James. *Puffin Rock.* Agincourt: The Book Society of Canada, 1980. Out of print.

—. *Goodbye, Carleton High.* Scholastic Canada, 1983. Out of print.

—. *Promises to Come.* Markham: Overlea House, 1988. Vancouver: Kits House, 1998 Paper 0- 9684300- 0-7.

—. *Blue.* Richmond Hill: Scholastic Canada, 1991 Paper 0-590-74044-X.

—. *The Case of the Marmalade Cat* (O'Brien Detective Agency Series). Richmond Hill: Scholastic Canada, 1992 Paper 0-590-73824-0.

—. *The Trail of the Chocolate Thief* (O'Brien Detective Agency Series). Richmond Hill: Scholastic Canada, 1993. Out of print.

—. *Torn Away.* New York: Viking, 1994. Out of print.

—. *The Mystery of the Gold Ring* (O'Brien Detective Agency Series). Richmond Hill: Scholastic Canada, 1995 Paper 0-590-24623-2.

—. *The Case of the Blue Raccoon* (O'Brien Detective Agency Series). Richmond Hill: Scholastic Canada, 1996 Paper 0-590-74044-X.

—. *Wish Me Luck.* New York: Farrar Straus and Giroux, 1997 Cloth 0-374-38453-3.

Awards

1994 Arthur Ellis Award for *Torn Away*

1997 Sheila A. Egoff Award for *Wish Me Luck*

Selected articles about James Heneghan

Hill, Mary Frances. "Brave Tales." *West Ender* 6 Nov. 1997: 9.

Jobe, Ronald. "Canadian Connections." *Journal of Adolescent and Adult Literacy* Apr. 1998: 596.

Oppel, Kenneth. "Humbly Yours, James Heneghan." *Quill and Quire* Feb. 98: 20, 43.

Pamela Mary Hickman
AUTHOR

Born
Cooksville, Ontario

School
Lorne Park P.S., White Oaks P.S., Queen Elizabeth Senior P.S., Lorne Park Secondary School; University of Waterloo, Waterloo, Ontario

Where I live now
Canning, Nova Scotia

My favourite books when I was young
"Historical fiction and biographies such as the *Little House on the Prairie* series or *Indian Captive*."

My favourite books now
"I still like biographies, but I also enjoy a good murder mystery (Gail Bowen), historical books (Robert MacNeil), short stories (Budge Wilson) and adventure (John Grisham)."

Career
"In high school I worked as a camp counsellor during the summers. In university, my summer jobs were science-related. I worked at the Horticultural Research Station in Simcoe, Ontario as a technician for one summer. I went to Alberta and worked on the province's mosquito control program in the wetlands. Another year, I worked at the Alberta Environment Centre as a technician. My first writing job was as the Education Coordinator for the Federation of Ontario Naturalists. I wrote educational kits about nature and the environment for teachers to use in their classrooms. I worked there for seven years. I am now a freelance writer."

Family
"I am married (since 1981) and have three daughters."

The room where I create
"I live in an old house that was built in 1763. Attached to it is the old barn which has been renovated inside to make it feel and look more like part of the house. My office is a room in the renovated part. It is small and usually quite messy with my reference books and papers all over. I have my computer on the same little wooden desk that I had when I was a young girl. I also have a bed in my office which doubles as a guest room when we have company!"

Spare time
"I love to garden. My family and I also spend a lot of time camping in the summer. Travelling is another one of my favourite things, although it is harder to fit in."

When I was growing up
"When I was young, my parents believed that it was important that my sister, my two brothers and I see all of Canada. They took us camping across Canada each summer until we had been to every province and its capital, as well as both northern territories. I have many memories of scenery and wildlife including bears, mountain sheep and elk."

My first book (and how it happened)
"While I was working for the Federation of Ontario Naturalists, I thought it would be fun to write a children's book about nature. One day I was at a teachers' conference showing them the education kits I had written. At other tables there were many children's book publishers. I walked over to one of them (Kids Can Press) and asked how I would go about writing a book for children. The woman asked for samples of my work and took them back to her office. A couple of months later they called and asked if I would be interested in writing a book on birds for children. That was how *Birdwise* started."

Where my ideas come from
"I usually choose subjects from things that interest me in nature. My publisher may also have an idea and ask if I would be interested in writing about it. The activities in my books come from different places. Sometimes I just figure out something and try it to

make sure it works; some activities are adapted from other books. I also get ideas from my children or their friends."

Who and what influenced me

"My experiences in the outdoors with my parents sparked my initial interest in nature. Some of my teachers and courses at university encouraged my love of science, as did my work at the Ontario Naturalists. My Grade 12 English teacher, Ms. Rosebrough, was very supportive and encouraged my enjoyment of writing."

How I work

"Before I start writing a book, I have to have a detailed outline of what will go into it. I begin my research for the outline by reading a lot of reference books and taking notes. When I actually write the text, I do it spread by spread. I do more research by contacting specialists who study plants and animals, checking facts and going out to do my own observations, when possible. My children often help me try out the activities."

Something nobody knew about me (until now)

"I collect great nature stuff to take with me when I go to talk to classes about my books. If I find a dead animal that is in good shape I put it in my freezer until I have time to take it to a taxidermist to get it stuffed. Right now I have a woodpecker and a star-nosed mole in my freezer!"

My favourite book that I've created

"One of my most special books is *A New Butterfly*. That's because the little girl in the book is my daughter, Connie. She inspired me to write the *My First Look at Nature* series when she was three years old, so I featured her in one of the books."

Pamela Mary Hickman

SELECT BIBLIOGRAPHY

Hickman, Pamela Mary. *Birdwise*. Toronto: Kids Can Press, 1988. Illustrations by Judie Shore. Out of print.

—. *Bugwise*. Toronto: Kids Can Press, 1990. Illustrations by Judie Shore. Out of print.

—. *Plantwise*. Toronto: Kids Can Press, 1991. Illustrations by Judie Shore. Out of print.

—. *Hands on Nature Series*. Markham: Pembroke Publishers, 1992. Illustrations by Judie Shore.
 Introducing Birds Paper 0-921217-93-5.
 Introducing Insects Paper 0-921217-92-7.
 Introducing Trees Paper 0-921217-91-9.
 Introducing Flowers Ferns Fungi and More Paper 0-921217-94-3.
 Introducing Reptiles Paper 0-921217-95-1.

—. *Habitats*. Toronto: Kids Can Press, 1993 Paper 1-55074-066-0. Illustrations by Sarah Jane English.

—. *Wetlands*. Toronto: Kids Can Press, 1993 Paper 1-55074-126-8. Illustrations by Judie Shore.

—. *The Kids Canadian Bird Book*. Toronto: Kids Can Press, 1995 Cloth 1-55074-196-9. 1996 Paper 1-55074-334-1. Illustrations by Heather Collins.

—. *The Kids Canadian Tree Book*. Toronto: Kids Can Press, 1995 Cloth 1-55074-198-5. 1996 Paper 1-55074-336-8. Illustrations by Heather Collins.

—. *The Kids Canadian Bug Book*. Toronto: Kids Can Press, 1996 1-55074-231-0. 1997 Paper 1-55074-329-5. Illustrations by Heather Collins.

—. *The Kids Canadian Plant Book*. 1996 Cloth 1-55074-233-7. 1997 Paper 1-55074-331-7. Illustrations by Heather Collins.

—. *The Night Book*. Toronto: Kids Can Press, 1996 Paper 1-55074-306-6; Cloth 1-55074-318- X. Illustrations by Suzanne Mogensen. ❧

—. *At the Seashore*. Halifax: Formac, 1996 Paper 0-88780-404-7. Illustrations by Twila Robar-DeCoste.

—. *The Jumbo Book of Nature Science*. Toronto: Kids Can Press, 1996 Paper 1-55074-317-1. Illustrations by Judie Shore.

—. *A Seed Grows: My First Look at a Plant's Life Cycle*. Toronto: Kids Can Press, 1997 Cloth 1-55074-200-0. Illustrations by Heather Collins.

—. *Hungry Animals: My First Look at a Food Chain*. Toronto: Kids Can Press, 1997 Cloth 1-55074-204-3. Illustrations by Heather Collins.

—. *A New Butterfly: My First Look at Metamorphosis*. Toronto: Kids Can Press, 1997 Cloth 1-55074-202-7. Illustrations by Heather Collins.

—. *Animal Senses: How Animals See, Hear, Taste, Smell and Feel*. Toronto: Kids Can Press, 1998 Cloth 1-55074-423-2. Illustrations by Pat Stephens.

—. *In the Woods*. Halifax: Formac, 1998 Paper 0-88780-412-8. Illustrations by Twila Robar-DeCoste.

—. *A New Duck*. Toronto: Kids Can Press, 1999 Cloth 1-55074-613-8. Illustrations by Heather Collins.

—. *A New Frog*. Toronto: Kids Can Press, 1999 Cloth 1-55074-615-4. Illustrations by Heather Collins.

Awards

1995 Lilla Stirling Memorial Award for *Habitats*

Selected articles about Pamela Hickman

Elliot, Wendy. "Canning Author Riding Wave of Interest in Kiddie Lit." *The Advertiser* [Kentville] 11 Sept. 1998.

Linda Holeman
AUTHOR

Born
December 24, 1949, Winnipeg, Manitoba

School
B.A., University of Winnipeg; B.Ed. and M.Ed., University of Manitoba, Winnipeg, Manitoba

Where I live now
"Winnipeg, in an old house on the banks of the Red River."

My favourite book when I was young
"I loved the Enid Blyton series; I also gobbled up non-fiction books or biographies of people who invented things."

My favourite book now
"Every year, I find one that I think must be my all-time favourite, but then the next wonderful one comes along."

Career
"Elementary teacher for 10 years, both in the classroom and as a special needs teacher. Now I write full-time, and teach writing."

Family
"My husband Jon, daughters Zalie and Brenna and son Kitt. We have a very small dog, Lewis, and a very hefty rabbit, Bobbie. We also have two Red-Eared Sliders (turtles) who have grown to the size of dinner plates, and will probably live forever. Their names are Cookie and Caramel."

The room where I create
"I finally got a 'room of one's own' about three years ago. It's on the third floor, which means that no one bothers to traipse all the way up to borrow my stapler! My office is cozy and cluttered, and I look out on the backyard, with its trees and the river. Lewis usually sleeps nearby."

Spare time
"My family loves exploring new places. I especially love finding unique bookstores on my travels. Of course my favourite spare time thing to do is read, but I also like doing things that have lots of pieces you have to fit together."

When I was growing up
"Because I was shy and liked to daydream, I found noisy, busy group activities stressful. I never wanted to be a Brownie or go to camp, but I envied the kids who seemed to fit into these situations. It took me awhile to realize that it was okay to like being alone or to be with one real friend.

"I had four siblings, and sometimes my grandmother lived with us, and for a long time my father ran his business out of the house as well, so my home was always full of bustle and activity. I dreamed of being all alone, just for a few hours. Maybe that's what drew me to the library; I spent most of my free time there. I loved books from my earliest school memory; it seems from the first day in Mrs. Anderson's Grade 1 class I started reading and never stopped. My parents weren't readers themselves, and we didn't have many books in our house, but they always encouraged their children to read."

My first book (and how it happened)
"The first stories I tried to write kept coming out in a teenager's voice. When I had written 10 (two had won contests) I sent off a query and a few of the stories to what was then Lester Publishing. Kathy Lowinger wrote back to say she'd like to see the rest of the stories. A few weeks later, she phoned — it was December 3, my son's third birthday; my husband and kids were waiting in the car watching me through the window as I signalled them to wait, jumping up and down with the phone in my hand.

"It was a moment I'd hardly dared to believe could ever happen, but if I had let myself indulge in a dream about having a book published, I saw myself celebrating in a glamorous setting, complete with champagne. As it turned out, I partied in a room with screaming kids jumping into a pit of plastic balls, drinking Coke, and visiting with a large mouse. It was perfect!"

Where my ideas come from

"The usual places — my imagination, and eavesdropping and watching the world around me in detail. A really good book will make me start dreaming about an idea; usually a character will come to me before a plot does. If a particular character keeps bothering me, telling me to listen even when I'm thinking, 'Go away! I'm too busy right now,' eventually I give in. Those persistent characters are the best ones to surround with a story."

Who and what influenced me

"I am always in awe of writers who can move me. I study how they do this, thinking about what they've done to capture a feeling so well. Good books were my first — and will always be the greatest — influence on my writing.

"The adults I grew up around also influenced me greatly — not necessarily to write, but to listen, and think. My mother is from a practical, hard-working Irish-Scottish background of farmers. My father's family were philosophers and dreamers who fled Russia in the first part of the century. The stories I heard!

"Right now my own three children influence me in huge ways. Being a witness and a part of their daily joy and pain as they struggle to grow up brings back my own joy and pain so clearly. It's definitely an asset having teenagers in the house when one is writing about and for them."

How I work

"The hardest work goes on in my head long before I start to write the book. It's only after months of jotting down snippets of dialogue, images of places, and 'what if' kinds of plotting that I take a deep breath and try to pull everything together. Once I begin the actual writing, it goes quite quickly. I never show my work-in-progress to anyone, and I try not to talk too much about it.

"I have no real work schedule. My home life is busy and rather unpredictable. The term I use for my work is 'creativity amidst chaos.' Somehow the work gets done; I'm very self-disciplined, and once I set a goal for myself I'm my own worst enemy. I make lots of lists, even in terms of what I hope to accomplish each week on the story or book I'm writing. That helps."

Something nobody knew about me (until now)

"I don't make any noise when I sneeze. Because I was so self-conscious when I was young, and was afraid of embarrassing myself with an explosive sneeze, I taught myself to hold it in! Now I can't sneeze out loud even if I want to. Don't try it. It must be hard on the ears."

My favourite book that I've created

"Just as I can't decide on my favourite book to read, I can't decide which book of mine I like best. Each of my books has something about it that I really like; each has something I wish I could change."

Tips for young creators

"There's something about noise that interferes with the voices and stories that are in our heads. See what happens if you get up before the rest of your family (I believe we're more creative and open in the morning) and sit at the kitchen table. Just sit there; don't eat, or read or turn on the radio. Listen. It may take a while, but some really interesting thoughts will come to you, thoughts that you can — if you write them down and try to understand them — turn into a story."

Linda Holeman

BIBLIOGRAPHY

Holeman, Linda. *Saying Good-Bye.* Toronto: Stoddart, 1995 Cloth 0-1-89555-47-7.

—. *Frankie on the Run.* Toronto: Boardwalk Books, 1995 Paper 1-895681-09-X.

—. *Flying to Yellow.* Winnipeg: Turnstone Press, 1990 Paper 0-88801-203-9.

—. *Promise Song.* Toronto: Tundra Books, 1997 Paper 0-88776-387-1.

—. *Mercy's Birds.* Toronto: Tundra Books, 1998 0-88776-463-0.

Selected articles about Linda Holeman

Jenkinson, Dave. "Profiles: Linda Holeman." *Resource Links* 2.1 (1996): 8-11.

Pendergast, Sara and Tom Pendergast. *St. James Guide to Young Adult Writers.* St. James Press, 1998.

Waxman, Sydell. "Introducing Linda Holeman." *CANSCAIP News* 19.4 (1997-8): 1-6.

Monica Hughes
AUTHOR

Born
November 3, 1925, Liverpool, England

School
London, England; Edinburgh, Scotland; Harrogate, England

Where I live now
Edmonton, Alberta

My favourite book when I was young
The Enchanted Castle by E. Nesbit (no contest!).

My favourite book now
The Tricksters by Margaret Mahy.

Career
Women's Royal Naval Service (WRNS) during World War II; dress designing in London; working in a dress factory and a bank, Zimbabwe; lab technician at National Research Council, Ottawa; writer.

Family
Husband, Glen; four children, Liz, Adrienne, Russell, Tom; three grandchildren, Melissa, Katherine and Sarah.

The room where I create
"In the living room, with a big bay window, trees outside and music on the CD player. After the 'creating', I work in my study with my word processor and books."

Spare time
"Read, swim, explore new (preferably distant) places, garden (not the heavy work), go to art exhibits, do cryptic crosswords, knit and sew, beachcomb on seaside beaches (which are unfortunately far from Alberta)."

When I was growing up
"I was born in Liverpool, England, but moved soon after with my parents to Cairo, Egypt, where we lived for the next five years. I learned to read before going to school and still remember some of my early books.

"On our return to England I went to a wonderful girls' school where I learned to write in ancient cuneiform symbols and Egyptian hieroglyphs. We were read aloud to: traditional myths and legends, and the Norse sagas. Here I discovered the works of E. Nesbit. In her wonderful blending of everyday life and the world of magic I found something that was to be tremendously important to me, especially when we moved, a couple of years later, to Edinburgh.

"There, the city and climate seemed grey to me, and education was no longer an adventure, but a grind directed towards the final exams. I reread E. Nesbit, holding onto her belief that 'there is a curtain, thin as gossamer, clear as glass, strong as iron, that hangs forever between the world of magic and the world that seems to us to be real. And when once people have found one of the little weak spots in that curtain — almost anything may happen'."

My first book (and how it happened)
"*Crisis on Conshelf Ten* happened as I was struggling to write stories for children and was searching for an idea. I saw a movie by Jacques Cousteau about an undersea house he had built to see if humans could live comfortably and safely underwater. The movie gave me a question

"What would it be like to be a child growing up under the sea? I thought, I don't know the answer, but what fun to find out! The public library gave me the answers, and out of my research came my first science fiction adventure."

Where my ideas come from
"From everywhere: a fact, an idea, a newspaper item, anything that stimulates a question. Finding the answer to the question gives me a story. I find it's very important to write down every possible idea that I find. Otherwise they can be lost — just as dreams are."

Who and what influenced me

"Definitely the books I've read. First, the memory of the great adventures I read as a child, which gave me the sense of story and purpose. Secondly, the children's and young adult books I deliberately read when I decided to become a children's writer in 1971. Those authors became my teachers. Through them, I learned how to write — I am still learning how to write."

How I work

"I pick the 'idea' I want to work on. I start thinking what it might become, where will it be set, who the characters are. As I begin to do necessary research, various incidents that will become part of the story begin to 'appear'. I think about the characters — where they come from, what they're like, until they start talking in their own voices. I often draw maps and plans of houses. Finally, I pick a title, put a disc in the player, pick up my black ballpoint and begin to write."

Something nobody knew about me (until now)

"When I was 12 years old, I was chosen to play Puck in Shakespeare's *A Midsummer Night's Dream*. I set out to learn the lines, getting more and more terrified as the time of the performance grew nearer. Nobody seemed to realize that I was petrified with stage fright. The week before the performance I got a severe ear infection and was off school for a month (there were no antibiotics back then). It was a drastic way of escaping. I've never acted in anything since."

My favourite books that I've created

Hunter in the Dark, Keeper of the Isis Light, The Story Box.

Tips for young creators

"Read good stuff! Keep a journal — not of events — but of people and how they seem to you, of the way in which events change you or your friends, descriptions of places and people. Keep your ears and eyes open and don't neglect your other senses. It will all be useful one day."

Monica Hughes

BIBLIOGRAPHY

—. *Gold Fever Trail: A Klondike Adventure* (Panda Books). Edmonton: J.M Lebel, 1974. Toronto: Stoddart, 1990 Paper 0-7736-7279-6.

—. *Crisis on Conshelf Ten*. London: Hamish Hamilton, 1975. London: Mammoth, 1992. Out of print.

—. *Earthdark*. London: Hamish Hamilton, 1977. London: Mammoth, 1991. Out of print.

—. *The Tomorrow City*. London: Hamish Hamilton, 1978. London: Mammoth, 1992. Out of print.

—. *The Ghost Dance Caper*. London: Hamish Hamilton, 1978. Toronto: General Publishing, 1993 Paper 0-7736-7407-1.

—. *Beyond the Dark River* (Irwin Young Adult). London: Hamish Hamilton, 1979. Toronto: Stoddart, 1992 Paper 0-7737-5522-5.

—. *The Keeper of the Isis Light*. London: Hamish Hamilton, 1980. London: Mammoth, 1991. Toronto: Tundra Books, 2000 Paper 0-88776-508-4.

—. *The Guardian of Isis*. London: Hamish Hamilton, 1980. North York: Houghton Mifflin Canada, 1993. Toronto: Tundra Books, 2000 Paper 0-88776-509-2.

—. *The Isis Pedlar*. London: Hamish Hamilton, 1982. London: Mammoth, 1991. Toronto: Tundra Books, 2000 Paper 0-88776-510-6.

—. *Hunter in the Dark*. Toronto: Clarke Irwin & Company, 1982. 1988 Paper 0-7725-1693-6. Toronto: General Publishing, 1989 Paper 0-7736-7405-5.

—. *Ring-Rise, Ring-Set*. London: Julie MacRae Books, 1982. London: Mammoth, 1992. Out of print.

—. *Beckoning Lights*. Edmonton: J.M Lebel, 1982. Toronto: General Publishing, 1990 Paper 0-7736-7280-X.

—. *Treasure of the Long Sault*. Edmonton: J.M. Lebel Publishing, 1990 Paper 0-7736-7277-X.

—. *Space Trap*. London: Julia MacRae Books, 1983. Toronto: Groundwood Books, 1994 Paper 0-88899-202-5.

—. *My Name is Paula Popowich!* Toronto: James Lorimer & Co., 1983 Paper 0-88862-689-4; Cloth 0-88862-690-8. Illustrations by Leoung O'Young.

—. *Devil on My Back*. Toronto: Bantam, 1986. Out of print.

. *The Dream Catcher*. Agincourt: Methuen, 1986. Toronto: Stoddart, 1988 Paper 0-416-052029.

—. *Sandwriter*. Agincourt: Methuen, 1986. Toronto: General Publishing, 1992 Paper 0-7736-7376-8.

—. *Blaine's Way*. Concord: Irwin Publishing, 1986. Toronto: Stoddart, 1996 Paper 0-7736-7445-43.

—. *Log Jam*. Concord: Irwin Publishing, 1987. Toronto: Stoddart, 1996 Paper 0-7736-7446-2.

—. *The Promise*. Toronto: Stoddart, 1989. 1994 Paper 0-7736-7408-X.

—. *The Refuge*. Toronto: Doubleday Canada, 1989. Toronto: General Publishing, 1992 Paper 0-7736-7377-6.

—. *Little Fingerling*. Toronto: Kids Can Press, 1989. 1992 Paper 1-55074-075-X. Illustrations by Brenda Clark.

—. *Invitation to the Game*. Toronto: HarperCollins, 1990. 1992 Paper 0-00-647414-4.

—. *The Crystal Drop*. Toronto: HarperCollins, 1992. 1993 Paper 0-00-647534-5.

—. *A Handful of Seeds*. Toronto: Lester Publishing, 1993 Cloth 1-895555-27-2. Illustrations by Luis Garay. Introduction by Sharon, Lois & Bram.

—. *The Golden Aquarians*. Toronto: HarperCollins, 1994 Cloth 0-00-224253-2.

—. *Castle Tourmandyne*. Toronto: HarperCollins, 1995 Cloth 0-00-224364-4. 1996 Paper 0- 00-648083-7.

—. *Where Have you Been, Billy Boy?* Toronto: HarperCollins, 1995 Cloth 0-00-224389-X. 1996 Paper 0-00-648133-7.

—. *Seven Magpies*. Toronto: HarperCollins, 1996 Cloth 0-00-224549-3. 1997 Paper 0-00- 648109-4.

—. *Jan's Big Bang*. Toronto: Formac, 1997 Paper 0-88780-384-9; Cloth 0-88780-385-7.

—. *The Faces of Fear*. Toronto: HarperCollins, 1997 Cloth 0-00-224560-4. 1998 Paper 0- 00-648160-4.

— ed. *What If...? Amazing Stories*. Toronto: Tundra Books, 1998 0-88776-458-4.

—. *The Story Box*. Toronto: HarperCollins, 1998 0-00-648051-9.

—. *The Other Place*. Toronto: HarperCollins, 1999 Paper 0-00-648176-0.

—. *Jan on the Trail*. Halifax: Formac, 2000. Paper 0-88780-502-7 Cloth 0-88780-503-5. Illustrations by Carlos Freire.

Awards

1981 Vicky Metcalf Award for a Body of Work

1981 Alberta Culture Juvenile Novel Award for *Hunter in the Dark*

1981 Canada Council Prize for Children's Literature for *The Guardian of Isis*

1982 Canada Council Prize for Children's Literature for *Hunter in the Dark*

1982 R. Ross Annett Award for Children's Literature for *Hunter in the Dark*

1983 R. Ross Annett Award for Children's Literature for *Space Trap*

1983 Vicky Metcalf Short Story Award for "The Iron Barred Door" in *Anthology 2*

1983 Canadian Library Association Young Adult Canadian Book Award for *Hunter in the Dark*

1986 Silver Feather Award (Germany) for *Hunter in the Dark*

1986 R. Ross Annett Award for Children's Literature for *Blaine's Way*

1987 Boeken Leeuw (Book Lion, Belgium) for *Hunter in the Dark*

1992 R. Ross Annett Award for Children's Literature for *The Crystal Drop*

2000 Phoenix Award for *The Keeper of the Isis Light*.

Selected articles about Monica Hughes

"Monica Hughes." In *Something About the Author: Autobiography Series*. ed. Joyce Nakamura. Detroit: Gale Research, vol. 11 (1991).

Gertridge, Allison. *Meet Canadian Authors and Illustrators*. Richmond Hill: Scholastic Canada 1994: 46-7.

Wishinsky, Frieda. "Strength from Solitude." *Books in Canada* 26.2 (1997): 36-7.

Bernice Thurman Hunter
AUTHOR

Born
November 3, 1922, Toronto, Ontario

School
Swansea Public School; Runnymede Collegiate Institute; both in Toronto, Ontario.

Where I live now
Scarborough, Ontario

My favourite book when I was young
Girl of the Limberlost

My favourite book now
The Stone Angel by Margaret Laurence.

Career
Writer

Family
"Two daughters, four grandkids, no pets (I wish I owned a horse)."

The room where I create
"A corner of my bedroom."

Spare time
"Go to movies, travel and read, read, read!"

When I was growing up
"I was a tomboy. I spent half the summer in the top branches of my Aunt Ellie's cherry tree (eating cherries!). I was also a storyteller. I would capture my audience, sit them along the curb, and tell them stories whether they liked it or not."

My first book (and how it happened)
"My first published book was *That Scatterbrain Booky*. In search of short story material, I began writing about my childhood. One memory triggered another, and I found I couldn't stop writing. So I ended up with a book instead of a short story."

That Scatterbrain Booky is the first in the *Booky* trilogy, all of which are based on Bernice's childhood memories of growing up during the Great Depression.

Where my ideas come from
"My ideas come from my memories, my friends' memories, and from my family's pioneer roots (*Lamplighter* is my father's story). I also eavesdrop — on the subway, and in line-ups at the bank and supermarket. You hear the darndest things!"

Who and what influenced me
"The books I read have a big influence on me. My Grade 8 teacher influenced my whole life with his praise and encouragement. His name was Mr. Carl Johnson. He was a fine teacher and a true gentleman. Also, my visit with L. M. Montgomery made me want to be a writer, just like her!"

Bernice didn't begin to write seriously until her fiftieth birthday. A columnist with the *Toronto Star* published a piece she wrote titled "A Grandchild Can Make Life Beautiful Again". Along with some fan mail, he sent her a letter, in which he said "I have never read a more beautiful description of a baby, anytime, anywhere. Keep writing!"

How I work
"A bit haphazardly, I'm afraid. I scribble ideas down constantly (my office area is strewn with notes). I try to write something every day, even if it's only one page. After all a page a day for a year makes a book!"

Bernice tries to work at least two hours a day on her writing. She begins a story by jotting ideas down in longhand at night, when she is least likely to be disturbed. The first chance she gets, she begins typing and retyping. She edits and revises her work until she is reasonably satisfied with it.

Something nobody knew about me (until now)
"Well, I think I spilled the beans in my *Booky* books. In fact, my brothers and sister have reprimanded me severely for giving away all our family secrets."

Tips for young creators

"Keep a journal or diary. Write about all the events in your life, whether they be sad or happy, scary or exciting, or just plain fun. Write, write, write."

My favourite book that I've created

"*Lamplighter*. It is based on my dear old dad's memories. The research that was necessary to recreate the pioneer life of my grandparents brought my roots vividly to life for me."

Bernice comes from pioneer stock on both sides of her family — her paternal great-grandparents settled in the wilds of Muskoka in the 1860s, and her maternal grandparents were among the first settlers of the village of Swansea (now a part of Toronto). They arrived from Cornwall, England in 1847.

Bernice Thurman Hunter

BIBLIOGRAPHY

Hunter, Bernice Thurman. *That Scatterbrain Booky*. Richmond Hill: Scholastic Canada, 1981 Paper 0-590-71082-6.

—. *With Love From Booky*. Richmond Hill: Scholastic Canada, 1983 Paper 0-590-73424-5.

—. *A Place For Margaret*. Richmond Hill: Scholastic Canada, 1984. 1990 Paper 0-590-73665-5.

—. *As Ever, Booky*. Richmond Hill: Scholastic Canada, 1985 Paper 0-590-71547-X.

—. *Margaret In The Middle*. Richmond Hill: Scholastic Canada, 1986. 1990 Paper 0-590-73666-3.

—. *Lamplighter*. Richmond Hill: Scholastic Canada, 1987 Paper 0-590-71373-6.

—. *Margaret On Her Way*. Richmond Hill: Scholastic Canada, 1988 Paper 0-590-73667-1.

—. *The Railroader*. Richmond Hill: Scholastic Canada, 1990 Paper 0-590-73421-0.

—. *The Firefighter*. Richmond Hill: Scholastic Canada, 1991 Paper 0-590-74051-2.

—. *Hawk and Stretch*. Richmond Hill: Scholastic Canada, 1993 Paper 0-590-74814-9.

—. *Amy's Promise*. Richmond Hill: Scholastic Canada, 1995 Paper 0-590-24621-6.

—. *Janey's Choice*. Richmond Hill: Scholastic Canada, 1998 Paper 0-590-12497-8.

—. *Two Much Alike*. Richmond Hill: Scholastic Canada, 2000 Paper 0-590-24844-8.

Awards

1981 IODE Book Award – Municipal Chapter of Toronto for *That Scatterbrain Booky*

1990 Vicky Metcalf Award for a Body of Work

1994 Toronto Historical Board Commendation for *Hawk and Stretch* and *The Firefighter*

1996 Scarborough Bicentennial Award of Merit for outstanding achievements

1998 Red Cedar Book Award for *Amy's Promise*

Selected articles about Bernice Thurman Hunter

"Hawk and Stretch." *Quill & Quire* Nov. 1993.

Hunter, Bernice Thurman. "Inspirations." *Canadian Children's Literature* 84 (1996): 87-9.

"Profile." *Quill & Quire* Oct. 1987.

Hazel Hutchins
AUTHOR

Born
August 9, 1952, southern Alberta

School
Strathmore, Red Deer Lake, and Calgary, all in Alberta

Where I live now
Canmore, Alberta

My favourite book when I was young
"Laura Ingalls Wilder's *Little House on the Prairie* series."

My favourite book now
The Diviners by Margaret Laurence

Career
Writer

Family
"One husband, three children, two cats, one dog and a herd of fish."

The room where I create
"My bedroom."

Spare time
Read, hike, bike, canoe, ski.

When I was growing up
"My home was a farm in southern Alberta and I loved it. I can remember walking across the fields singing at the top of my lungs just to hear my voice alive on the prairie air. Living on a farm was fun, but I must have been lonely sometimes, for as a young child I invented several imaginary friends to entertain me while my older sisters and brother were at school. I named my friends Valerie, Barette and Witch Hazel. And I used to daydream. When I became old enough to go to school I left my imaginary friends at home but I took the day-dreaming with me. I remember sitting at my desk and staring out the window lost in another world entirely. My first book grew out of some of those daydreams."

My first book (and how it happened)
"My first book was *The Three and Many Wishes of Jason Reid*. To write it I sat down and tried to remember how I had felt and what had interested me when I was 11 years old. I remembered my class daydreams — one of them was what I would do if I had three wishes. I also remembered our school baseball games. When I put the two ideas together the story began to happen."

Where my ideas come from
"Ideas arrive from a thousand different places in a thousand different ways — objects around my house, things my children say and do, family stories from my parents, remembrances of my own childhood, scraps of conversations, interesting bits of history, other people's stories, exaggeration and just plain playing around with 'what if'. A notebook is handy for keeping story ideas safe until I have time to work on them. And, once started, a strong story will grow ideas all on its own.

"The story *Tess* grew from a magazine article written by my aunt about gathering cow patties for fuel on the prairies many years ago. The novel *Within a Painted Past* began when I imagined a painting on the blank wall before me, a painting so realistic that the snow was falling from the canvas onto my bedroom carpet below.

"People sometimes think the most important thing a writer needs is a computer. It's not. The most important thing a writer needs is a love of stories well told, and a lively, inquiring imagination."

Who and what influenced me
"All the time I was growing up I loved books. My mom read to us often. My dad liked to recite Robert Service poems. I read whatever I came across. A few of the things I remember reading and enjoying at various stages of my life are *Just Mary* stories, *Dana Girls* mysteries, the Laura Ingalls Wilder series, my dad's Zane Grey westerns and Hemingway."

How I work
"Initially, I write my stories long-hand. Later I put them into a computer to edit and print. The cat who adopted us one cold January morning, sleeps on top of the printer. Whenever I want to

print a story I have to remove her furry being and even then she has been known to try to climb back on her perch while paper is reeling through. One day she is going to get her tail caught in the works and I'll have to dismantle the machine to rescue her."

Something nobody knew about me (until now)

"I like Jersey Milk chocolate bars, people with a sense of humour, Canadian folk music and blues from any country, garden peas, wild birds, friends who forgive, high alpine lakes and Indian summer."

My favourite book that I've created

"My favourite book is always the one I'm working on at the moment. I always think I've just come across the best idea yet and I always want to do justice to it by working it into the *best story ever*. If I ever lose that feeling about my work, I'll know it's time to stop."

Tips for young creators

"Don't *tell* people your stories — write them down. Talking about a story idea often causes it to mysteriously slip away. But if you can get it on paper you'll find it builds instead of fades. Most writers will tell you to write about things you know, and that's very true, but you must also be sure to write about things which intrigue you and catch your own imagination. You also have to be prepared to rewrite. And rewrite. And rewrite. Sigh."

Hazel Hutchins

BIBLIOGRAPHY

Hutchins, Hazel. *The Three and Many Wishes of Jason Reid* (Annick Young Novels Series). Toronto: Annick Press, 1983 Paper 0-920236-61-8. Illustrations by John Richmond.

—. *Anastasia Morningstar and the Crystal Butterfly* (Annick Young Novels Series). Toronto: Annick Press, 1984 Paper 0-920236-95-2. Illustrations by Barry Trower. ✤

—. *Leanna Builds a Genie Trap.* Toronto: Annick Press, 1986 Paper 0-920303-55-2; Cloth 0-920303-54-4. Illustrations by Catharine O'Neill. ✤

—. *Ben's Snow Song: A Winter Picnic.* Toronto: Annick Press, 1987 Paper 0-920303-90-0; Cloth 0-920303-91-9. Illustrations by Lisa Smith.

—. *Norman's Snowball* (Annick Toddler Series). Toronto: Annick Press, 1989 Paper 1-55037-050-2; Cloth 1-55037-053-7. 1996 Annikin Paper 1-55037-494-X. Illustrations by Ruth Ohi.

—. *Casey Webber The Great* (Annick Young Novels Series). Toronto: Annick Press, 1988 Paper 1-55037-022-7; Cloth 1-55037-023-5. Illustrations by John Richmond.

—. *Nicholas at the Library.* Toronto: Annick Press, 1990 Paper 1-55037-132-0; Cloth 1-55037-134-7. Illustrations by Ruth Ohi.

—. *Katie's Babbling Brother.* Toronto: Annick Press, 1991 Paper 1-55037-156-8; Cloth 1-55037-153-3. 1996 Annikin Paper 1-55037-496-6. Illustrations by Ruth Ohi.

—. *A Cat of Artimus Pride* (Annick Young Novels Series). Toronto: Annick Press, 1991 Paper 1-55037-199-1. Illustrations by Ruth Ohi. ✤

—. *And You Can Be the Cat.* Toronto: Annick Press, 1992 Paper 1-55037-216-5; Cloth 1-55037-219-X. 1996 Annikin Paper 1-55037-495-8. Illustrations by Ruth Ohi.

—. *The Best of Arlie Zack* (Annick Young Novels Series). Toronto: Annick Press, 1993 Paper 1-55037- 315-3. Illustrations by Ruth Ohi.

—. *The Catfish Palace.* Toronto: Annick Press, 1992 Paper 1-55037-317-X; Cloth 1-55037-316-1. Illustrations by Ruth Ohi.

—. *Within a Painted Past* (Annick Young Novels Series). Toronto: Annick Press, 1994 Paper 1-55037- 989-5; Cloth 1-55037-369-2. Illustrations by Ruth Ohi.

—. *Tess.* Toronto: Annick Press, 1995 Paper 1-55037-394-3; Cloth 1-55037-395-1. Illustrations by Ruth Ohi.

—. *Believing Sophie.* Morton Grove: Ill.: Albert Whitman & Co., 1995 Cloth 0-8075-0625-7. Illustrations by Dorothy Donahue.

—. *Yancy and Bear.* Toronto: Annick Press, 1996 Paper 1-55037-502-4; Cloth 1-55037-503-2. Illustrations by Ruth Ohi.

—. *The Prince of Tarn.* Toronto: Annick Press, 1997 Paper 1-55037-438-9; Cloth 1-55037-439-7. Illustrations by Ruth Ohi.

—. *Shoot for the Moon, Robyn.* Halifax: Formac Publishing, 1997 0-88780-388-1; Cloth 0-8878-389-X. Illustrations by Yvonne Cathcart.

—. *It's Raining, Yancy and Bear.* Toronto: Annick Press, 1998 Paper 1-55037-528-8; Bound 1-55037- 529-6. Illustrations by Ruth Ohi.

—. *Robyn's Want Ad.* Halifax: Formac, 1998. 0-88780-458-6. Illustrations by Yvonne Cathcart.

—. *One Duck.* Toronto: Annick Press, 1999 Paper 1-55037-560-1. Illustrations by Ruth Ohi.

—. *Robyn Looks for Bears.* Halifax: Formac, 2000 Paper 0-88780-496-4 Cloth 0-88780-497-7. Illustrations by Yvonne Cathcart.

Awards

1987 White Ravens Selection of the International Youth Library, Munich for *Leanna Builds a Genie Trap*

1988 Parenting Magazine's Reading Magic Award for *The Three and Many Wishes of Jason Reid*

1991 R. Ross Annett Award for Children's Literature for *A Cat of Artimus Pride*

1996 Storytelling World Award for *Tess*

1998 R. Ross Annett Award for Children's Literature for *The Prince of Tarn*

Selected articles about Hazel Hutchins

"Hazel Hutchins." *Something about the Author: Autobiography Series.* Vol. 81 (1995): 145-161.

Hutchins, Hazel. "Pulled into the Past." *Canadian Children's Literature* 83 (1996): 92-94.

For more information about Hazel, visit her Web site at www.inkspot.com/author/hutchins

Sharon Jennings
AUTHOR

Born
January 21, 1954, Toronto, Ontario

School
"I went to schools in Toronto and Ottawa."

Where I live now
Toronto, Ontario

My favourite books when I was young
"Pierre Berton's *The Secret World of Og*, the *Anne* books, the *Little House* books, anything by Noel Streatfield (e.g. *Ballet Shoes*) and Geoffrey Trease (e.g. *Cue for Treason*). Anything with an orphan."

My favourite book now
"I have tons of favourite books. Here's a few: *Uncle Ronald*, by Brian Doyle, everything by Robertson Davies, *Zen and the Art of Motorcycle Maintenance* by Robert Pirsig."

Career
"I was an editor with a couple of publishers for 11 years. At first I worked on high school text-books. That was okay — but then I got a job that turned my life around. I was hired to be the senior editor of a primary language arts series. I was surrounded all day with stories and art for children; work was fun! Now I write at home and I do lots of school visits and volunteer work for writing and literacy organizations."

Family
"My husband Tony and I have three children, Adrian, Guy and Mia."

The room where I create
"...is also the room where my children create and watch TV and play on the computer. Every now and then my husband yells about not having any desk space but we just ignore him. I have lots of children's book posters on the walls and lots of books on the shelves and lots of piles of stuff on the floor. One day I will clean it all up."

Spare time
"In my spare time I cook, eat, read, and walk. And, of course, I am my children's chauffeur."

When I was growing up
"I wrote plays and put them on in the backyard. I was the writer, producer, director, and star. I wrote stories all the time, and whenever I finished reading a book that I really liked, I made up more of that story in my head. I belonged to children's theatre groups and I loved performing for an audience. I also played the accordion. (So does Mrs. Ming! Coincidence? I think not.)"

My first book (and how it happened)
"When I got my job working with primary language arts textbooks, I had just had my first child. I was surrounded all day at work, and all night at home, with information and ideas about kids and books. I started having ideas. I wrote *Jeremiah and Mrs. Ming* because I lived with a little boy who didn't want to go to bed. It took me two years to get the courage to send it to a publisher."

How I get my ideas
"I spy on my children. I listen to the way they talk and what they talk about. I remember many, many details of how I felt growing up. Sometimes I'll hear something or remember something and I'll see an entire picture book in my head. Writing it out is the hard part."

Who and what influenced me
"Books influence me. Remembering how I escaped into books as a child and lived in them, becoming part of them, I want to do that for others."

How I work
"I'm not as organized as I'd like to be. I wish I could get up every morning and get straight to work. If I have an idea, I'll work

like crazy. No laundry gets done, no meals are cooked, I forget I have children. I get so caught up in my own story that, when I stop writing, I feel as if I am in a time-warp. I get my best ideas just before falling asleep at night and when I first wake up."

Something nobody knew about me (until now)

"You have to promise not to tell my mother. When I was a little kid I wanted to be an orphan. In books, orphans (or children with parents so far away that they might as well have been orphans) had the best adventures: Anne Shirley, Orphan Annie, Susannah of the Mounties, Rebecca of Sunnybrook Farm, Jane Eyre, Mary Lennox, Heidi. I believed life would be better if I wasn't stuck with my parents."

My favourite book that I've created

"I have a soft spot for my first book. I'll never forget opening that letter from Annick Press, and reading that they wanted *Jeremiah and Mrs. Ming*. This was a turning point in my life."

Tips for young creators

"If you like writing, just do it. No one will say to you, 'You should be a writer when you grow up.' It's something you have to do for yourself. Write about things you like. Write the kind of book you like to read."

Sharon Jennings

BIBLIOGRAPHY

Jennings, Sharon. *Jeremiah and Mrs. Ming*. Toronto: Annick Press, 1990 Paper 1-55037-078-2; Cloth 1-55037-079-0; Big Book 1-55037-124-X. Illustrations by Mireille Levert.

—. *When Jeremiah found Mrs. Ming.* Toronto: Annick Press, 1992 Paper 1-55037-234-3; Cloth 1-55037-237-8. Illustrations by Mireille Levert.

—. *Sleep Tight, Mrs Ming.* Toronto: Annick Press, 1993 Paper 1-55037-325-0; Cloth 1-55037- 322-6. Illustrations by Mireille Levert.

—. *The Bye-Bye Pie.* Markham: Fitzhenry and Whiteside 1999 Cloth 1-55041-405-4. Illustrations by Ruth Ohi.

—. *Into My Mother's Arms.* Markham: Fitzhenry and Whiteside, 2000 Cloth 1-55041-538-6. Illustrations by Ruth Ohi.

Selected articles about Sharon Jennings

Ellis, Sarah. "News from the North." *Horn Book* Jan./Feb. 1991: 110.

Sybesma, Jetske. "Overt and Covert Content in Current Illustrated Children's Books." *Canadian Children's Literature* 62 (1991): 99-100.

Julie Johnston
AUTHOR

Born
Smith Falls, Ontario

School
U. of T. 1963, occupational therapy; Trent University 1984, Honours English Lit.

Where I live now
Peterborough and Rideau Lake, both in Ontario

My favourite books when I was young
All L.M. Montgomery's books, all of Louisa May Alcott's books.

My favourite book now
Howard's End by E.M. Forster and *Possession* by A.S. Byatt

Career
"I worked as an occupational therapist with handicapped children and adults from 1963 to 1968. I am now writing full time."

Family
"I have a husband and four grown-up daughters as well as one granddaughter and two grandsons."

The room where I create
"I have two work places. In Peterborough, my study is painted a passionate brick colour. It's crammed with books, plants, mementos, photos, a bulletin board scattered with addresses, cartoons and memos. I have a fireplace that doesn't work, brief-cases, and a wastebasket chock full of junk. At the lake, in my cottage I have windows on nearly every side. I'm up high among the trees and overlook the lake. From here, besides writing, I can keep an eye on my wildlife visitors — loons, ducks, Canada geese, deer, raccoons and chipmunks. This is where I do my writing all summer and sometimes for short spells during the winter."

Spare time
"I grow vegetables, flowers and weeds. I like to go puttering about in my old leaky boats. Apart from that, I like to walk, hike, bike and read books."

When I was growing up
"As a child I loved climbing trees, exploring in the woods, swimming, boating, riding horses, painting pictures and writing stories."

My first book (and how it happened)
"When I first decided to branch out and write something longer than the short stories, articles and plays I had been writing, I knew that I had to write about something very close and familiar to me. At the time, I had been keeping track of dreams and stray thoughts in a journal, many of them about my own childhood. I think I felt that the character I knew best was the child I once was. Although *Hero of Lesser Causes* is not in any way autobiographical, the time frame (late 1940s and early 1950s) seemed carved in my memory. Those memories allowed me to get inside my story.

"That first novel, *Hero of Lesser Causes*, took six years from completion to publication. It was a time filled with many disappointments and a lot of frustration, but in many ways it was worth it. I learned a great deal about rewriting and a great deal about having patience. I was fortunate to have a wonderful editor, Kathy Lowinger, who taught me a great deal about how a novel is put together. When it actually won the Governor General's Award in 1992, I couldn't believe it. I had to keep telling myself it was true. The excitement and thrill on that occasion was exceeded only by winning the award again with my second novel in 1994."

Where my ideas come from
"Life, the past, characters I meet, books, movies, songs.

"Sometimes people ask me why I write for young teens. Part of the reason is that I still feel close to my own childhood and adolescence. Many of my strongest feelings about life come from my past. Also, I think people become conscious of themselves being in the world at around the age of 11 or 12. It's at about this time that we say, 'Yes, there's more to the world than home, family and school.' We start looking at life on a broader scale and we start making choices and decisions that will affect our future lives. To me it is the starting point of people's stories, of their struggles to find a way of belonging in the world."

Who and what influenced me
"Family, friends, books, especially those by Margaret Laurence."

How I work
"I think out my plot and then I scribble it down fast. I listen for each character to speak to me and I study her or him to discover the most earnest needs. Then I set to work on Chapter 1, page 1. Each day I revise and then add a little more.

"When I started my second book, *Adam and Eve and Pinch-Me*, I once again found a strong connection to a certain period in my own life. I had been struggling for years to get *Hero* published but with no luck. To keep my spirits up I began a new book set in the present. Sara, the main character, emerged as an angry, frustrated person who didn't seem to fit in anywhere. I have a strong suspicion that my own prevailing mood of anger and frustration had a lot to do with her creation.

"My third book was very different. For one thing, the main character is a boy. It was a challenge to try to get inside a boy's life but I found a way to help me do it. I concentrated on the stories my father had told me about his childhood. He once told me that he had been badly teased by his uncle for wearing a wrist watch at a time when it was manly to wear a pocket watch. Out of that incident I began to form Fred's personality. *The Only Outcast* is based on real people and a real diary, but the personalities of the characters are my own invention. While I was writing the book, I was given a clue about what Fred's little sister Bessie might have been like. I know a woman, in her nineties now, who had known Bessie and described her as 'quite the gal.' Not much to go on, I admit, but it was something. Bessie, in the book, definitely has a mind of her own as I think she must have had in real life."

Something nobody knew about me (until now)
"My life is an open book."

My favourite book that I've created
The Only Outcast

Tips for young creators
"Never say 'this is impossible.' Analyze everything about life. Ask questions. Read books."

Julie Johnston

BIBLIOGRAPHY

Johnston, Julie. "Mirrors." *The Blue Jean Collection.* Saskatoon: Thistledown Press, 1992 Paper 0- 920633-94-3.

—. *Hero of Lesser Causes.* Toronto: Lester Publishing, 1992 Cloth 1-895555-22-1. 1996 Paper 0- 7737-5850-X.

—. *Adam and Eve and Pinch-Me.* Toronto: Lester Publishing, 1994. Toronto: Stoddart, 1996 Paper 0-7737-5839-9.

—. *The Only Outcast.* Toronto: Tundra, 1998 Cloth 0-88776-441-X Paper 0-88776-488-6.

—, ed. *Love Ya Like a Sister: from the Journals of Katie Ouriou.* Toronto: Tundra Books, 1999 Paper 0-88776-454-6.

Awards
1992 Governor General's Literary Award for *Hero of Lesser Causes*

1993 IODE Canada Violet Downey Book Award for *Hero of Lesser Causes*

1994 Joan Fassler Memorial Book Award for *Hero of Lesser Causes*

1994 Governor General's Literary Award for *Adam and Eve and Pinch-Me*

1995 Ruth Schwartz Children's Book Award for *Adam and Eve and Pinch-Me*

1995 Canadian Library Association Young Adult Book Award for *Adam and Eve and Pinch-Me*

Selected articles about Julie Johnston
Jenkinson, Dave. "Profiles: Julie Johnston." *Resource Links* 1.3 (1996): 104.

Lewis, Amanda. "Turning the Pages of Cottage Life." *Cottage Life,* October 1998: 74.

Little, Jean. "Julie Johnston: an Exciting New Voice." *Canadian Children's Literature* 77 (1995): 33.

Ross, Val. "The Lives of a Writer." *The Globe and Mail* 15 November 1994: C1.

Welwyn Wilton Katz
AUTHOR

Born
June 7, 1948, London, Ontario

School
Orchard Park Public School, Oakridge Secondary School, University of Western Ontario; all in London, Ontario

Where I live now
London, Ontario

My favourite book when I was young
Swallows and Amazons by Arthur Ransome.

My favourite book now
"Too many to list, but *The Last Unicorn* by Peter S. Beagle is up there."

Career
Writer

Family
Husband, Doug Bale; daughter, Meredith Katz; cat, Perdy.

The room where I create
"My office — a converted bedroom in the upstairs of my house."

Spare time
"Read, play the flute and the recorder, garden, and cook with herbs."

When I was growing up
"As a child, I read a lot and was encouraged by my family to read a lot. My favourite books were mysteries and adventure stories, especially those by Arthur Ransome. But I never considered writing. My family, like many, did not consider writing a real career. I wrote my first story when I was 10 and it won a prize at a local hobby fair. I was also a teenage correspondent for the local city newspaper. The first time I actually experienced the thrill of writing that flowed was in a Grade 11 English composition exam. Humble beginnings for someone who is now a full-time writer."

Working with an editor
"I've learned that the role of an editor is very important in the development of a writer's skill and in his or her ego. With my book *Sun God, Moon Witch*, I rewrote it several times and each time the publisher refused it. I was convinced I was a bad writer and couldn't go on. It was only the help of my editor, who kept calling and encouraging me to finish the work and let me know that these were just temporary setbacks, that enabled me to finish the book.

"Eventually, the manuscript was accepted and I feel good about the final version."

Where my ideas come from
"The world around us is full of ideas. People are the primary source — feelings, needs, fears, wants. I'm also interested in the idea that the past is never really over and done with. A lot of my ideas for books come from that belief."

Who and what influenced me
"Studying mathematics at university helped me to be a strong structuralist. Great writers like Diana Wynne Jones, Margaret Mahy and J.R.R. Tolkien also influenced both my choice of writing fantasy for young people and my need to become a better writer with each book I write (because they are such good writers themselves)."

How I work
"I combine the writing, researching, planning and revising of my books with giving talks and teaching courses in creative writing. I try to write as much and as often as possible. I do all my writing on the computer and print out each day's work so that I always have a hard copy because I have a constant fear of my computer failing in some way!"

Something nobody knew about me (until now)
"Scary music in movies terrifies me. I can't watch horror movies because of it."

My favourite book that I've created

"*Whalesinger* (though that's a little like asking a mother her favourite baby!)"

Tips for young creators

"Read more books than junk and write every day!"

Welwyn Wilton Katz

BIBILIOGRAPHY

Katz, Welwyn Wilton. *The Prophecy of Tau Ridoo*. Edmonton: Tree Frog Press, 1983. Out of print.

—. *False Face*. Toronto: Groundwood Books, 1987 Paper 0-88899-063-4.

—. *The Third Magic*. Toronto: Groundwood Books, 1990 Paper 0-88899-126-6.

—. *Witchery Hill*. Toronto: Groundwood Books, 1990. 1995 Paper 0-88899-245-9.

—. *Sun God, Moon Witch*. Toronto: Groundwood Books, 1990. 1995 Paper 0-88899-246-7.

—. *Whalesinger*. Toronto: Groundwood Books, 1990 Cloth 0-88899-113-4. 1993 Paper 0-88899-191-6.

—. *Come Like Shadows*. Toronto: Penguin Books Canada, 1993. Out of print.

—. *Time Ghost*. Toronto: Groundwood Books, 1994 Paper 0-88899-275-0; Cloth 0-88899-216-5.

—. *Out of the Dark*. Toronto: Groundwood Books, 1995 Paper 0-88899-241-6. 1996 Paper 0- 88899-262-9.

—. *Beowulf*. Toronto: Groundwood Books, 1999 Cloth 0-88899-365-X. Illustrations by Laszlo Gal.

Awards

1987 International Children's Fiction Contest winner for *False Face*

1988 Governor General's Literary Award for *The Third Magic*

1988 Max and Greta Ebel Memorial Award for Children's Writing for *False Face*

1994 Vicky Metcalf Award for a Body of Work

Selected articles about Welwyn Wilton Katz

The Canadian Who's Who. Toronto: Trans-Canada Press.

Micros, Marianne. "'My Books Are My Children': An Interview with Welwyn Wilton Katz." *Canadian Children's Literature* 90 (1998): 51-65.

"Welwyn Wilton Katz." *Something about the Author: Autobiography Series*. Detroit: Gale Research, vol. 25 (1997).

Who's Who in Canadian Literature 1994-95. Toronto: Reference Press.

Richardo Keens–Douglas
AUTHOR

Born
Grenada (The Isle of Spice) West Indies

School
Presentation College, Grenada; Dawson College Theatre School, Montreal, Quebec

Where I live now
"Toronto, Canada, and I spend lots of time in Grenada."

My favourite books when I was young
"Mystery, spy books, tales and comics."

My favourite book now
"I don't really have one; I tend to read all kinds of books, but I love to read inspirational books — books that make you feel good about life and yourself."

Career
"I am an actor, dancer, singer and writer. I give workshops for teachers and students all over North America on self-esteem and using the imagination. I performed for the Stratford Shakespearean Festival, aboard the *HMS Britannia* for Princess Diana, at the famous Apollo Theatre in New York. I have had my own national radio show on CBC.

"Right now I am writing a TV series called *Cocoa Roots*. And my new musical *The Nutmeg Princess* opened at Young Peoples Theatre in March, 1999."

Family
"I come from a really big family: seven kids (five boys and two girls). I am the last. I had a great Mom and Dad. They have both passed on now, and I miss them very much."

The room where I create
"I have no special room to create. I create everywhere and anywhere: on the beach, in the park, in bed. But I love quiet when I create. Sometimes I even put on music to inspire me when I am writing."

When I was growing up
"When I was growing up, I would spend most of my time outside, playing on the beach, or going into the country to swim in the rivers."

My first book (and how it happened)
"I never really thought I would be writing books, I was more interested in telling my stories live, because I grew up in the oral tradition. One day, I was telling a story to a group of young people, and a little black girl with a Whoopi Goldberg hairdo put her hand up and asked me if I knew a story of a black princess. At the time I didn't. This little girl wanted to hear a story of a princess that looked like her. She wanted all her friends to know that there are black princesses and princes too. So I decided to go and write a story about a black princess, and I wrote *The Nutmeg Princess*."

Where my ideas come from
"A perfect example is the story I told you about how I came to write *The Nutmeg Princess*. Ideas are constantly coming. Something you could say, or something I read in a newspaper, or maybe there is a message I would like to pass on, I would put it into a story. Like my book, *Grandpa's Visit*. I wanted to talk about how we look at too much TV and don't spend enough time together as a family, so I worked it into a story. Or I make up all kinds of wild and wonderful stories. I really try and use my imagination."

Who and what influenced me
"My Mom and Dad. They were a very positive force in my life. There were also great story-tellers, so in a way they were also my books. Also I am very spiritual; I believe in God very much."

How I work
"I tend to do my stories orally first; my style always has the feel of storytelling. That's why I

always like people to read my stories out loud. After, I write them down, and then I put them on the computer for editing. Before I publish any of my stories I must try them out on a live audience. I like to get human feedback, so I find it very helpful when I can get an immediate response from the listener. I also do a lot of on-the-spot editing as well. That's the best way, because right then and there you can see what works and what doesn't."

Something nobody knew about me (until now)

"When I was 14 years old and living on the island of Grenada, I got all my friends together and I formed a dance group called The Spice Follies. And in Grenada, when the tourist boats would come to visit us, we would go onto the boats and put on a show to make some money for pocket change. It was a lot of fun."

My favourite book that I've created

"I love all my books. Each one is so special. They each have their own little magic to them."

Tips for young creators

"Never stop laughing. Never be afraid to be creative and to try things. Sometimes things will get very tough, but that's when you have to smile and keep going. As the Nutmeg Princess says, 'If you believe in yourself all things are possible.'"

Richardo Keens-Douglas

BIBLIOGRAPHY

Keens-Douglas, Richardo. *The Nutmeg Princess*. Toronto: Annick Press, 1992 Paper 1-55037-236-X; Cloth 1-55037-239-4. Illustrations by Annouchka Galouchko.

—. *La Diablesse and the Baby*. Toronto: Annick Press, 1994 Paper 1-55037-992-5; Cloth 1-5037-993-3. Illustrations by Marie Lafrance. ✿

—. *Freedom Child of the Sea*. Toronto: Annick Press, 1995 Paper 1-55037-372-2; Cloth 1-55037-373-0. Illustrations by Julia Gukova.

—. *Grandpa's Visit*. Toronto: Annick Press, 1996 Paper 1-55037-488-5; Cloth 1-55037-489-3. Illustrations by Frances Clancy.

—. *The Miss Meow Pageant*. Toronto: Annick Press, 1998 Paper 1-55037-536-9; Cloth 1-55037-537-7. Illustrations by Marie Lafrance.

—. *Mama God, Papa God*. Vancouver: Tradewind Books, 1999 Paper 1-896580-16-5.

Awards

1995 American World Storytelling Award for *La Diablesse and the Baby*

Gordon Korman
AUTHOR

Born
October 23, 1963, Montreal, Quebec

School
Thornhill High, Thornhill, Ontario; New York University, (BFA), New York, U.S.A

Where I live now
"I divide my time between Great Neck, New York where I live with my wife, Michelle, and Thornhill."

My favourite book when I was young
Dr. Seuss's Sleep Book

My favourite book now
Catch-22 by Joseph Heller

Career
Novelist and lecturer

My family
"Father, Charles; mother, Bernice; and my pet."

The room where I create
"On planes, in hotel rooms and in all of my various homes. My favourite is Mom's living room in Thornhill, Ontario."

Spare time
"I love music and all sports, and I'd do anything to spend time on an ocean beach! Also movies."

When I was growing up
"It was my ambition to be a dog, specifically a black Labrador retriever. When I got older, my ambitions ranged from astronaut (of course!) to hockey star. Careerwise I was vague. My best subjects at school were math and science."

My first book (and how it happened)
"*This Can't Be Happening at Macdonald Hall* was written by mistake when I was in Grade 7. Our teacher asked for what he called a 'novelette.' What he wanted, he later told me, was something that didn't end after the first page. He asked for an outline the first week, and a chapter a week after that. I really got into it and accidentally wrote a story I called 'Bruno and Boots.' Almost to justify having done so much work for school, I conned my Mom into typing it for me, and sent it to Scholastic. They liked it, published it, and the rest all happened from that one English project."

Where my ideas come from
"My ideas come from plain old hard work, and a lot of thinking and planning. Sometimes I pick up the thread of an idea from a group of students I've talked to. I often discuss the ideas I'm working on with family and friends. A new viewpoint can often be helpful, but there are no blinding flashes of inspiration; it's work."

Who and what influenced me
"We are all influenced by every person and/or event that comes our way. The strongest influences in my life have always been my parents, especially my mother, who is a writer too, and who collaborated with me on two poetry books. Now that I live away from my folks, other influences, mostly of friends, come into play as well."

How I work
"I work on a portable computer when I'm travelling. I work on a desk-top computer at home. I still work in longhand on a clipboard when the going gets tough. My favourite way to write is to dictate to my Mom; she writes in longhand while I kick a Nerf ball around the living room, and toss it through a small basketball hoop!"

Something nobody knew about me (until now)
"I can cook when I have to and my swimming, while not pretty, would probably win an endurance test. I like classical music, if you exclude opera, and I really enjoy spending time with kids. I only just discovered these things myself!"

My favourite book that I've created
"I don't have a true 'favourite'. However, I'm usually most 'into' the newer releases."

Tips for young creators

"Read a lot, and write a lot too. Those two activities develop a smoothness in your language. And, chances are, if it is written fluently, it will read that way too. ALWAYS plan before you start to write. And lastly, enjoy what you're writing. If you like it, it's possible that others will too!"

Gordon Korman

SELECT BIBLIOGRAPHY

Korman, Gordon. *This Can't Be Happening at Macdonald Hall!* (Bruno and Boots Series), 1978. Richmond Hill: Scholastic Canada, 1980 Paper 0-590-44213-9.

—. *Go Jump in the Pool!* (Bruno and Boots Series). Richmond Hill: Scholastic Canada, 1979. 1991 Paper 0-590-44209-0. Illustrations by Lea Daniel.

—. *Beware the Fish* (Bruno and Boots Series). Richmond Hill: Scholastic Canada, 1980 Paper 0-590-44205-8. Illustrations by Lea Daniel.

—. *Who is Bugs Potter?* Richmond Hill: Scholastic Canada, 1980 Paper 0-590-44207-4. Illustrations by Dino Kotopoulis.

—. *I Want to Go Home.* Richmond Hill: Scholastic Canada, 1981 Paper 0-590-44210-4. Illustrations by Constantine Zottas.

—. *Our Man Weston.* Richmond Hill: Scholastic Canada, 1982 Paper 0-590-43755-0.

—. *The War with Mr. Wizzle* (Bruno and Boots Series). Richmond Hill: Scholastic Canada, 1982 Paper 0-590-44206-6.

—. *Bugs Potter Live at Nickaninny.* Richmond Hill: Scholastic Canada, 1983. 1990 Paper 0-590-73625-6.

—. *No Coins, Please.* Richmond Hill: Scholastic Canada, 1984 Cloth 0-590-71429-5; Paper 0-590-44208-2.

—. *A Semester in the Life of a Garbage Bag.* Richmond Hill: Scholastic Canada, 1987. Out of print.

—. *Son of Interflux.* Richmond Hill: Scholastic Canada, 1988. 1995 Paper 0-590-24513-9.

—. *The Zucchini Warriors.* Richmond Hill: Scholastic Canada, 1990 Paper 0-590-44174-4.

—. *Losing Joe's Place.* Richmond Hill: Scholastic Canada, 1990 Paper 0-590-42769-5.

—. *Radio 5th Grade.* Richmond Hill: Scholastic Canada, 1991 Paper 0-590-41928-5; Cloth 0-590-41927-7.

—. *Macdonald Hall Goes Hollywood* (Bruno and Boots Series). Richmond Hill: Scholastic Canada, 1991 Cloth 0-590-43940-5. 1992 Paper 0-590-43941-3.

—. *The Twinkie Squad.* New York: Scholastic Inc., 1992. Richmond Hill: Scholastic Canada, 1994 0-590-45250-9.

—. *The Toilet Paper Tigers.* Richmond Hill: Scholastic Canada, 1993. 1995 Paper 0-590-46231-8.

—. *Why Did the Underwear Cross the Road?* Richmond Hill: Scholastic Canada, 1994 Cloth 0-590-47501-0. 1996 Paper 0-590-47502-9.

—. *Something Fishy at Macdonald Hall* (Bruno and Boots Series). Richmond Hill: Scholastic Canada, 1995 Cloth 0-590-25521-5.

—. *The Chicken Doesn't Skate.* Richmond Hill: Scholastic Canada, 1996 Cloth 0-590-85300-7.

—. *Liar, Liar Pants on Fire.* New York: Scholastic Press, 1997 Cloth 0-590-27142-3. Illustrations by Joann Adinolfi.

—. *Quarterback Exchange: I Was John Elway.* New York: Hyperion Paperbacks, 1997 Paper 0-7868-1236-2.

—. *Running Back Conversation: I was Barry Sanders.* New York: Hyperion Paperbacks, 1997 Paper 0-7868-1237-0.

—. *Super Bowl Switch: I was Dan Marino.* New York: Hyperion Paperbacks, 1997 Paper 0-7868-1238-9.

—. *Heavy Artillery: I Was Junior Seau.* New York: Hyperion Paperbacks, 1997 Paper 0-7868-1259-1

—. *Ultimate Scoring Machine: I Was Jerry Rice.* New York: Hyperion Paperbacks, 1998 Paper 0-7868-1270-2.

—. *The Sixth Grade Nickname Game.* Richmond Hill: Scholastic Canada, 1998.

— et al. *NFL Rules!* New York: Hyperion Books, 1998 Paper 0-7868-1271-0.

—. *Slapshots #1: The Stars from Mars.* Richmond Hill: Scholastic Canada, 1999 Paper 0-590-70619-5.

—. *Slapshots #2: The All-Mars All-Stars.* Richmond Hill: Scholastic Canada, 1999 Paper 0-590-70620-9.

—. *Slapshots #3: The Face-Off Phony.* Richmond Hill: Scholastic Canada, 2000 Paper 0-590-70629-2.

Korman, Gordon and Bernice Korman. *The D-Minus Poems of Jeremy Bloom.* Richmond Hill: Scholastic Canada, 1992 Paper 0-590-44819-6.

—. *The Last Place Sports Poems of Jeremy Bloom.* Richmond Hill: Scholastic Canada, 1996 Paper 0-590-25516-9.

Awards

1981 Canadian Authors Association Air Canada Award for authors under the age of thirty-five

1986 International Reading Association Children's Choice Award for *I Want to Go Home*

1986 American Library Association Young Adult Services Division Best Book for *Son of Interflux*

1987 International Reading Association Children's Choice Award for *Our Man Weston*

1987 American Library Association Young Adult Service Division Best Book for *A Semester in the Life of a Garbage Bag*

1991 Manitoba Young Readers Choice Award for *The Zucchini Warriors*

Selected articles about Gordon Korman

Jenkinson, David. "Portraits." *Emergency Librarian* 20.3 (1993): 66-70.

Rae, Arlene Perly. "Children's Books." *The Toronto Star*, 23 Oct. 1993.

Slopen, Beverly. "Book World." *The Toronto Star*, 20 Nov. 1993.

Paul Kropp

AUTHOR

Born

February 22, 1948, Buffalo, New York, U.S.A.

School

Columbia College of Columbia University, B.A., New York City, U.S.A.; University of Western Ontario, M.A., London, Ontario

Where I live now

Toronto, Ontario

My favourite book when I was young

The Little Engine That Could

My favourite book now

The Ciderhouse Rules by John Irving

Career

Writer and teacher

Family

Wife, Gale Bildfell; five children

The room where I create

"Office on the second floor, over the kitchen."

Spare time

"Read fiction and newspapers (I'm an addict: two or three a day), play croquet and tennis, dabble at the piano (Mozart, mostly), attend opera and symphony concerts."

When I was growing up

"I began writing in Miss Jackman's class in Grade 1. At the time, we were expected to illustrate our stories and this proved to be a considerable handicap for me. Unlike my arch-rival Toby, I couldn't draw bunnies or spiders or people; I could only manage to draw World War II combat aircraft. As a result, most of my stories involved a B-52 bomber, some fighter aircraft and a few exploding civilians. Miss Jackman always said, 'Paul, why can't you write nice stories like Toby's?' Toby, who wrote stories about friendly bunnies, went on to become a doctor. I continued to do my bomber stories, at least until I didn't have to draw pictures anymore, and went on to become a writer."

My first book (and how it happened)

"My first book was *Burn Out* and I created it for the students I was teaching at a vocational high school in Hamilton, Ontario. I had been using the books available at the time for these young men (which ranged from *Scruffy the Tugboat* to *Terry and Sid, Lorry Drivers*) but decided I could write something more appropriate myself. I wanted to write something realistic, with characters based on kids I knew, with high-action plots that would pull the reader into the story and drag him right through to the end."

Where my ideas come from

"Ideas come from everywhere: kids write to me, I stumble across them in schools, they pop into my mind while driving, I see them in the newspaper, my own children generate some of them. Developing ideas requires a special place for me: the shower. There's nothing like a good half-hour shower to develop plot or character ideas, or resolve that nagging problem in Chapter Two."

Who and what influenced me

"My early teachers influenced me a good deal. I recall Mr. C. Reid Sanders in high school announcing at the beginning of a Grade 11 English class that we had 20 minutes to write something beautiful. He put an Andres Segovia recording on the old phonograph, sat back with a wry smile, and let us write. In my case, it was a paragraph about waves pounding the shore and dappling moonlight. A day later, he held me up after class and said, 'I enjoyed what you wrote yesterday, Paul. I too thought it was beautiful.' It was my first inkling that I could actually write something someone else might enjoy.

"When I began to write fiction, there were no creative writing classes so I had to teach myself how to write. My self-education project involved taking the masters of young adult writing, like Paul Zindel and M.E. Kerr, and adult writing, like John Updike and Graham Greene, and carefully studying their style and technique. I even copied over whole chapters to get a feel for their writing. Eventually I mastered the Paul Kropp voice because it was so unlike everyone else's."

How I work

"At seven thirty in the morning I grab a shower and think about what I'm going to write that day. Then, at eight o'clock, I turn on my computer and I start to write. I always write regardless of whether I'm feeling good or ill, inspired or bedraggled. If I get stuck, I hit the shower again. By noon, I'm usually ready to call it quits for the day, though I sometimes keep going until one or two o'clock if I'm feeling inspired or a deadline is looming. Then I grab another shower and turn to other work: letters, consulting, returning phone calls."

Something nobody knew about me (until now)

"The first time I ever appeared on the radio was on CBC's *As It Happens* in 1973. I was interviewed as Canada's top croquet player. This was hardly a significant achievement, since only a dozen people in all North America played serious croquet at the time, but it gave me my first ten minutes on air."

My favourite book that I've created

"I love them all, especially *Moonkid and Liberty*, probably because I'm a Moonkid at heart, and the three junior novels, *Fast Times with Fred, Cottage Crazy* and *Ski Stooges* because my own kids are in them."

Tips for young creators

"Read tons of stuff: good, bad and in-between. Keep a diary or journal. Steal ideas and techniques from the best writers out there. Expect rejection; then keep on writing. Remember that the two most important activities for a professional writer are research and revision. When you forget that, remember that writing is like an iceberg: only the final draft appears on the surface — what keeps everything afloat is five drafts of revision down below sea level."

Paul Kropp

SELECT BIBLIOGRAPHY

Kropp, Paul. *Wilted*. New York: Dell, 1980. Rev. ed. rpt. as *You've Seen Enough*. Toronto: Prentice Hall, 1992. Out of print.

—. *Justin, Jay-Jay and the Juvenile Dinkett*. Richmond Hill: Scholastic Canada, 1986. Out of print.

—. *Getting Even*. New York: Bantam, 1986. Out of print.

—. *Death Ride* (Series 2000). Toronto: Maxwell Macmillan Canada, 1986 Paper 0-02-947360-8.

—. *Jo's Search* (Series 2000). Toronto: Maxwell Macmillan Canada, 1986 Paper 0-02-947370-5.

—. *Not Only Me* (Series 2000). Toronto: Maxwell Macmillan Canada, 1987 Paper 0-02-953500-X.

—. *Under Cover* (Series 2000). Toronto: Maxwell Macmillan Canada, 1987 Paper 0-02-953501-8.

—. *Cottage Crazy*. Richmond Hill: Scholastic Canada, 1988 Paper 0-590-71955-6.

—. *Moonkid and Liberty*. Toronto: Stoddart, 1988. 1996 Paper 0-7736-7442-X.

—. *Baby Blues* (Series 2000). Toronto: Maxwell Macmillan Canada, 1989 Paper 0-02-953546-8. ❧

—. *The Rock*. Toronto: Stoddart, 1989 Paper 0-7737-5313-3; Cloth 0-7737-2366-8. 1996 Paper 0-7736-7450-0.

—. *Fast Times with Fred*. Richmond Hill: Scholastic Canada, 1990. Out of print.

—. *We Both Have Scars* (Series 2000). Toronto: Maxwell Macmillan Canada, 1990 Paper 0-02-953984.

—. *The Victim Was Me* (Series 2000). Toronto: Maxwell Macmillan Canada, 1991 Paper 0-02-954008-9.

—. *Ellen/Eléna/Luna*. Toronto: Prentice Hall, 1992 Paper 0-02-954137-9.

—. *Ski Stooges*. Richmond Hill: Scholastic Canada, 1992 Paper 0-590-74062-8.

—. *Riot on the Street* (Series 2000). Toronto: Maxwell Macmillan Canada, 1993 Paper 0-02-954208-1.

—. *The Reading Solution: Making Your Child a Reader for Life*. Toronto: Random House, 1993 Paper 0-349422-266-0.

—. *Moonkid and Prometheus*. Toronto: Stoddart, 1997 Paper 0-7736-7465-9.

Paul Kropp is also the author of 19 "Series Canada" titles published by Prentice Hall.

Selected articles about Paul Kropp

Brandon, Paul. "Paul Kropp: 100,000 Teenagers Can't Be Wrong." *Quill & Quire* (April 1992).

Gertridge, Allison. *Meet Canadian Authors and Illustrators*. Richmond Hill: Scholastic Canada, 1994: 56-57.

Hancock, Pat "Introducing Paul Kropp." *CANSCAIP News* 15.1 (1993): 1-2.

—. "Paul Kropp." *Behind the Story*. Ed. Barbara Greenwood. Markham: Pembroke Publishers, 1995: 56-9.

For more information about Paul Kropp, visit his Web site at www.clo.com/~author/

Michael Arvaarluk Kusugak
AUTHOR

Born
"Contrary to popular belief, I was born at Cape Fullerton, NWT, not Repulse Bay."

School
Chesterfield Inlet, Rankin Inlet, Nunavut; Yellowknife, Northwest Territories; Churchill, Manitoba; Saskatoon, Saskatchewan

Where I live now
"I list my home as Rankin Inlet, Nunavut but I do so much travelling I sometimes feel that I have no permanent home. Right now I am visiting friends in Water Valley, Alberta. Sometime this summer I intend to return home to Rankin Inlet. Next fall, I start to look for a new home. I think I will try living in the Maritimes or Newfoundland for awhile."

My favourite books when I was young
"There were no books written in Inuktitut and I did not speak any other language. When I finally learned to read in English, I was completely engrossed with Jack London, Robert Service, Pearl Buck and John Steinbeck. In school, I read all those books about Cowboy Sam and Curious George with great enthusiasm."

My favourite book now
"*The Canterbury Tales* by Geoffrey Chaucer is my all-time favourite.

He was a great storyteller who told stories about real people. I also really like *Les Miserables* by Victor Hugo, almost all of Dickens' work and *What's Bred in the Bone* by Robertson Davies."

Career
Storyteller/writer

Family
"I have four boys: Qilak, Ka'lak, Nathaniel and Bubsy, and a grandson, Justin."

The room where I create
"I create wherever I am. My favourite place is my shed with my office in it. I also like the serenity of my cabin in the wilderness. I wrote *Who Wants Rocks?* in the Berton House (with Robert Service's cabin across the street and Jack London's old cabin down a little ways) in Dawson City, Yukon."

Spare time
"I read. I traipse around Baltimore, Indianapolis, Amsterdam or wherever I happen to be. My favourite spare time activity is to bob up and down in my 24-foot wooden boat on Hudson Bay watching seals, whales and other animals of the sea."

When I was growing up
"We lived in igloos and sod huts in winter and in tents in summer. We hunted seals, walrus, whales,

caribou and all kinds of animals to feed ourselves. We travelled by dog team all winter and boat in summer. I loved bannock and peanut butter that we got from the Hudson's Bay Company store. I loved to play ball with a red, white and blue rubber ball. We played soccer on the sea ice. And I loved the stories my grandmother told us to put us to sleep."

My first book (and how it happened)
"One night, I was putting my boys to bed and, as they always did, they said 'Dad, can you read us a story?' I said 'OK.' They got a book and I started to read, but it was one I had read so many times that I finally said, 'I am not going to read you this book anymore.' I put it away and told them a story about these creatures that live under the sea ice called qallupilluit. They said 'Dad, why don't you write it down?' I wrote it down and, then, Bob Munsch and I worked on it together. It was published in 1988 as *A Promise is a Promise*."

Where my ideas come from
"I get my ideas from the stories my grandparents and my parents told me. I also work from my own childhood experiences. I like to think about what it must have been like when we knew no

people other than Inuit. How did people live? What kinds of stories did they tell and why? How did we survive in this harsh land? Did we even think about being cold? Who invented the igloo? Who designed the first snowknife? There are so many interesting questions. I try to find the answers and write about them."

Who and what influenced me

"My grandmother (her name was Tuurngaq, 'the spirit of the shaman') and my uncles, who told me the stories of my people. My mother and father who warned me about the creatures under the sea ice and the hide-and-seek creatures and who told me about the beauty of the northern lights."

How I work

"I walk a lot thinking about the stories in my mind. I tell them to myself over and over until they begin to flow like stories that come from a storyteller. I draft outlines. I write my first drafts with a fountain pen on plain paper because I like to watch ink flow onto paper like a good story should. I tell the stories to my sons, my nieces and nephews. I type my drafts into a computer. Then I edit and rewrite my stories over and over. I read them out loud, trying to make them sound as if they come from the greatest storytellers I know. I e-mail the stories to trusted friends and ask for their comments. I rewrite and submit my work to my publisher. And then the editing begins."

My favourite book that I've created

"*Northern Lights: The Soccer Trails* is still my favourite book. I still get more feedback from this book than I do from any other, from both children and adults.

For example, I received a letter from an 11-year-old girl in Alberta who says her mother used to read the book to her when she was little. Now her mother has MS and it affects her eyes. Now she reads it to her mother. It is so touching to hear your own stories touch people that way."

Tips for young creators

"I think of it this way: A story is beautiful when it is first born because you know you made it all on your own.

"After you write it down, put it away for awhile and do something else. Read it and you will see that something could be better. Maybe something is missing. Maybe you could tell it in a slightly different way. Rewrite it. The next time, you might find something that could be added. Reread it and you find something that could be changed to make it flow better. Eventually, it becomes too long, disjointed and unwieldy. Redraft it, thinking about all the things you really want to say. Get rid of the stuff that gets in the way and rewrite it again. Before you know it, you have a story you can be proud to read and tell to other people.

"The greatest stories have been told for hundreds of years and, with each retelling, they improve. Every time you rewrite your story, it gets better. It is hard work but maybe a hundred years from now, someone will read your story and say 'This is the best story I have ever read.' That is what I hope people will say about my stories someday. That is why I rewrite again and again, trying to make my stories sound like they have been told over and over. Happy writing. It is the most wonderful job in the world."

Michael Arvaarluk Kusugak

BIBLIOGRAPHY

Kusugak, Michael Arvaarluk. *Baseball Bats for Christmas.* Toronto: Annick Press, 1990 Paper 1-55037-144-4 Cloth 1-55037-145-2. Illustrations by Vladyana Langer Krykorka.

—. *Hide and Sneak.* Toronto: Annick Press, 1992 Paperback 1-55037-228-9 Cloth 1-55037-229-7. Illustrations by Vladyana Langer Krykorka.

—. *Northern Lights: The Soccer Trails.* Toronto: Annick Press, 1993 Paper 1-55037-338-2 Cloth 1-55037-339-0. Illustrations by Vladyana Langer Krykorka.

—. *My Arctic 1,2,3.* Toronto: Annick Press, 1996 Paper 1-55037-504-0 Cloth 1-55037-505-9. Illustrations by Vladyana Langer Krykorka.

—. *Arctic Stories.* Toronto: Annick Press, 1998 Paper 1-55037-452-4 Cloth 1-55037-453-2. Illustrations by Vladyana Langer Krykorka.

—. *Who Wants Rocks?* Toronto: Annick Press, 1999 Paper 1-55037-588-1 Cloth 1-55037-589-X. Illustrations by Vladyana Langer Krykorka.

— and Robert Munsch. *A Promise is a Promise.* Toronto: Annick Press, 1988 Paper 1-55037-008-1 Cloth 1-55037-009-X. Illustrations by Vladyana Langer Krykorka.

Awards

1994 Ruth Schwartz Children's Book Award for *Northern Lights: The Soccer Trails*

1995 CNIB Tiny Torgi Award for *Northern Lights: The Soccer Trails*

Julie Lawson
AUTHOR

Born
November 9, 1947, Victoria, British Columbia

School
University of Victoria, British Columbia

Where I live now
East Sooke on Vancouver Island, British Columbia

My favourite book when I was young
Anne of Green Gables by L.M. Montgomery.

My favourite book now
"Any good historical fiction or suspense thriller and mysteries."

Career
"I have worked as a library clerk and camp counsellor, but mostly as an elementary school teacher. Now I'm a full-time author."

Family
"I live with my husband, Patrick. I used to have a dog, chickens and ducks, but now my pets are the wild deer that graze in my yard and the grey squirrel that comes to my deck for peanuts."

The room where I create
"I write in an upstairs tower where every window looks out at the forest. From my desk I can also see the waterfall that flows into our pond. It's a perfect place for writing and daydreaming."

Spare time
"Curl up with a good book, hike in East Sooke Park, make quilts with thousands of pieces of material, row in the Sooke Basin, travel, spend time with friends. I also love to cook — and eat."

When I was growing up
"Summer was the best time. We'd pack everything into the car and head for the family cabin on the Sooke Basin — Mom, Dad, my brother, two canaries, two dogs and me. One summer there were eight puppies as well. We spent the time fishing, digging for clams, rowing, swimming, exploring the islands in the Basin, building tree forts, picking huckleberries, roasting marshmallows over beach fires, searching for arrowheads... There were no other kids to play with, so I often created stories in my mind and acted them out. There was no television, so at night or on rainy days my whole family would sit by the fire and read.

"The rest of the year I was in Victoria, going to school and taking piano lessons. I loved acting in plays at school. One Christmas, my grandfather gave my family a typewriter. I typed my first stories on that Royal typewriter — in red ink on yellow typewriting paper."

My first book (and how it happened)
"When I was a kid I loved writing stories, and dreamed that one day I'd become an author. I became a teacher instead, but figured I'd be an author during the summer holidays and in my spare time. I procrastinated for years, then finally decided to stop thinking about it and do it. So, in 1989 I took a six month leave of absence and seriously started to write.

"One day, I heard someone talking about 'sifting sand'. I liked the sound of those words and scribbled in my notebook 'old man sifts sand, tells stories...' and forgot about it. Then one day I was on a beach, watching the sand trickle through my fingers, and thought, what if every grain of sand held a story? And what if someone were able to tell those stories, by sifting the sand? The *Sand Sifter* came to life. Published in 1990, it weaves together adaptations of Pacific Rim folklore, while telling the tale of a mysterious old man and the children who come to love him and his stories."

Where my ideas come from
"My ideas come from found objects, overheard conversations and strange-sounding words. They can be triggered by a

nursery rhyme, a fairy tale, or an ancient folktale. Many of my ideas come from actual places and experiences. Travelling in China, hearing about a bear on a train in the Rockies, exploring Victoria's Chinatown, seeing the lava flow into the sea on the big island of Hawaii — these experiences have all worked their way into stories."

Who and what influenced me

"I have been tremendously influenced by reading the best in Canadian children's literature — picture books, juvenile fiction and young adult novels."

How I work

"A story usually begins with an idea jotted down in a notebook. Maybe a phrase, a sentence, an opening paragraph, a situation... I carry a notebook with me wherever I go.

"Eventually, one idea will push itself to the front of my mind and nag and nag until I can't do anything but go along with it. I'll take that initial idea to the computer and develop it, writing whatever comes to mind. This is the exciting part — new unexpected ideas surface, characters come to life and a structure begins to take shape.

"When this first draft is complete, I print a copy for the revising and editing. Changes are written in longhand. Then back to the word processor, making the changes and discovering new possibilities. I repeat these steps several times — writing, printing, revising, polishing — until I get it right. I'm always working on several stories at the same time, so if I get bogged down on one, I can switch to another."

Tips for young creators

"Read as much as you can. Write something every day, even if it's just scribbling down a idea. Keep an idea file with newspaper clippings or pictures or story starters. Ask 'What if...' questions to stimulate your imagination. Always be on the lookout for story possibilities."

Julie Lawson

BIBLIOGRAPHY

Lawson, Julie. *The Sand Sifter*. Victoria: Beach Holme, 1990 Paper 0-88878-288-8. Illustrations by Anna Mah.

—. *A Morning to Polish and Keep*. Red Deer: Red Deer College Press, 1992 Cloth 0-88995-082-2. Illustrations by Sheena Lott.

—. *My Grandfather Loved the Stars*. Victoria: Beach Holme, 1992 Cloth 0-88878-304-3. Illustrations by Judy McLaren.

—. *Kate's Castle*. Toronto: Oxford/Stoddart Kids, 1992 Paper 0-19-541001-7. Illustrations by Frances Tyrrell.

—. *The Dragon's Pearl*. Toronto: Oxford/Stoddart Kids, 1992. 1995 Paper 0-7737-5717-1; Cloth 0-7737-2882-1. Illustrations by Paul Morin.

—. *White Jade Tiger*. Victoria: Beach Holme, 1993 Paper 0-88878-332-9.

—. *Blown Away*. Red Deer: Red Deer College Press, 1995 Paper 0-88995-119-5. Illustrations by Kathryn Naylor.

—. *Fires Burning*. Toronto: Stoddart Kids, 1995 Paper 0-7736-7430-6.

—. "So, Tell Me." *The First Time*. Vol. 2. Victoria: Orca Book Publishers, 1995 Paper 1-55143-039-8.

—. *Whatever You Do, Don't Go Near That Canoe!* Richmond Hill: Scholastic Canada, 1996 Cloth 0-590-24429-9. Illustrations by Werner Zimmermann.

—. *Cougar Cove*. Victoria: Orca Book Publishers, 1996 Paper 1-55143-072-X.

—. *Too Many Suns*. Toronto: Stoddart Kids, 1996 Cloth 0-7737-2897-X. Illustrations by Martin Springett.

—. *Goldstone*. Toronto: Stoddart Kids, 1997 Paper 0-7737-5891-7.

—. *Emma and the Silk Train*. Toronto: Kids Can Press, 1997 Cloth 1-55074-388-0. Illustrations by Paul Mombourquette.

—. *Turns on a Dime*. Toronto: Stoddart Kids, 1998 Paper 0-7737-5942-5.

—. *In Like a Lion*. Richmond Hill: Scholastic Canada, 1998 Cloth 0-59024938-X. Illustrations by Yolaine Lefebvre.

—. *Midnight in the Mountains*. Victoria: Orca Book Publishers, 1998 Cloth 1-55143-113-0. Illustrations by Sheena Lott.

Awards

1993 U.S. National Parenting Publication Award for *The Dragon's Pearl*

1994 Sheila A. Egoff Children's Book Prize for *White Jade Tiger*

1997 CNIB Tiny Torgi Award for *Whatever You Do, Don't Go Near that Canoe!*

Selected articles about Julie Lawson

Campbell, Marie "Some Key Actors on Kids' Scene." *Quill & Quire* (Oct. 1992).

Heiman, Carolyn "Children's Book Author on Roll of Successes." *Victoria Times-Colonist* 25 Oct. 1992.

McFarlane, Sheryl. "Introducing Julie Lawson." *CANSCAIP News* 19.1 (1997): 1-4.

Dennis Lee
AUTHOR

Born
August 31, 1939, Toronto, Ontario

School
University of Toronto, Toronto, Ontario

Where I live now
Toronto, Ontario

My favourite book when I was young
"If I liked a book, I would live inside it until I finished it. So my favourite book was usually the one I was reading at the time. It felt more real than anything else."

My favourite book now
"All kinds of things. My favourite children's book is *The Wind in the Willows.*"

Career
Poet and editor

Family
Three grown children. One grandchild.

Spare time
"When words are coming, I don't seem to have any spare time. I may write for six or 10 hours, but my brain is on call the rest of the day as well. So I seldom do much reading or going out when stuff is coming through."

When I was growing up
Writing poetry has always come naturally to Dennis. A poem he wrote when he was seven was published in the children's magazine *Wee Wisdom*. From then until he graduated from the University of Toronto, he considered a variety of careers — perhaps he would become a magician, or perhaps a minister.

"Then, in my twenties, I was beginning to write seriously and think I might become a writer. I had to spend almost 10 years fidgeting around before I wrote anything good — even though I published one book of adult poetry first."

My first book (and how it happened)
"When I started reading nursery rhymes to my children, I quickly developed a twitch. All we seemed to read about were jolly millers, pigs, and queens."

So Dennis began composing rhymes and chants with a Canadian context, mixing the familiar with the fabulous. He spent nine years on this project. Part way through, in 1970, 14 of the poems were published as *Wiggle to the Laundromat.*

But the manuscript kept growing, until in 1974 it was divided in two. Poems for older children appeared as *Nicholas Knock*;

poems for younger children, as *Alligator Pie.* And *Alligator Pie* went on to become one of the most popular books for children ever published in Canada.

Where my ideas come from
"The ideas for my verses seem to wiggle in from anywhere. Sometimes it's a character I get fascinated with, sometimes a rhyme or a phrase or an even vaguer itch. All I know is that whatever I start with almost never ends up being the final subject of the poem.

"I try to encompass quite a broad range — from delicate lyrical pieces to rambunctious rude ones, from stories to broad jokes to expressions of fear or tenderness or aspiration. Poem by poem, I try to include as many of the strains of being human as I can. So then a whole book is a kind of birthday party to which all these aspects of ourselves are invited."

Writing for children
"Like everyone, I have more than one child in me," he explains. "I'm a two-year-old, I'm a five-year-old, I'm a ten-year-old. Those kids are excited by scary things, or silly things, or whatever. Ideally, what excites them will get written with the craft of the adult, under the direction of the child."

Writing songs

Dennis's unique way with words led him in a new direction: writing song lyrics. "I did the words for most of the songs in 'Fraggle Rock' with Phil Balsam writing the melodies." "Fraggle Rock" was co-produced by Jim Henson and CBC Television, and has been shown in nearly 100 countries around the world.

Dennis and Phil also wrote songs for the stage adaptation of *Jacob Two-Two Meets the Hooded Fang* and *Jacob Two-Two and the Dinosaur*, both based on the books by Mordecai Richler.

How he works

Working alone and in complete quiet in the study of his Toronto home, Dennis prefers to write his poems in longhand, typing and re-writing them as he goes along. Some of the four-line poems may be reworked as many as 30 times, the longer ones as many as 50 times.

Who and what influenced me

"As a children's poet I've been most influenced by Mother Goose, Lewis Carroll, and A.A. Milne. But after a while, you find a voice of your own."

Tips for young creators

"Write the thing that your heart knows. Don't be afraid to rewrite. My poetry for children is all in the older style — with rhyme, regular rhythms, and set stanza forms. But there's another way to write poetry, called 'free verse,' and for most kids it's a better place to begin. You're less likely to crank out artificial stuff, just to fill out the pattern. Your teacher or librarian or parents can show you how to do it."

Dennis Lee

BIBLIOGRAPHY

Lee, Dennis. *Alligator Pie*. Toronto: Macmillan Canada, 1974 Cloth 0-7715-9591-3. 1987 Paper 0-7715-9566-2. Illustrations by Frank Newfeld.

—. *Nicholas Knock and Other People*. Toronto: Macmillan Canada, 1974. Illustrations by Frank Newfeld. Out of print.

—. *Garbage Delight*. Toronto: Macmillan Canada, 1977 Cloth 0-7715-9592-1. 1988 Paper 0-7715-9541-7. Illustrations by Frank Newfeld.

—. *The Ordinary Bath*. Toronto: Magook, 1979. Illustrations by Jon McKee. Out of print.

—. *Wiggle to the Laundromat*. Toronto: New Press, 1980. Illustrations by Charles Pachter. Out of print.

—. *Jelly Belly*. Toronto: Macmillan Canada, 1983 Cloth 0-7715-9776-2. 1994 Paper 0-7715-9420-8. Illustrations by Juan Wijngaard.

—. *Lizzy's Lion*. Don Mills: Stoddart, 1984 Cloth 0-7737-0078-1. Paper 0-7736-7397-0. Illustrations by Marie-Louise Gay.

—. *The Dennis Lee Big Book*. Toronto: Macmillan Canada, 1985 Cloth 0-7715-9692-8. Illustrations by Barb Klunder.

—. *The Difficulty of Living on Other Planets*. Toronto: Macmillan Canada, 1987. Illustrations by Alan Daniel. Out of print.

—. *The Ice Cream Store*. Toronto: HarperCollins, 1991 Cloth 0-00-223749-0. 1996 Paper 0-00-647951-0. Illustrations by David McPhail.

—. *Ping and Pong*. Toronto: HarperCollins, 1993 Cloth 0-00-223996-5. Illustrations by David McPhail.

—. *Dinosaur Dinner (With a Slice of Alligator Pie)*. Ed. Jack Prelutsky. New York: Knopf, 1997 Cloth 0-679-87009-1. Illustrations by Debbie Tilley.

Awards

1974 IODE Book Award – Municipal Chapter of Toronto for *Alligator Pie*

1975 Canadian Library Association Book of the Year Award for Children for *Alligator Pie*

1978 Canadian Library Association Book of the Year Award for Children for *Garbage Delight*

1978 Ruth Schwartz Children's Book Award for *Garbage Delight*

1986 Vicky Metcalf Award for a Body of Work

1991 Mr. Christie's Book Award for *The Ice Cream Store*

1994 The Order of Canada

Selected articles about Dennis Lee

O'Brien, Leacy. "If Food be the Music of Poetry, Play on: Dennis Lee." *CM* 20.3 (1992): 137-8.

Pyper, Andrew. "The Fabulously Lucky Dennis Lee." *Quill and Quire* July 1996: 46.

Loris Lesynski
AUTHOR/ILLUSTRATOR

Born
Eskilstuna, Sweden, March 16, 1949

Where I live now
"Partly in the country, partly in Toronto."

My favourite books when I was young
"Anything British."

My favourite book now
"My notebook! Or else whatever I'm reading at the moment."

Career
"I've always been a graphic designer (I designed *this* book) and illustrator. Many of the 'spot' illustrations in spellers, French series and math books were done by me. But I always wanted to write and illustrate my own books for kids. It took me an incredibly long time to learn how because I just couldn't get it through my head that rough drafts and revisions are necessary for everyone; I thought if it didn't work right away it was a sign that it wasn't any good, and wouldn't ever be.

"Now I actually enjoy revising a story or polishing up a poem; now I'm pretty confident that somehow, some way, some day, it will turn out well.

"These days my 'job' is almost all about writing, illustrating and designing picture books and poems for kids, and going places to talk to children, teachers and librarians. I tell them what I've discovered about capturing ideas, and show them artwork from the rough sketches to the final stage, sometimes doing quick cartoons of the kids as ogres. I really like brainstorming with a group of kids, all of us blurting out our most original ideas and then writing a rhyming story together on the spot."

The room where I create
"…is the one between my ears. One of the great things about writing is that you can do it almost anywhere — on the bus, in a hammock, at the dentist."

Spare time
"My spare time, work time and play time are all kind of mixed up together. I'm always mulling over my stories and poems. My favourite other way to spend time is talking with people I like — the kind of talking where you laugh a lot and bounce ideas back and forth. I love reading and bring home bagfuls of books from the library. I also like listening to music, writing letters (and e-mails) and taking photographs."

When I was growing up
"I drew pictures for other kids all the time, such as cartoon portraits on the backs of their clipboards. I've always liked writing just about anything — letters, diaries, poems, stories. I started writing longer funny rhyming poems around Grade 6."

My first book (and how it happened)
"One day the title *Boy Soup* came into my head and I thought it was the funniest title I'd ever heard. The first line I wrote was:

> *'The boys cooked the carrots, the boys boiled the peas.'*

I adored how 'boys' and 'boiled' sounded together. That's a line in the middle of the book. Then I wrote backwards to the front and frontwards to the end, all the time making sketches of the Giant. It took a lot of fixing and changing, rewriting and revising, to get it right, but by the time I finished I really understood that reworking a story is a normal part of writing it, and can even be fun.

"The members of my writing group — Teresa, Ann, Susan and Nancy, all writers for children — are so tough. They won't let me get away with even one word that's crummy or just not quite right. It's like having four editors. But it works."

Where my ideas come from
"Not so much 'where' as 'how'. By staying open-minded and

open-hearted. Often by trying to avoid boring chores. Sometimes by connecting things that don't go together (like *boy* and *soup*). Most of all by trying to keep myself amused. Now that I know how to hear them, I notice wordplay, poems and stories hurtling around in my head all the time."

Who and what influenced me

"E. Nesbit, e.e. cummings, Dennis Lee, Lewis Carroll, Robert Service, Maurice Sendak. I really like the way Roald Dahl jumps right into a story."

How I work

"I'm usually working on a bunch of different drawings, poems, and story ideas at the same time. This isn't all that organized but it's exciting. Right now I'm putting together a book of poems called *Nothing Beats a Pizza* and another one called *Ummm....* To take a break from other writing, I'm working on a book of poems just for kindergarten kids — with maybe *Zigzag* for the title. For me, a picture book story can take four or five years to cook; right now I have several ideas I like a lot that are at the simmering stage (one is about a girl that turns to stone, and another will be called *Princess Camp*)."

Something nobody knew about me (until now)

"I often work in my flannelette pajamas. That's why they have ink spots and paint splotches all over them."

Tips for young creators

"Find books you enjoy and read them. Write whenever you feel like it, scribble down your story ideas, and make notes of your observations. Nobody can write about your experiences, your impressions or your point of view better than you can.

"Rewriting — fixing and revising and improving your writing — is as important as a good idea. I know, I know, nobody likes it at first, but once you get over that, it's so much fun and you really get good at it. Hardly anybody's story or poem is just right the first time it goes down on paper.

"If you like to draw, find art lessons somewhere while you're still a kid, just to learn the basics and try out different art supplies. (If you can't find classes, ask someone who draws and paints to spend a little time showing you how they do their work.)

"I hope you'll find a good box or bag in which to save some of your favourite drawings and writing. You'll love looking at it all when you're older.

"Most of all, hang on tightly to your own creativity. The world today always wants you to buy other people's stories, songs, artwork — even really dopey art 'kits' — so you have to be strong and say, 'No, I want to do this myself, no matter how it turns out.' What I most hope you'll want to do after reading my poems and stories is write some of your own."

Loris Lesynski

BIBLIOGRAPHY

Lesynski, Loris. *Boy Soup.* Toronto: Annick Press, 1996 Paper 1-55037-416-8; Cloth 1-55037-417-6. Illustrations by the author.

—. *Ogre Fun.* Toronto: Annick Press, 1997 Paper 1-55037-446-X; Cloth 1-55037-447-8. Illustrations by the author.

—. *Catmagic.* Toronto: Annick Press, 1998 Paper 1-55037-532-6; Cloth 1-55037-533-4. Illustrations by the author.

—. *Dirty Dog Boogie.* Toronto: Annick Press, 1999 Paper 1-55037-572-5; Cloth 1-55037-573-3. Illustrations by the author.

— *Night School.* Toronto: Annick Press, 2000. Paper 1-55037-584-9; Cloth 1-55037-585-7. Illustrations by the author.

Awards

"Nobody has given me any prizes or awards yet. If you would like to be the first, please call."

Selected articles about Loris Lesynski

Ceballo, Valerie. "Soup's On!" *The Lazy Writer* 1.3 (Fall 1997): 22-24.

Jean Little
AUTHOR

Born
January 2, 1932, Taiwan

School
University of Toronto, Toronto, Ontario

Where I live now
"Near Elora, Ontario in an old stone farmhouse. We have ten acres on a windy hilltop."

Career
Writer

Family
"My sister, Pat deVries, her granddaughter Jeanie and grandson Ben share the house with me. We also have three dogs: Ritz, my Seeing Eye dog who is a black Lab; Tobias, a tiny Papillon; and Hershey who is part Irish wolfhound. We have adopted a stray orange tabby cat who came meowing to our door. His name is Roughie (because he is orange and his story of his princely past is fishy). We also have a blue-eyed stray called Frankie and a black kitten called Spooky."

When she was growing up
Since birth, Jean's vision has been severely limited. She had an extremely supportive family and a good deal of credit for her achievements — surviving the teasing of schoolmates, success in school and university, teaching disabled children in Canada and the U.S., and the triumphs of her writing career — must rest with them.

When the Littles moved to Guelph, Ontario, from Taiwan, they found there were no special classes available for students with visual disabilities. Even though her parents, both doctors, knew that young Jean would never have more than 10 per cent vision, they decided to send her to a regular school. At home, she had no special privileges and was expected to participate in family life to the same degree as her two brothers and sister.

School
After her difficulties in seeing the blackboard in elementary and high school, Jean found university lectures a pleasure. She graduated first in her class from Victoria College, University of Toronto, then trained in the United States to be a teacher of disabled children. She began her teaching career at the Crippled Children's Centre in Guelph.

Books and writing
Despite her visual disability, books were an important part of Jean's life from an early age. She discovered that through reading, she could live lives other than her own. And books, unlike some of her young schoolmates, "were more accepting." By the time she was in her teens, she came to realize that the next best thing to escaping through reading was escaping through writing.

Jean's father encouraged her to write, and he sent two of her poems to *Saturday Night* magazine when she was just 17. The magazine decided to publish the poems, and when a $30 cheque arrived, Jean was so excited she didn't realize what the money was for — she certainly hadn't expected to be paid.

Her first book (and how it happened)
While Jean was attending a seminar in Utah on teaching handicapped children she met a published author of children's novels, Virginia Sorensen. With that meeting, Jean began considering a career as a writer. This ambition received a mighty boost when, in 1961, she took her manuscript for *Mine for Keeps* to a friendly librarian. The librarian suggested that Jean submit it for the Little, Brown Canadian Children's Book Award. The company would pay the winner $1,000, and publish the winning manuscript.

Jean took the librarian's advice — and won! Looking back, Jean confesses some embarrassment as to the ease with which her first novel was published: "When I'm travelling and people ask me whether I had any trouble getting my first book published, I almost hate to answer — they get so mad!"

How she works

While she is enormously enthusiastic about her career as a writer, Jean's limited vision makes the physical act of writing a complicated process. To write, Jean uses a talking computer — she types her manuscripts into the computer, and it reads back to her what she has written.

That relatively simple method is a far cry from the way she wrote one of her most popular novels, *Mama's Going to Buy You a Mockingbird*. She dictated her manuscript, punctuation and all, onto many cassette tapes. After it was typed, her editor, Shelley Tanaka, read the manuscript back to her and both suggested revisions. It took Jean seven and a half years to complete the book, and it went on to win the Canadian Library Association Book of the Year Award for Children, and was made into a feature-length film shown on CBC Television.

Jean Little

BIBLIOGRAPHY

Little, Jean. *Mine for Keeps*. Toronto: Little Brown, 1962. Toronto: Penguin Books, 1994 Cloth 0- 670-85967-2. 1996 Paper 0-14-037686-0.

—. *Home From Far*. New York: Little Brown, 1965. Illustrations by Jerry Lazare. Out of print.

—. *Spring Begins in March*. Toronto: Little, Brown, 1966. Toronto: Penguin Books, 1996 Paper 0-14-038084-1. Illustrations by Lewis Parker.

—. *Take Wing*. Toronto: Little, Brown, 1968. Out of print.

—. *When the Pie Was Opened*. Toronto: Little, Brown, 1968. Out of print.

—. *One to Grow On*. Toronto: Little Brown, 1969. Toronto: Penguin Books Canada, 1991. Paper 0-14-034667-8.

—. *Look Through My Window*. New York: HarperCollins, 1970. 1995 Paper 0-00-648078-0. Illustrations by Joan Sandin.

—. *Kate*. New York: HarperCollins, 1971. 1995 Paper 0-00-648073-X..

—. *From Anna*. New York: HarperCollins, 1972. Markham: Fitzhenry and Whiteside, 1977. 2nd Ed. Paper 0-88902-373-5. Illustrations by Joan Sandin.

—. *Stand in the Wind*. New York: HarperCollins, 1975. Toronto: Penguin Books, 1995 Paper 0-14-038056-6. Illustrations by Emily A. McCully.

—. *Listen for the Singing*. New York: E.P. Dutton, 1977. Toronto: Stoddart, 1989 Paper 0-7737- 5327-3.

—. *Mama's Going to Buy You a Mockingbird*. Toronto: Penguin Books Canada, 1984 Cloth 0-670-80346-4. 1985 Paper 0-14-031737-6.

—. *Lost and Found*. Toronto: Penguin Books Canada, 1985 Paper 0-14-031997-2.

—. *Different Dragons*. Toronto: Penguin Books Canada, 1986 Cloth 0-670-80836-9. 1988 Paper 0-14-031998-0.

—. *Hey World, Here I Am!* Toronto: Kids Can Press, 1986 Paper 1-55074-036-9. Illustrations by Sue Truesdell.

—. *Little By Little*. Toronto: Penguin Books Canada, 1987 Cloth 0-670-81649-3. 1989 Paper 0-14-032325-2.

—. *Invitations to Joy: A Celebration of Canada's Young Readers and the Books They Love*. Toronto: The Canadian Children's Book Centre, 1989. Out of print.

—. *Stars Come Out Within*. Toronto: Penguin Books Canada, 1990 Cloth 0-670-82965-X. 1992 Paper 0-14-034714-3.

—. *Jess Was the Brave One*. Toronto: Penguin Books Canada, 1991. Illustrations by Janet Wilson. Out of print.

—. *Revenge of the Small Small*. Toronto: Penguin Books Canada, 1992 Cloth 0-670-844471-3. 1995 Paper 0-14-055563-3. Illustrations by Janet Wilson.

—. *His Banner Over Me*. Toronto: Penguin Books Canada, 1995 Cloth 0-670-85664-9. 1996 Paper 0-14-037761-1.

—. *Jenny and the Hanukkah Queen*. Toronto: Penguin Books Canada, 1995. Illustrations by Suzanne Mogensen.

—. *Gruntle Piggle Takes Off*. Toronto: Penguin Books Canada, 1996 Cloth 0-670-86340-8. Illustrations by Johnny Wales.

—. *The Belonging Place*. Toronto: Penguin Books Canada, 1997 Cloth 0-670-87593-7.

—. *What Will the Robin Do Then?* Toronto: Penguin Books Canada, 1999 Paper 1-14-130152-X.

—. *Emma's Magic Winter*. Toronto: HarperCollins, 1998 Paper 0-00-648081-0 Cloth 0-06-025389-4.

continued

—. *I Know An Old Laddie.* Toronto: Penguin Books Canada, 1999 Cloth 0-670-88085-X. Illustrations by Rose Cowles.

—. *Willow and Twig.* Toronto: Penguin Books Canada, 2000 Cloth 0-670-88856-7.

Little, Jean, and Maggie deVries. *Once Upon a Golden Apple.* Toronto: Penguin Books Canada, 1991 Cloth 0-670-82963-3. 1993 Paper 0-14-054164-0. Illustrations by Phoebe Gilman.

Mackay, Claire, and Jean Little. *Bats About Baseball.* Toronto: Penguin Books Canada, 1995. Cloth 0-670-85270-8. Illustrations by Kim LaFave.

Awards

1961 Little, Brown Canadian Children's Book Award for *Mine for Keeps*

1974 Vicky Metcalf Award for a Body of Work

1977 Canada Council Children's Literature Prize for *Listen for the Singing*

1981 Deutscher Jugendliteraturpreis (Germany)

1985 Canadian Library Association Book of the Year for Children Award for *Mama's Going to Buy You a Mockingbird*

1985 Ruth Schwartz Children's Book Award for *Mama's Going to Buy You a Mockingbird*

1988 Boston Globe/Horn Book Honour Book Award for *Little By Little*

1991 The Order of Canada

Honorary Doctorates from University of Guelph and Nipissing University

Selected articles about Jean Little

"In Person: Blind Author Spreads Glory of Reading Children's Books." *The Globe & Mail* 9 Dec. 1991.

Frazer, Frances. "Something on Jean Little." *Canadian Children's Literature* 53 (1989): 33-39.

Greenwood, Barbara. "Introducing Jean Little." *CANSCAIP News* 7.3 (1985): 2-3.

Hart, Diane. "Author Knows How an Outsider Feels." *The Toronto Star* 2 Nov. 1997: E1.

Ross, Catherine "An Interview with Jean Little." *Canadian Children's Literature* 34 (1984): 6-22.

Celia Barker Lottridge
AUTHOR

Born
April 1, 1936, Iowa City, Iowa, U.S.A.

School
Illinois (kindergarten); California (Grades 1 to 4, two schools); Massachusetts (Grades 5 to 6); Kansas (Grades 7 to 12, two towns); university in California, New York City and Toronto, Ontario.

Where I live now
Toronto, Ontario

My favourite book when I was young
Swallows and Amazons by Arthur Ransome.

My favourite book now
"Any book I'm in the middle of reading."

Career
"I've done a lot of things but the common thread in all of my work has been children, books and stories. First I was a children's librarian, then a teacher-librarian, then I worked at the Children's Book Store in Toronto. Now I am a writer and a storyteller and Director of the Parent-Child Mother Goose Program where we teach parents to share stories and rhymes with their young children."

Family
"I have a grown-up son named Andrew. For 17 years I had a brown dog named Vanya. Someday I'll have another dog, but right now I travel too much."

The room where I create
"After years of writing in the kitchen I have a third-floor study with a slanting ceiling, a desk with a computer on it, and shelves and shelves of books. When I need inspiration I take a notebook to a café or art gallery. The people and the pictures seem to jog my imagination."

Spare time
"I love to travel by car, train or plane. When I arrive in a new place I walk for miles and look at things — which is exactly what I do when I'm at home. I also read, go to art galleries, swim and listen to other storytellers."

When I was growing up
"When I was a kid we moved often. I saw a lot of wonderful country but I got tired of having to make new friends. Books were very important to me because they were like friends who could travel with me wherever I might go. I also had a brother, a sister and a dog. My brother was fun to play with most of the time, my sister (who is seven years younger than I) loved to listen to stories I told her, and our dog was friendly and funny (she was a daschund). We had other animals, too, especially after we settled down in a small town when I was 12. We had a cat, pigs, chickens, ducks, a lamb and, for a little while, a horse who used to run away a lot because she missed the farm where she was born. Finally we took her back to stay."

My first book (and how it happened)
"My first book happened because I always wanted to make up stories and write them down. I dreamed of having a book with my name on it in a library. But for a long time it was only a dream because I had horrible handwriting when I was young and I couldn't spell very well either, so no one encouraged me to write stories. They just corrected my mistakes. When I finally learned to write properly I was in high school and I was in the habit of telling stories, not writing them. Years later it occurred to me that I could write down one of the stories I told. I did that and it became my first book, *Gerasim and the Lion*."

Where my ideas come from
"I get ideas from watching people in my neighbourhood,

from remembering things that happened to me, from stories people have told me about their lives, and from folk tales I tell in schools and libraries."

Who and what influenced me

"My parents told me many stories about what happened to them when they were young. My father also made up adventure stories and told them to us on our many car trips. And when we weren't on car trips, my mother read aloud to us every night after supper while we did the dishes. So stories were always an important part of my life. A later, very important influence was the children who talked to me about the books they love and don't love and all the children I have told stories to for over 30 years. Every time I go to a school or library this influence is at work."

How I work

"Many of my books are based on folk tales or true stories I have heard, so I often tell them to people before I write them down. Since I visit schools as a storyteller I have plenty of chances to do this. When a story feels right being told, then it is ready to be written. That's the first draft.

"I rewrite my stories 10 or 20 times after that. The most important thing is to give the story a rest between drafts. I try not to even think about it while it is resting, so when I go back to it, I read it with a fresh eye and can see what needs to be changed."

Something nobody knew about me (until now)

"I love the pictures that artists have made up for my stories, but the truth is, inside my head, I have a completely different set of pictures — the ones I had in

my mind as I wrote the story. Since I am not an artist those pictures will always be my own secret."

Tips for young creators

"Read, read, read. Take time to daydream. Let your mind wander. That lets story ideas take shape in your mind. See the story in your mind's eye while you write. Read your story aloud to yourself, your dog or a friend. You will probably hear places that don't sound quite the way you want them too. Make a few changes and there's your second draft!"

Celia Barker Lottridge

BIBLIOGRAPHY

Lottridge, Celia Barker. *The Juggler*. Richmond Hill: Scholastic Canada, 1985. Illustrations by Ariadne Ochrymovych. Out of print.

—. *One Watermelon Seed*. Don Mills: Stoddart/Oxford University Press, 1986. 1997 Paper 0-7737-5944-1. Illustrations by Karen Patkau.

—. *Mice* (Nature's Children). Toronto: Grolier, 1986. Out of print. ✦

—. *The Name of the Tree*. Toronto: Groundwood Books, 1989 Cloth 0-88899-097-9. Illustrations by Ian Wallace.

—. *Ticket to Curlew*. Toronto: Groundwood Books, 1992 Cloth 0-88899-163-0. 1994 Paper 0-88899-221-1. Illustrations by Wendy Wolsak.

—, ed. *The Moon is Round and Other Rhymes to Play with Your Baby*. Toronto: Vermont Square, 1992 Paper 0-9681462-0-1. Illustrations by Bud Fujikawa.

—. *Ten Small Tales*. Toronto: Groundwood Books, 1993 Cloth 0-88899-156-8. Illustrations by Joanne Fitzgerald.

—. *Something Might Be Hiding*. Toronto: Groundwood Books, 1994 Cloth 0-88899-176-2. Illustrations by Paul Zwolak.

—, comp. *Letters to the Wind: Classic Stories and Poems for Children*. Toronto: Key Porter Books, 1995 Cloth 1-55013-631-3.

—. *The Wind Wagon*. Toronto: Groundwood Books, 1997 Paper 0-88899-234-3. Illustrations by Clifford Daniel.

—. *Wings to Fly*. Toronto: Groundwood Books, 1997 Paper 0-88899-280-7; Cloth 0-88899-293-9. Illustrations by Jack McMaster.

—. *Music for the Tsar of the Sea*. Toronto: Groundwood Books, 1998 Cloth 0-88899-328-5. Illustrations by Harvey Chan.

Lottridge, Celia Barker, and Sandra Carpenter-Davis. *Bounce Me, Tickle Me, Hug Me: Lap Rhymes and Play Rhymes from Around the World*. Toronto: Parent-Child Mother Goose Program/Groundwood Books, 1997 Paper 0-9681462-2-8.

Lottridge, Celia Barker, and Alison Dickie, comp. *Mythic Voices, Reflections in Mythology*. Scarborough: Nelson Canada, 1990 Paper 0-17-603713-6.

Lottridge, Celia Barker, and Susan Horner. *Prairie Dogs* (Nature's Children). Toronto: Grolier, 1985. Out of print. ✦

Awards

1993 IODE Book Award – Municipal Chapter of Toronto for *Ten Small Tales*

1993 Canadian Library Association Book of the Year for Children Award for *Ticket to Curlew*

1993 Geoffrey Bilson Award for Historical Fiction for Young People for *Ticket to Curlew*

1998 IODE Violet Downey Book Award for *Wings to Fly*

1999 Ruth Schwartz Children's Book Award for *Music for the Tsar of the Sea*

Janet Lunn
AUTHOR

Born
"December 28, 1928, Dallas, Texas, U.S.A. (We moved to Vermont when I was an infant.)"

School
Norwich, Vermont; Rye, New York; Montclair, New Jersey; Queen's University, Kingston, Ontario

Where I live now
"An old farm house in rural Ontario beside a small Lake Ontario bay. When we moved into this house in 1968, it had a leaking roof, no furnace, no plumbing, and crumbling plaster on all its walls. The only soul who seemed to care a button for it was the ghost of an old woman who appeared to some of us on the stairs and in the big downstairs bedroom."

My favourite book when I was young
"*The Secret Garden* by Frances Hodgson Burnett. (I also loved *Heidi*, *Little Women* and all of Nesbit)."

My favourite book now
"Still *The Secret Garden* but I read all the time and some of Jane Gardam's books are serious contenders."

Career
"Mother (five children), writer, reviewer, lecturer. To answer a most-often-asked question, I write only for children."

Family
"One brother and two sisters (all living in the U.S.A.); five kids, all grown; six grandchildren; two step-great-grandchildren; four step-grandchildren; one inside cat and one outside cat (a stray who boards here but does not room)."

The room where I create
"The room where I work was, a hundred years ago, a child's bedroom. Out of its window I can see the back yard and, through the trees, the bay beyond. My work room is crammed full of stuff, the back yard is full of birds and animals and I love it."

Spare time
"All summer I garden but when the garden settles down for the winter, I hibernate. I like to listen to music (classical and folk), I like movies and I'm a compulsive reader, talker and visitor. I travel a lot."

When I was growing up
"I dreamed all the time, making sequels to all the books I read. I drew and I painted (not very well) and I loved dolls — I still have the dollhouse I had when I was small (and my mother had when she was small). My children had it later, but it is too old and fragile for their children so it is in my home where they visit. One sister and I used to make up stories together — now we are working on a history of our family.

"We lived in an eighteenth-century farm house in Vermont; I loved the tales about the Abenakis' battles that gave our brook the name 'Blood Brook' and about the pioneer family's baby buried under the old pine tree outside my bedroom window. I used to lie in bed at night listening to the wind, making up stories about those battles, about that baby, and about pioneer times and the American Revolution. In those stories I always saved my whole (imaginary) family from certain death by some incredibly brave deed. And not only did I conjure up the exciting events, I pictured every detail of the log cabin and the clothes my story people wore."

My first book (and how it happened)
"*Double Spell* (1968) was written when I got to know a pair of identical twins. I discovered that they didn't always love being twins. I'd always wanted to be a twin (in my head I was often many people) so this fascinated me — and so the story began. As stories will do, it grew and

changed, shrank, grew and changed some more. I wrote whole chapters that I couldn't use, created characters who never appeared in the final writing. It still seems strange to me that my long daydream is lodged between book covers for other people to read."

Where my ideas come from

"Ideas come from all over. *Amos's Sweater* came to be because of a cantankerous old ram I met at my friend Peg Fraser's farm near Norwich, Vermont. I thought he was funny and I liked him, so I made up a story for him. *The Root Cellar* came to be as a result of moving into this old house and *Shadow in Hawthorn Bay* and *The Hollow Tree* followed after, each one a different period of the island's history. *One Hundred Shining Candles* was because I love Christmas."

Who and what influenced me

"I've been influenced by everything that has happened to me, everyone I've ever known or read about. Chief among these influences are a childhood in rural Vermont (I am a true country person), the books I have loved that have fed my all-too-active imagination, two wonderful English teachers, and my late husband whose love for his home brought me to the countryside where I live and about which I write."

How I work

"With great difficulty. When I have a new book to write I do anything and everything to avoid it. When I finally sign a contract with a publisher saying that I will have the story ready at a certain time, I make myself set to work. Once I've started, I can't think of anything else until it's finished. I live almost more in the world of my story than in the

world where I eat and sleep. Bits of writing are all over the house, reference books are everywhere. The cat does not like finding maps, books and parts of chapter five on his favourite sleeping place."

Something nobody knew about me (until now)

"When I'm really tired or I can't write (because everything I write seems wrong) I like to colour colouring books. I'm glad there are colouring books of birds and wildflowers, complicated ones in which I have to think hard about the colours. Colouring books help my thinking in winter — in summer, gardening does."

My favourite book that I've created

"My favourite book is always the one I'm working on because I'm living so deeply in that world. I do find though, that I feel the greatest pleasure when people tell me they like *One Hundred Shining Candles*. I think it is because I love Christmas. I really enjoy reading that story aloud."

Tips for young creators

"Find your own way of working. We are all different and need to discover for ourselves how we work best. The important thing is to make yourself work even when you don't feel like it. It's amazing how once you get started, you want to work!"

Janet Lunn

BIBLIOGRAPHY

Lunn, Janet. *Double Spell*. Toronto: Penguin Books Canada, 1966. 1986 Paper 0-14-031858-5.

—. *Larger Than Life*. Toronto: Press Porcépic, 1979. Out of print.

—. *The Twelve Dancing Princesses*. Toronto: Methuen, 1979. Illustrations by Laszlo Gal. Out of print.

—. *The Root Cellar*. Toronto: Penguin Books Canada, 1986. 1996 Paper 0-14-038036-1. Illustrations by Scott Cameron.

—. *Amos's Sweater*. Toronto: Groundwood Books, 1988 Cloth 0-88899-074-X. 1994 Paper 0-88899-208-4. Illustrations by Kim LaFave. ✽

—. *Shadow in Hawthorn Bay*. Toronto: Penguin Books Canada, 1988 Paper 0-14-032436-4.

—, ed. *The Canadian Children's Treasury*. Toronto: Key Porter Books, 1988 Cloth 1-55013-066-8. 1994 Paper 1-55013-507-4.

—. *Duck Cakes for Sale*. Toronto: Groundwood Books, 1989 Paper 0-88899-094-4. 1992 Paper 0-88899-157-6. Illustrations by Kim LaFave.

—. *One Hundred Shining Candles*. Toronto, Lester Orpen and Dennys/ Key Porter, 1990 Cloth 0-88619-185-8. 1994 Paper 1-55013-636-4. Illustrations by Lindsay Grater.

—, comp. *The Unseen: Scary Stories Selected by Janet Lunn*. Toronto: Lester Publishing, 1994 Cloth 1-895555-42-6. 1996 Paper 0-7737-5845-3.

—. *The Hollow Tree*. Toronto: Alfred A. Knopf Canada, 1997 Cloth 0-394-28074-1. 1998 Paper 0-676-97143-7.

—. *Come to the Fair*. Toronto: Tundra Books, 1997 Cloth 0-88776-409-6. Illustrations by Gilles Pelletier. ✽

—. *Charlotte*. Toronto: Tundra Books, 1998 Cloth 0-8776-383-9. Illustrations by Brian Deines.

continued

—. *The Umbrella Party*. Toronto: Groundwood Books, 1998 Cloth 0-88899-298-X. Illustrations by Kady MacDonald Denton.

Lunn, Janet, and Christopher Moore. *The Story of Canada*. Toronto: Key Porter Books/Lester Publishing, 1992 Cloth 1-895555-32-9. Rev. ed. 1996 Third ed. 2000 Paper 1-55263-150.8. Illustrations by Alan Daniel.

Awards

1979 IODE Book Award – Municipal Chapter of Toronto for *The Twelve Dancing Princesses*

1982 Canadian Library Association Book of the Year for Children Award for *The Root Cellar*

1982 Vicky Metcalf Award for a Body of Work

1986 Canada Council Children's Literature Prize for *Shadow in Hawthorn Bay*

1987 Canadian Library Association Book of the Year for Children Award for *Shadow in Hawthorn Bay*

1987 IODE Violet Downey Book Award for *Shadow in Hawthorn Bay*

1987 Saskatchewan Library Association Young Adult Book of the Year Award for *Shadow in Hawthorn Bay*

1989 Ruth Schwartz Children's Book Award for *Amos's Sweater*

1992 IODE Book Award – Toronto Chapter for *The Story of Canada*

1992 Honorary Doctorate, Queen's University

1993 Honorary Diploma, Loyalist College

1993 Information Book Award for The Story of Canada

1993 Mr. Christie's Book Award for *The Story of Canada*

1996 Order of Ontario

1997 Order of Canada

Selected articles about Janet Lunn

The International Who's Who of Women. London: Europa Publications, 1992.

Reed, Brenda. "Canadian History from Cows to Catalogues: Janet Lunn." *CM* 20.6 (1992): 294-297.

Something About the Author. Ed. Anne Commire. Detroit: Gale Research, vol. 4.

Who's Who in Canadian Literature 1992-93. Toronto: Reference Press, 1992.

Roy MacGregor
AUTHOR

Born
June 4, 1948, Whitney, Ontario

School
Early education in Huntsville, Ontario, then Laurentian University and University of Western Ontario

Where I live now
Kanata, Ontario

My favourite books when I was young
Thornton W. Burgess' animal books, Jack London, *The Hardy Boys, Wind in the Willows*, Scott Young's hockey books

My favourite book now
As I Lay Dying by William Faulkner

Career
Columnist with the *The National Post*, previously sports columnist with *The Ottawa Citizen*, general columnist with *The Toronto Star*

Family
Married to Ellen, four children: Kerry, Christine, Jocelyn, Gordon

The room where I create
"A main-floor office in our home, with a window looking out onto the street. I have a computer, a CD player and hundreds of books in the room."

Spare time
"I walk the dog, play hockey three times a week, and spend summers at a cottage on the edge of Algonquin Park, near where I grew up."

When I was growing up
"I was always into sports, playing hockey, lacrosse and baseball at the competitive level. I was lucky to play against Bobby Orr for many years when we were of minor hockey age. He was great; I was a fringe player. I also took up golf around age 13 and became quite interested in it. I did well at school, then badly enough to fail Grade 12, then well enough to pass the rest of the way."

My first book (and how it happened)
"My first book was for adult readers, a novel about the life of painter Tom Thomson. There was a family connection to the story, and it had interested me all my life. My first book for young readers came much later, and was done at the suggestion of my publisher, Douglas Gibson of McClelland & Stewart."

Where my ideas come from
"From imagination, from research, and from luck."

Who and what influenced me
"I am influenced by everyone I have met and everywhere I have been, but mostly by family, both the one in which I grew up and the one in which I now live."

How I work
"I research each Screech Owls book by actually going to where the book will be set. Then I organize it, working out the plot very carefully. Then I start to write — and I never can tell what's going to happen."

Something nobody knew about me (until now)
"When I go to a new place, I pretend I'm one of my characters — Nish —and see if there is material there for him to use. He is always in trouble, so I look for it."

My favourite book that I've created
"For grownups, *Chief: The Fearless Vision of Billy Diamond*, about the Crees of northern Quebec. For young readers, *The Screech Owls' Northern Adventure*, which is also the story of the Crees of northern Quebec, only told differently."

Tips for young creators
"Plan your plots, then get to work. Even if nothing seems to be happening, it soon will and you won't even be aware of it until you suddenly stop, sweating and breathless, and wonder where the time went."

Roy MacGregor

BIBLIOGRAPHY

MacGregor, Roy. *Mystery at Lake Placid*. Toronto: McClelland & Stewart, 1995 Paper 0-7710-5625-7.

—. *The Night They Stole the Stanley Cup*. Toronto: McClelland & Stewart, 1995 Paper 0-7710-5626-5.

—. *The Screech Owls' Northern Adventure*. Toronto: McClelland & Stewart, 1996 Paper 0-7710-5628-1.

—. *Murder at Hockey Camp*. Toronto: McClelland & Stewart, 1996 Paper 0-7710-5629- X.

—. *Kidnapped in Sweden*. Toronto: McClelland & Stewart, 1997 Paper 0-7710-5615-X.

—. *Terror in Florida*. Toronto: McClelland & Stewart, 1997 Paper 0-7710-5616-8.

—. *The Quebec City Crisis*. Toronto: McClelland & Stewart, 1998 Paper 0-7710-5617-6.

—. *The Screech Owls' Home Loss*. Toronto: McClelland & Stewart, 1998 Paper 0-7710-5618-4.

—. *Nightmare in Nagano*. Toronto: McClelland & Stewart, 1998 Paper 0-7710-5619-2.

—. *Danger in Dinosaur Valley*. Toronto: McClelland & Stewart, 1999 Paper 0-7710-5620-6.

—. *The Ghost of the Stanley Cup*. Toronto McClelland & Stewart 1999 Paper 0-7710-5622-2.

Awards

1998 Manitoba Young Reader's Choice Award for *Mystery at Lake Placid*

Roy MacGregor has also won numerous awards for his adult work.

For more information about Roy MacGregor, visit his Web sites at
www.umanitoba.ca/cm/profiles/mcgregor.html
or
www.screechowls.com

Claire Mackay
AUTHOR

Born
"December 21, 1930 in a little second-floor flat above a pool hall in Toronto, Ontario."

School
Jarvis Collegiate, University of Toronto, both in Toronto, Ontario; postgraduate work at University of British Columbia, Vancouver, British Columbia; further studies, University of Manitoba, Winnipeg, Manitoba.

Where I live now
Toronto, Ontario

My favourite books when I was young
Og, Son of Fire; Emily of New Moon.

My favourite book now
"Far too many favourites to list; the Narnia books and Susan Cooper's *Dark is Rising* series are some I love."

Career
Writer

Family
"One husband, three sons, five grandchildren including twin girls. No pet now, but our last one was a huge tomcat named Darth Vader who challenged a motorcycle to a duel and lost."

The room where I create
"Large, many-windowed, slanted-ceiling, third-floor room where raccoons and cardinals perch outside and observe me."

Spare time
"Go bird-watching; read dictionaries; solve extremely difficult cryptic crossword puzzles; watch baseball games; and read."

When I was growing up
"I was born and my father lost his job at the beginning of the Depression. I was painfully shy and turned to books for comfort, friendship, and even oblivion. I read constantly, up to 20 books a week. I started a newspaper at age eight, spying on neighbours for news items. I adored words, language, poetry and read aloud to my mother even though she didn't listen. I hated the telephone because it interrupted my reading. At age 10, I got a job in the public library (10 cents an hour)."

My first book (and how it happened)
Claire's writing career began with a story she wrote to please her 11-year-old son.

"I said to myself, 'I'll try this, though it will never see print.' There was a certain therapy in describing the father-son conflict because of the tension in our own family at that time. In a way *Mini-Bike Hero* was the result of a very practical resolve to start, continue, and finish a fairly lengthy writing project — with no thought of publication. When it was finished, though, I saw an ad in a magazine and sent the story in. Of course I thought I'd get it right back."

But Scholastic liked the manuscript and decided to publish it. Even then, Claire thought she had reached the end of a process rather than the start of a career. "I thought it would be a little book nobody would notice and a few kids would read."

The first printing sold out in four months, and fan letters started arriving. "You're sure on our side!" wrote one of her young readers. A teacher wrote: "The kids feel you're a personal friend of theirs. We've never had an author who had that kind of personal impact." Claire believes her first book made such an impact because "I championed the idea of kids making their own choices about their own activities."

Where my ideas come from
"My own experiences as a child — and my children's and grandchildren's experiences. Unexplored events in history. Any experience which surprises, delights or enlightens me, giving me the sudden exquisite knowledge of what it is to be human."

Who and what influenced me

"My Grade 8 teacher, Mr. Newton, who taught me that the only failure is not trying again. My professor at U.B.C., Frances McCubbin, who encouraged me to write when, at age 37, I had all but abandoned the dream of doing so. Jean Little and Katherine Paterson, fine writers and excellent friends. To be in their company is an education, a keen pleasure, and a privilege. They have made me believe I can write when I was sure I couldn't."

How I work

"Slowly! Usually in the morning, when my brain is less torpid than usual. I revise endlessly. Sometimes pages go through 30 drafts but I like revising. It means I've got a story to work on!"

Something nobody knew about me (until now)

"I am terrified of moths, the big furry-bodied kind that rattle at the windows. Confront me with moths and I would betray my mother, my children and my native land."

My favourite book that I've created

"I like them all, or parts of them all for different reasons: *Mini-Bike Hero* because it got me started writing for publication; *The Minerva Program* because it's the best-written; *Exit Barney McGee* because Barney's emotional life was like mine as a child; and all the non-fiction books because they are subjects close to my heart."

Tips for young creators

"Read all the time, and everything. Write every day if you can. Watch other people and how they behave. Listen to find out why people behave as they do. Learn the tools of the writing trade."

Claire Mackay

BIBLIOGRAPHY

Mackay, Claire. *Mini-Bike Hero*. Richmond Hill: Scholastic Canada, 1974. Rev. ed. 1991 Paper 0-590-73636-1. ✢

—. *Mini-Bike Racer*. Richmond Hill: Scholastic Canada, 1976. Rev. ed.1991 Paper 0-590-73637-X.

—. *Exit Barney McGee*. Richmond Hill: Scholastic Canada, 1979. Rev. ed. 1992 Paper 0-590-71863-0.

—. *Mini-Bike Rescue*. Richmond Hill: Scholastic Canada, 1982. Rev. ed. 1991 Paper 0-590-73638-8. ✢

—. *The Minerva Program*. Toronto: James Lorimer & Co., 1984 Paper 0-88862-716-5; Cloth 0-88862-717-3. ✢

—. *Pay Cheques and Picket Lines: All About Unions in Canada*. Toronto: Kids Can Press, 1987. Paper 0-921103-34-4; Cloth 0-921103-32-8. ✢

—. *The Toronto Story*. Toronto: Annick Press, 1990 Paper 1-55037-135-5; Cloth 1- 55037-137-1. Illustrations by Johnny Wales.

—. *Touching All the Bases: Baseball for Kids of All Ages*. Richmond Hill: Scholastic Canada, 1994 Paper 0-590-24200-8. Illustrations by Bill Slavin.

— ed. *Laughs: Funny Stories*. Tundra Books, 1997 Paper 0-88776-393-6.

Hewitt, Marsha, and Claire Mackay. *One Proud Summer*. Toronto: Penguin Books Canada, 1981 Paper 0-88961-048-7. ✢

Mackay, Claire, and Jean Little. *Bats About Baseball*. Toronto: Penguin Books Canada, 1995 Cloth 0-670-85270-8. Illustrations by Kim LaFave.

Awards

1982 Ruth Schwartz Children's Book Award for *One Proud Summer*

1983 Vicky Metcalf Award for a Body of Work

1988 Vicky Metcalf Short Story Award for "Marvin and Me and the Flies" in *Canadian Children's Annual* No. 12

1990 Parenting Publications of America Award of Excellence

1992 City of Toronto Civic Award of Merit

Selected articles about Claire Mackay

Barbara Greenwood, ed. *The CANSCAIP Companion*. Rev. ed. Markham: Pembroke Publishers, 1994.

Michasiw, Barbara. "Freeing the Creative Imagination." *Canadian Children's Literature* 64 (1991).

Something About the Author: Autobiography Series. Detroit: Gale Research, vol. 25 (1998).

Kevin Major

AUTHOR

Born
September 12, 1949,
Stephenville, Newfoundland

School
Amalgamated Schools,
Stephenville; Memorial
University, St. John's; both in
Newfoundland.

Where I live now
St. John's, Newfoundland

My favourite book when I was young
The Old Man and the Sea by
Ernest Hemingway.

My favourite book now
The Remains of the Day by
Kazuo Ishiguro.

Career
Junior and senior high school
teacher 1970-74; substitute
teacher 1974-89; writer since
1974.

Family
Wife, Anne; two sons; no pets.

The room where I create
"I have worked in a basement, a
cottage by the sea, a laundry
room, the kitchen table and now I
have a new second-storey space!"

Spare time
"I like to read, spend time with
my family, visit art galleries and
spend time in the garden and
canoe."

When I was growing up
"I was the youngest of seven
children, the only one born after
Newfoundland became the
tenth province of Canada. My
father was fond of calling me 'the
only Canadian in the family'.

"My family had moved to
Stephenville from a small out-
port community when the United
States built an air force base
there during World War II. My
father continued to fish in the
summertime, as he had done
before, but also worked at various
jobs for the Americans and
operated a restaurant for several
years. It was a very interesting
place to spend my youth: I was a
new Canadian, yet very much a
Newfoundlander, and surrounded by American culture.

"With seven years' difference
between myself and the next
youngest in the family, I spent
my teenage years almost as an
only child. I was shy and spent a
lot of time alone. Although I
remember liking books from an
early age, I didn't spend endless
hours reading everything I could
get my hands on. And even
though I wrote poems and
stories for contests and school
yearbooks, it was only as I
neared the end of high school
that I started to think of myself
as having a special interest in
writing. I remember a Grade 10
teacher saying he thought that
someday I would write a book."

My first book (and how it happened)
"I went to Memorial University
in St. John's and studied pre-med
for three years with the intention
of becoming a doctor. I was
accepted for medical school, but
at that point I decided that I
might not be doing the right
thing. In the back of my mind
was the urge to write. I decided
to take a year away from
studying and try to make up my
mind about what exactly I wanted to do with my life.

"I spent several months
travelling through the West
Indies and Europe with very
little money but lots of enthusiasm. It was great fun. When I
returned to university the next
year, I went into the faculty of
education, and became a teacher.
I taught junior high and high
school in various small coastal
communities in Newfoundland.
One of the things I noticed was
that there were very few novels
available for my students to read
that were set in such places. I
was writing some poetry and
short stories at the time, and I
decided to try my hand at writing a novel.

"That first effort was never
published (and I'm glad now
that it wasn't!), but the second

try resulted in *Hold Fast*, published in 1978. By that time I had given up full-time teaching and was devoting most of my time to writing. I continued to substitute teach over the years, but I never went back to the classroom full-time. Now I don't teach at all, I write full-time."

Where my ideas come from

"I draw material from many different sources — life around me, the drama in Newfoundland history, my own experiences of growing up, a newspaper article or something I've seen on television. Creating fiction for me is a matter of combining bits and pieces from many different sources into a unified and interesting story."

Who and what influenced me

"Writers Ernest Hemingway and Mark Twain, my family, reading the biographies of well-known authors and discovering what struggles they had."

How I work

"My early works were written first in long-hand and then typed. Now I use a word processor. The part of writing I like best is the very beginning — thinking through a story and seeing that it could work, the first imagining of a world that has never been created before. It's very exciting. The computer eliminates many of the less interesting aspects of getting words neatly to paper, and helps this excitement to continue all the way through the year or so of the actual writing and rewriting of the manuscript. I work fairly steadily from 9:00 a.m. to 3:00 p.m., with some work in the evenings and maybe weekend early mornings."

Something nobody knew about me (until now)

"I have a great weakness for desserts, especially crème caramel."

Tips for young creators

"Read, read, read. Plan your stories before writing. Write only about subjects which hold a strong interest for you. And remember, most writers are adults before they are published."

Kevin Major

BIBLIOGRAPHY

Major, Kevin. *Hold Fast* (Irwin Young Adult). Toronto: Clarke Irwin & Company, 1978. Toronto: Stoddart, 1991 Paper 0-7737-5429-6. 1995 Paper 0-7736-7438-1.

—. *Far From Shore* (Irwin Young Adult). Toronto: Clarke, Irwin & Company, 1980. Toronto: Stoddart, 1991 Paper 0-7737-5428-8. 1995 Paper 0-7736-7439-X.

—. *Thirty-Six Exposures*. New York: Delacorte Press, 1984. Toronto: Doubleday Canada, 1994 Paper 0-385-25464-4.

—. *Dear Bruce Springsteen*. Toronto: Doubleday Canada, 1987. 1994 Paper 0-385-25459-8.

—. *Blood Red Ochre*. Toronto: Doubleday Canada, 1989. Toronto: Seal Books, 1996 Paper 0-7704-271700.

—. *Eating Between the Lines*. Toronto: Doubleday Canada, 1991 Paper 0-385-25293-5. Toronto: Seal Books, 1995 Paper 0-7704-2705-7.

—. *Diana: My Autobiography*. Toronto: Doubleday Canada, 1993 Paper 0-385-25413-X. Toronto: Seal Books, 1995 Paper 0-770-42702-2.

—. *No Man's Land*. Toronto: Doubleday Canada, 1995 Cloth 0-385-25503-9. 1996 Paper 0-385-25579-9.

—. *Gaffer.* Toronto: Doubleday Canada, 1997 Paper 0-385-25667-1.

—. *The House of Wooden Santas.* Red Deer: Red Deer College Press, 1997 Cloth 0-88995-166-7. Wood carvings by Imelda George. Photographs by Ned Pratt.

Awards

1978 Canada Council Children's Literature Prize for *Hold Fast*

1979 Canadian Library Association Book of the Year for Children Award for *Hold Fast*

1979 Ruth Schwartz Children's Book Award for *Hold Fast*

1981 Canadian Library Association Young Adult Book Award for *Far From Shore*

1992 Ann Connor Brimer Award for *Eating Between the Lines*

1992 Canadian Library Association Book of the Year Award for Children for *Eating Between the Lines*

1992 Vicky Metcalf Award for a Body of Work

1998 Mr. Christie's Book Award for *The House of Wooden Santas*

1998 Ann Conner Brimer Award for *The House of Wooden Santas*

Selected articles about Kevin Major

Gertridge, Allison. *Meet Canadian Authors and Illustrators*. Richmond Hill: Scholastic Canada, 1994: 72-3

McNaughton, Janet. "Major's Moves." *Quill and Quire* Apr. 1993: 1

For more information about Kevin Major, visit his Web site at www4.newcomm.net/kmajor

Ainslie Manson
AUTHOR

Born
October 31, 1938, Montreal, Quebec

School
"After high school in Montreal I took university courses and credits wherever I happened to be living. I don't have a specific degree from one university, but bits and pieces (mostly creative writing and history) from many."

Where I live now
West Vancouver, British Columbia

My favourite books when I was young
"Books were scarce because of the war, so I read whatever came my way. A few of my earliest favourites were *Lassie Come Home, Anne of Green Gables, My Friend Flicka* and scores of horse stories (I was horse crazy!)."

My favourite book now
"That's too difficult! When I'm not near the book I love, I love the book I'm near! I couldn't possibly choose a best – that would be like saying I love one of my children more than another!"

Career
"When I lived in Montreal I worked for the McGill Graduate Society and for a public relations company. Later I worked in London, England and then in the U.S. at Yale University for the Master of one of the undergraduate colleges. More recently I worked as a freelance journalist for a Vancouver newspaper. Now I write full time."

Family
"I have been married for 36 years to David Manson. He's a doctor. We have three sons, Graeme, Murray and Gavin. Graeme is a writer now too. He is writing for film and television. The other two are into the sciences like their dad."

The room where I create
"My writing room is in an out-of-the-way corner of the house. It is a peaceful room with a view of the sea and I love it. On the walls I have book posters and a few treasured illustrations from my picture books. 'Old Bear' from *Just Like New* sits on a cluttered bookshelf and a funny dressed-up toy horse sits beside my computer reminding me to get on and finish a horse story I am working on. The room is usually messy with overflowing baskets of filing and work to be done. Sometimes when too many other activities get in the way of my precious writing time, I am drawn in the door. I stand wistfully in the centre of the room, feel the creative juices flowing, and long to sit down at my desk."

Spare time
"I enjoy riding, kayaking, canoeing, and cross-country skiing. At quieter times I like to curl up with a good book. I watch very little television but, when I do, I am always quilting."

When I was growing up
"I rode a lot as a child. I grew up in the country and we lived across the road from a wonderful woman who gave riding lessons on her farm. I was always there! Taking riding lessons, or as I grew older, helping. I would catch the horses for her, and saddle them up, and I'd take people out on trail rides. I wasn't paid but all my riding was free. I thought it was a great arrangement!"

My first book (and how it happened)
"My first book was *Mr. McUmphie of Caulfeild Cove*, a story I made up for my boys. It was all about them but I changed it a fair amount when I finally wrote it down. I made poor Murray into a girl because I felt I needed a girl in the story. And Gavin became twins, known as the Horrible Howlers! Someone came up to Gavin when he was in Grade 7 and said, 'Oh hey, I know who *you* are… you're the horrible howlers!' My poor sons… what I put them through!"

Where my ideas come from

"My stories are often history-connected — bits and pieces from long ago that have fascinated me. Or I start with a real incident from my own life, and then go a little wild with it. I also keep an 'idea box'. It's a wonderful wooden box into which I stuff magazine articles, photos, title ideas, etc. With this box I will never be at a loss for a story idea. In fact I think I'll have to live till I'm about 150 years old in order to tell all the stories I want to tell!"

Who and what influenced me

"A number of my books are history-connected and I think I was lured into my love of history by a teacher I had in high school. She made history fun, and she made it come alive. I don't think one particular author has influenced me, but I've probably absorbed a little of many of the books that I've read. My husband, David, hasn't exactly influenced my writing, but he has certainly encouraged it."

How I work

"The process is different for me with every book. I wrote *A Dog Came, Too* completely in my head because I was longing to get to it and I was too busy working on another book. I'd think about Alexander Mackenzie's dog each morning as I walked my own dogs. When I finally did get a chance to start writing the story, the words just came flowing out of my finger tips. It was ready for the publisher in 10 days. That was wonderful — but it rarely happens. Usually I make false starts trying to find the direction I want, and I have to do many rough drafts before I'm satisfied.

"I always recommend making organized outlines... because by using outlines you can avoid so many pitfalls — but I have to confess that I'm not an outline-expert myself. The story has to take me where I'm going — and that destination is often a complete surprise and one of the most exciting things about writing."

Something nobody knew about me (until now)

"I was desperately shy when I was a child. I was so shy it was almost impossible for me to go to my best friend's house for dinner. It wasn't until I was nearly 50 that I learned to stand up comfortably and talk in front of a crowd. I think it was talking to kids in schools about books and writing that finally cured me! I can't resist sharing my enthusiasm about books!"

My favourite book that I've created

"*Just Like New*, I think — because it's the most fun to read in schools. But often my favourite book will be the book I'm working on."

Tips for young creators

"Try to write every day. Keep a journal that is just for you. Not only is this great writing practice but it's an excellent future source of story ideas. Keep an idea box. And read, read, read."

Ainslie Manson

BIBLIOGRAPHY

Manson, Ainslie. *Mr. McUmphie of Caulfeild Cove*. Winnipeg: Queenston House, 1981. Illustrations by Janet Stethem.

—. *Alexander Mackenzie*. Toronto: Grolier, 1988. Out of print.

—. *Simon Fraser* (Pathfinders Series). Toronto: Grolier, 1990. Out of print.

—. *A Dog Came Too*. Toronto: Groundwood Books, 1992 Cloth 0-88899-187-8. 1993 Paper 0- 88899-187-8. Illustrated by Ann Blades.

—. *Just Like New*. Toronto: Groundwood Books, 1996 Cloth 0-88899-228-9. Illustrated by Karen Reczuch.

—. *Baboo: The Story of Sir John A. Macdonald's Daughter*. Toronto: Groundwood Books, 1998 Cloth 0-88899-329-3. Illustrations by Bill Ward.

—. *Ballerinas Don't Wear Glasses*. Vancouver: Orca Book Publishers, 2000 Paper 1-55143-176-9 Cloth 1-55143-158-0. Illustrations by Dean Griffiths.

Awards

1996 Five Owls Book of Merit for *Just Like New*

Selected articles about Ainslie Manson

"Meet Ainslie Manson." *Cornerstones 4A*. Gage Educational Publishing Co., 1998.

Carol Matas
AUTHOR

Born
November 14, 1949, Winnipeg, Manitoba

School
Winnipeg, Manitoba

Where I live now
Winnipeg, Manitoba

My favourite book when I was young
"The entire *Wizard of Oz* series by Frank Baum."

My favourite book now
"Anything by Doris Lessing."

Career
Writer

Family
Husband, Per Brask; children, Rebecca and Sam; dog, Tara.

The room where I create
"A desk in my bedroom."

Spare time
"Read, watch baseball, see movies, watch sci-fi shows on television and, in the summer, go for walks."

When I was growing up
"I loved to read but I wanted to grow up to be an actress. I especially loved to read out loud to the class. At the age of 20, I went to London, England to study acting, and then I worked professionally in Toronto. It was only when I was working in the theatre that I fell into writing."

My first book (and how it happened)
"My first book has never been published. It's in a box somewhere (I hope) and I decided to write it when I was pregnant with Rebecca and couldn't work as an actress. Everyone I showed it to loved it, so I decided to write another one. And a third. And finally, the third one, *The D.N.A. Dimension*, was accepted for publication. Somehow by then, I wasn't interested in acting anymore, I just wanted to write."

Where my ideas come from
"A conversation, a television show, a movie, a book, a view, a dream, a stray thought... and suddenly I think, that's a great idea for a book!

"For me, different books have begun in different ways. My first books dealt with subjects that were in my mind at the time: nuclear war, genetic engineering, big business, the greenhouse effect, ecology... each book was about a specific idea, and the social themes became the backdrops. *The Fusion Factor* is a book about personal responsibility. In *The D.N.A. Dimension* I wanted to consider a Hitler figure, a person who thought he was making a perfect world but who, in fact, was doing just the opposite. The idea for *Lisa* came to me after I read a non-fiction book about the rescue of the Danish Jews; the idea for the sequel came from talking to my in-laws. Ideas can come from many different quarters, and I always have at least three different ideas for new books circulating in my head."

Who and what influenced me
"The *Oz* books I'm sure were a great influence — not in terms of style, for I write very differently and often on very serious subjects, but I always strive to give my reader the same sense of wonder, delight and excitement from reading that I enjoyed when I read those books.

"My theatre training has helped me in that I can 'hear' the way people talk to each other. I write with very little description of surroundings or people's thoughts, letting the dialogue convey the characters' emotions."

How I work
"In multiple drafts. The first draft is the most fun — and the period of months just before I start to write the least. I can spend months or years thinking of a story, what I want to say, the rough plot, the central character, before I even begin to write. And just before I put pen to paper (yes, I write longhand) I'm always sure it'll never work. Once I get

going though, I can't stop. Then I give it to my friend and critic, Perry Nodelman who critiques it for me and I do a major rewrite. Then off to the publisher. Another large rewrite. Then a smaller one, and more corrections until four or five or six drafts later, we have a finished book."

Something nobody knew about me (until now)
"I'm a baseball fanatic — fan is too tame a word. I also love science fiction and any kind of mystery."

Tips for young creators
"Don't try to be perfect. Just get down to your story. Try to write about something you really care about and then revise and fix it up later. Don't be afraid. Fear is what stops you from putting those words down. Throw away all caution and write."

Carol Matas

BIBLIOGRAPHY
Matas, Carol. *The D.N.A. Dimension*. Toronto: Gage Publishing, 1982. Out of print.

—. *The Fusion Factor*. Saskatoon: Fifth House, 1986. Rpt. as *It's Up to Us*. Toronto: General Publishing, 1991 Paper 0-7736-7335-0.

—. *Zanu*. Saskatoon: Fifth House, 1986. Toronto: General Publishing, 1991 Paper 0- 7736-7338-5.

—. *Me, Myself and I*. Saskatoon: Fifth House, 1987. Toronto: General Publishing, 1991 0- 7736-7340-7.

—. *Lisa*. Toronto: Lester & Orpen Dennys, 1987 Paper 0-88619-163-7. Richmond Hill: Scholastic Canada, 1994 0-590-24189-3.

—. *Jesper*. Toronto: Lester & Orpen Dennys, 1989 Paper 0-88619-109-2. Richmond Hill: Scholastic Canada, 1994 0-590-24188-5.

—. *Adventure in Legoland*. Richmond Hill: Scholastic Canada, 1992 Paper 0-590-74260-4.

—. *The Race*. Toronto: HarperCollins, 1991. 1993 Paper 0-00-647430-6.

—. *Sworn Enemies*. Toronto: HarperCollins, 1993 Cloth 0-00-223897-7. 1994 Paper 0- 00-647490-X.

—. *Safari Adventure in Legoland*. Toronto: Scholastic Canada, 1993 Paper 0-509-74600- 6. Illustrations by Elroy Freem.

—. *Daniel's Story*. Toronto: Scholastic Canada, 1993 Paper 0-590-46588- 0; Cloth 0-590-46920-7.

—. *The Lost Locket*. Richmond Hill: Scholastic Canada, 1994 Paper 0-590-74587-5.

—. *The Burning Time*. Toronto: HarperCollins, 1995 Paper 0-00-647954-5; Cloth 0-00- 224268-0.

—. *The Primrose Path*. Winnipeg: Bain and Cox, 1995 0-921368-55-0.

—. *After the War*. Richmond Hill: Scholastic Canada, 1996 Paper 0-590-12384-X; Cloth 0-590-24758-1.

—. *The Freak*. Toronto: Key Porter Books, 1997 Paper 1-55013-852-9.

—. *The Garden*. Richmond Hill: Scholastic Canada, 1997 Paper 0-590-12490-0; Cloth 0- 590-12381-5.

—. *Telling*. Toronto: Key Porter Books, 1998 Paper 1-55013-933-9.

—. *Greater Than Angels*. Richmond Hill: Scholastic Canada, 1998 Cloth 0-590-12498-6.

—. *In My Enemy's House*. Richmond Hill: Scholastic Canada, 1999 Cloth 0-590-51570-5.

—. *Cloning Miranda*. Richmond Hill: Scholastic Canada, 1999 Paper 0-590-1458-X.

Matas, Carol, and Perry Nodelman. *Of Two Minds*. Winnipeg: Bain and Cox, 1994 Paper 0-921368-44-5. Toronto: Scholastic Canada, 1998 Paper 0-590-39468-1.

— and Perry Nodelman. *More Minds*. New York: Simon & Schuster, 1996 Paper 0-68980-388-5 Richmond Hill: Scholastic Canada, 1998 Paper 0-590-39469-X.

Awards
1988 Geoffrey Bilson Award for Historical Fiction for Young Readers for *Lisa*

1989 Sydney Taylor American Librarians Award for *Lisa's War* (U.S. title)

1993 Sydney Taylor American Librarians Award for *Sworn Enemies*

1994 Silver Birch Award for *Daniel's Story*

1996 Manitoba Young Reader's Choice Award for *Daniel's Story*

1996 Jewish Book Award for *After the War*

Selected articles about Carol Matas
Nodelman, Perry. "Good, Evil, Knowledge, Power: A Conversation between Carol Matas and Perry Nodelman." *Canadian Children's Literature* 82 (1996): 57-68.

Tye, Judy. "*Daniel's Story* by Carol Matas Wins First Ontario Silver Birch Award — 'the Children's Choice.'" *The Teaching Librarian* 3.1 (1995): 39-40.

Sheryl McFarlane

AUTHOR

Born

1954, Pembroke, Ontario (in the Ottawa Valley)

School

Tempe Elementary and Junior School, McClintock High School, all in Tempe, Arizona, U.S.A.; University of British Columbia, Vancouver, British Columbia.

Where I live now

Victoria, British Columbia

My favourite book when I was young

"I didn't read much until I hit my teenage years. *The Lord of the Rings* and *The Catcher in the Rye* were the first books I fell in love with."

My favourite books now

"This is impossible to answer! I love picture books, but I also love books like *The Giver, Chasing Redbird, The Tent*, and anything by Katherine Patterson, Timothy Findley and Doris Lessing. Reading *Fugitive Pieces* by Ann Michaels was an incredible experience, and I think that Alice Munro is a genius."

Career

"I have been a tree planter, farm hand, research technician for Agriculture Canada, daycare worker and teacher. These days, I write children's books. I also give talks on writing, children's literature and family literacy at conferences, schools and libraries."

Family

"I am married and have three daughters, Ali, Chloe and Katie."

The room where I create

"I have a tiny unheated office in a rambling old house. My office is a terrible, terrible mess, with stray cups of cold tea and shrivelled apple cores buried under books, files, messages, magazines, and notes. Sometimes I have to work at the kitchen table or in the living room because I can't fight my way through the clutter that blocks the door to my office."

In my spare time

"I love to garden, go for walks on the beach, kayak, and read."

When I was growing up

"I was never the sort of kid you'd imagine becoming a writer. I didn't even read much until I hit my teen years. I was too busy building forts in the cottonwood trees that lined the irrigation ditch near my home, playing hide and seek in the orange groves and cotton fields, playing pick-up baseball with the neighbourhood kids, or building skateboards out of discarded baby carriage wheels and scrap wood.

"Junior High opened up a new and unexpected world for me: the work of books. For the first time, I stepped beyond the boundaries of my neighbourhood, and I loved it. I travelled to distant places, met fascinating people, and lived in a multitude of pasts and a wealth of possible futures. I was convinced that authors must be an exotic species indeed, to be able to achieve such feats of wonder."

My first book (and how it happened)

"*Waiting for the Whales* began when my grandfather died many years ago. My grandfather had never seen the ocean, let alone a whale. But, when I was a child, I used to follow him around in his wonderful garden. I realized how much about gardening he had taught me. A few years later, my 75-year-old friend Roy died. Like my grandfather, Roy passed on a lifetime of wisdom to family and friends. The grandfather in my story combines some of the things I loved about both of these men. The story was set on the West Coast because it's the place in the world I love most.

"In *Waiting for the Whales* I tried to honour the unique friendship that I had shared with my grandfather and with Roy. I also wanted to show some of the ways that people live on even after they die. They live in our hearts, in our memories, and in the things they have taught us. And perhaps even in the spirit of the whales, as one Coastal Salish elder told me. Now my grandfather and Roy also live between the pages of *Waiting for the Whales*."

Where my ideas come from

"I get ideas from all sorts of places — from things I hear on the radio and read in the paper, from things I overhear, from memories of when I was little (like following my grandfather around in his garden), from things I do with my own children."

Who and what influenced me

"If I hadn't become a reader, I wouldn't have become a writer, so probably the most important influence was Mrs. Smith, my Grade 9 English teacher. She encourage me to read, and she was the very first person to encourage me to write.

"Even with Mrs. Smith's encouragement, I think I would not have become a writer if it weren't for Canadian author Robert Kroetsch. He was the first author I'd ever met and he was just a normal sort of person who liked writing, but worked at it too. From then on, I stopped thinking of authors as super-human. If authors were normal people who worked at their writing, it didn't seem quite so far-fetched to want to be one."

How I work

"I have to mull things over in my head until I know who the characters are, where they're going, what makes them tick. Once they're real for me, I don't usually have problems with the plot. I always work with pencil and paper to start. Once I have the bare bones of the story on paper, I start playing around with it on the computer. Computers are great for editing, but sometimes it's too easy to change things or delete them before you're really sure of what you want.

"Another important part of writing for me, is research. Even though my stories are fictional, they have a lot of facts built into them, and I usually have to do quite a lot of research, about whales, bald eagles, moonsnails, or how judging is done at the fall fair. I may write between seven and fourteen drafts for each book, and often spend between six months to a year doing it."

Something nobody knew about me (until now)

"My favourite place to work is in bed, with a lovely cup of hot tea in one hand and all of my books and paper spread out around me."

My favourite book that I've created

"This is like asking which of my three children is my favourite. Each book has something special about it. I love my first book because it reminds me of the special times I had with my grandfather. I love *Eagle Dreams*, because the language in that book has the rhythms of the ocean. I love *Jessie's Island* because it's about all the things I have done with my own children. I love *Tides of Change* because it's about the place in the world I most cherish. I love *Going to the Fair* because it is like revisiting the excitement of fall fairs."

Tips for young creators

"Read, read, read. And, of course, write. You learn how to write not by talking about it or thinking about it, but by doing it. Keeping a journal is a good way to start. It also gives you the opportunity to become an observer, which is what writers often are. Finally, give equal time to your imagination. One of the things I have most in common with other writers is the time we spent as children imagining. I was constantly told to stop daydreaming. If I had, I probably wouldn't be a writer today."

Sheryl McFarlane

BIBLIOGRAPHY

McFarlane, Sheryl. *Waiting for the Whales*. Victoria: Orca Book Publishers, 1991. 1993 Paper 0-920501-96-6. Illustrations by Ron Lightburn.

—. *Jessie's Island*. Victoria: Orca Book Publishers, 1992 Paper 0-920501-76-1. Illustrations by Sheena Lott.

—. *Eagle Dreams*. Victoria: Orca Book Publishers, 1994 Paper 1-55143-016-9. Illustrations by Ron Lightburn.

—. *Moonsnail Song*. Victoria: Orca Book Publishers, 1994 Cloth 1-55143-008-8. Illustrations by Ron Lightburn.

—. *Tides of Change: Faces of the Northwest Coast*. Victoria: Orca Book Publishers, 1995 Cloth 1-55143-040-1. Illustrations by Ken Campbell.

—. *Going to the Fair*. Victoria: Orca Book Publishers, 1996 Paper 1-55143-062-2. Illustrations by Sheena Lott.

Awards
1992 IODE Violet Downey Book Award for *Waiting for the Whales*

For more information about Sheryl McFarlane, visit her Web site at www.islandnet.com/~sheryl/

Janet McNaughton
AUTHOR

Born
November 29, 1953, Toronto, Ontario

School
Honours B.A., York University; M.A. and Doctorate in folklore, both from Memorial University of Newfoundland

Where I live now
"I live in St. John's, Newfoundland in a small, Victorian house with no closets."

My favourite books when I was young
Pippi in the South Seas by Astrid Lindgren, *The Book of Three* by Lloyd Alexander, and *Half Magic* by Edward Eager.

My favourite book now
The Secret Garden

Career
"I am a full-time writer. I review books for *Quill & Quire* and other magazines, and write for adult literacy programs when I am not writing stories."

Family
"My husband, Michael Wallack, teaches political science at Memorial University. My daughter, Elizabeth, plays soccer, piano and French horn and is interested in composing music."

The room where I create
"I work in the small, middle bedroom of my house. There are books all over the place, and my desk is usually a mess. In winter, I grow hydroponic vegetables in pots and trays all over the room. The big bulletin board in front of my desk is covered with photographs of children and gardens, work of my favourite illustrators and things that remind me of the book I'm writing at the moment."

Spare time
"I try to keep up with the wonderful books of other writers and illustrators. I garden and take long walks."

When I was growing up
"I was shy and awkward. I couldn't spell, was bad at arithmetic and didn't do well in school. The only thing I was good at was the annual public speaking competition. I spent a lot of time alone, reading and daydreaming. When I was with other kids, I mostly watched them. Watching and daydreaming and reading all helped to make me a writer. I failed Grade 9; after that, my marks got better every year."

My first book (and how it happened)
"When I graduated with my Ph.D, I thought I would try to write a book. Because books were so important to me when I was young, I decided to write for young readers. *Catch Me Once, Catch Me Twice* was based on ideas arising from my doctoral dissertation, the big essay you write before they give you a Ph.D. I was writing about midwives, women who helped other women have babies in the days when there were few doctors in Newfoundland. I thought, 'There could be a girl whose grandfather was a doctor, and a boy whose grandmother was a midwife, and they could be friends even though they would come from very different circumstances.' I set the story in St. John's during World War II because many exciting changes happened then. When the book was rejected by larger publishers on the mainland, I decided to send it to a small, Newfoundland publisher who does a very good job. He accepted the novel right away."

Where my ideas come from
"From the imagination. People who want to be writers should exercise their imaginations every day."

Who and what influenced me
"Astrid Lindgren taught me that girls did not have to be well-behaved in stories. Lloyd

Alexander taught me that a girl could be smart and active. Lucy Maud Montgomery taught me it was okay to use really big words. I am still learning from other writers. When I read Tim Wynne-Jones and Sarah Ellis, I long to write as beautifully as they do. When I read Kit Pearson, I hope I can make my characters as vivid and real as she does.

"I belong to a group of writers who meet regularly to share their work. Some of these writers have helped me greatly, especially Bernice Morgan and Helen Porter."

How I work

"I usually have an idea in my head for a few years before I begin to write. I do any research I can to develop the idea of the book. For my historical books, I used old newspapers, photographs and magazines. For the science fiction book I'm working on now, I read journals like *New Scientist* and *Nature*.

"My way of working is unusual. I sit down and write the story from beginning to end. Every day, I read what I wrote the day before and make changes, then I try to take the story forward. The order of events often gets changed around while I write; my ideas about what will happen next change too. If I get stuck, I go back to research materials until I can see a way forward. I try not to criticize my work too much in the first draft. The idea is just to get everything down on paper.

"When that's done, I breathe a sigh of relief, and then I start to revise. When I am as happy with the book as I can be, I give it to another writer whom I trust, and she gives me her feedback. Then I rewrite again. When I am satisfied, I give the book to a publisher, who gives me an editor and we begin to rewrite

again. It usually takes me about six months to write a first draft, but two years or more before the book is ready to be published. I always use a computer, partly because I'm a bad speller and the computer helps (although I still use a dictionary sometimes), and partly because I tend to lose notebooks and paper, but computer files stay put."

Something nobody knew about me (until now)

"I never thought I could be a writer because stories do not come easily to me. It turns out that doesn't matter as much as I thought it would. If I start with a character I really care about, and put that character in an interesting situation, the story just grows."

My favourite book that I've created

"I hate to say I have one favourite. But I'm glad I wrote *To Dance at the Palais Royale* because it draws upon the story of how my mother's family came to Canada. If I hadn't written that book, no one would know what my aunts went through when they came to Canada alone as teenage domestic servants. They were very brave to make that journey, and I wanted to make sure their stories were not forgotten. But every time I write a new book, I hope it will be better than the one before, and that I will learn something new about writing."

Tips for young creators

"Daydream. Keep a journal. Write your daydreams and your night dreams, your ideas, names of the books you are reading and how you feel about them. When you feel a powerful emotion, write it down. One day, you'll want to make a character feel that emotion and your journal

will help you remember.

"There is almost always one perfect word for anything you are trying to say. Always reach for that word to say things in the best possible way."

Janet McNaughton

BIBLIOGRAPHY

McNaughton, Janet. *Catch Me Once, Catch Me Twice*. St. John's: Tuckamore Books, 1994. Toronto: Stoddart Kids, 1996 0-7736-7449-7.

—. *To Dance at the Palais Royale*. St. John's: Tuckamore Books, 1996 Paper 1-895387-38-8. Toronto: Stoddart Kids, 1998 0-7736-7473-X.

—. *Make or Break Spring*. St. John's: Tuckamore Books, 1998 1-895387-93-0.

Awards

1997 IODE Violet Downey Award for *To Dance at the Palais Royale*

1997 Ann Connor Brimer Award for *To Dance at the Palais Royale*

1997 Geoffrey Bilson Award for Historical Fiction for Young People for *To Dance at the Palais Royale*

1998 Writers' Alliance of Newfoundland and Labrador/Hibernia Children's Literature Award for *To Dance at the Palais Royale*

Selected articles about Janet McNaughton

Smulders, Marilyn. "Digging Up Bones: Canadian Writers are Revisiting the Past for Inspiration." *The Daily News* [Halifax] 11 October 1996.

For more information about Janet McNaughton, visit her Web site at www.avalon.nf.ca/~janetmcn/

Sylvia McNicoll
AUTHOR

Born
September 30, 1954, Ajax, Ontario

School
B.A. (in English, minor in economics) at Concordia University, Montreal, Quebec

Where I live now
Burlington, Ontario

My favourite books when I was young
"*Grimm's Fairy Tales, Nancy Drew* mysteries, the *Little House on the Prairie* series, and any basketball story."

My favourite book now
"There is no favourite. I get a kick out of picture books, first chapter, junior and young adult novels. I love the optimism and energy of stories for young people."

Career
"Before writing, I was a senior clerk for the corporate cash department of Canadian International Paper. I began my writing career free-lancing for the *Burlington Post*."

Family
"I have three children: Jennifer, Craig, and Robin. and a husband, Bob McNicoll, whom I married when I was 19. My wildly creative children provide me with lots of ideas and test read my work."

The room where I create
"My office is divided in two, my writing base and the family computer side. My desk suffocates under piles of books, binders, and notes; my portable notebook computer perches precariously near the edge. Whoever is working on the family computer will act as my consultant, listening to bad sentences, answering spelling questions, or playing 'what's-that-word-that-means...?'"

Spare time
"There's very little spare time; often the research for a project becomes my recreation for that time period. While I was writing a Stage School series, for example, I went to the ballet, mime shows, laugh festivals and many amateur performances.

"I do love the outdoors, camping, swimming, rollerblading, hiking, canoeing, cross-county skiing. And I love curling up with a good book or watching a movie with my family."

When I was growing up
"I was the class clown, the only girl who was ever sent into the hall. In Grade 3, I remember the teacher reading a cliffhanger mystery where the villain suddenly accosted the main character. I gasped, loudly I guess, and was sent to the coat closet for the rest of the story. To be honest, this was one of the few times I didn't deserve the punishment. It always amazes me that teachers invite me back into the classroom today for what probably got me in trouble when I was young. I usually make an effort to speak to the 'bad kids' in the hall whenever visiting schools."

My first book (and how it happened)
"*Blueberries and Whipped Cream* was a project for a Writing for Children course given by Paul Kropp. He challenged me to write an outline for the second class and then presumed out loud that I couldn't finish the novel within the time slot of the course. That was all it took. I wrote in the early morning and late at night when my three toddlers were asleep. A year later the novel was published by Gage Publishing and then Macmillan Australia. I also sold a film option for it and Paul, of course, gave me an A+."

Where my ideas come from
"Twenty or so years later, I'm still the kid standing in the hall. I feel like an outsider or alien, always observing the classroom and world in amazement and with a keen sense of the absurdity of it all. My ideas arise from my observations."

Who and what influenced me
"Great teachers! When they weren't annoyed with me, my teachers praised my writing and told me I was talented. Later on, Paul Kropp

influenced me. While taking his course was a catalyst to writing a publishable novel, reading Paul's work prior to the course inspired me to accept my own style.

"The first editor who ever liked my work, Sharon Siamon, helped me place *Blueberries and Whipped Cream*. I worked with her later on many projects, most recently as co-writers under the pseudonym Geena Dare in the Stage School Series. Working with young people, reading their stories and coaching them electronically or in person — it's all very inspiring."

How I work

"First, some fragment of an idea intrigues me but I resist for a while. Then I start writing and rewriting a beginning in my head, becoming part of the main character. I think about the climax and finally I create an ending. By the time I sit down and write the first three chapters I've bonded with the character and story. Occasionally, my books are bought or rejected on the basis of these chapters and an outline. The characters that are rejected still haunt me.

"Then I write, often researching as I go along. On good days I go into a dream world and emerge with seven pages written. On bad ones, I agonize over every word and force myself to write three pages. One third of the way through a story, I'm convinced it's awful. Two thirds of the way through, I'm living my life through the story and while I want it to end, I fear it too. When I finish the draft, I feel exhilarated — for perhaps two hours.

"Finally I rewrite. I give my manuscript to my writing group and test it on young readers. I gather comments and change accordingly. After about three rewrites, I mail it to an editor and rewrite again according to her suggestions. By the time the book is published, I'm fairly sick of it and can't bring myself to read it for awhile."

Something nobody knew about me (until now)

"Principals still scare me. While standing in the hall as a young person, I narrowly escaped getting the strap from our patrolling principal. The bell rang in the nick of time. Today, when I know a principal is in my audience or even when I get introduced at the beginning of a visit, deep down I feel I'm going to get in trouble again and this time the bell won't save me."

My favourite book that I've created

"*Bringing Up Beauty* is my favourite because I wrote it slowly, at a time when I was convinced no one wanted to read my work. I did it exactly how I wanted because I thought no one cared. There was very little rewriting or editing — *Bringing Up Beauty* feels like it's me."

Tips for young creators

"Learn about yourself, find out what you like and what you're good at. This means trying out new things, whether it's sampling octopus, bungee jumping or just reading a different kind of story. Being good at something doesn't mean you've won a prize or even praise from the teacher for it. It means you satisfy something inside yourself."

Sylvia McNicoll

BIBLIOGRAPHY

McNicoll, Sylvia. *Blueberries and Whipped Cream*. Toronto: Gage, 1988 0-7715-7017-1. Illustrations by Vlasta van Kampen.

—. *The Tiger Catcher's Kid*. Toronto: Nelson, 1989 Paper 0-17-602592-8.

—. *Jump Start*. Toronto: Maxwell Macmillan, 1989 Paper 0-02-953928-5.

—. *More than Money*. Toronto: Nelson, 1990 Paper 0-17-603058-1.

—. *Project Disaster*. Richmond Hill: Scholastic Canada, 1990 Paper 0-590-73742-2. ✦

—. *Facing the Enemy*. Toronto: Nelson, 1992 Paper 0-17-603064-6.

—. *Bringing Up Beauty*. Toronto: Maxwell Macmillan, 1994 Paper 0-02-954257-X; Cloth 0-02-954256-1.

—. *The Big Race*. Richmond Hill: Scholastic Canada, 1996 Paper 0-590-24908-8. ✦

—. *Walking a Thin Line*. Richmond Hill: Scholastic Canada, 1997 Paper 0-590-12379-3.

— (As Geena Dare). *Dan Clowning Around*. Orchard Books, 1998 1-86039-646-1.

— (As Geena Dare). *Matt Heartbreak Hero*. Orchard Books, 1998 1-86039-647-X.

—. *Smoky and the Gorilla*. Richmond Hill: Scholastic Canada, 1999 Paper 0-590-54238-9. Illustrations by Susan Gardos.

—. *Double Dribble*. Richmond Hill: Scholastic Canada, 1999 Paper 0-590-50798-2. Illustrations by Susan Gardos.

Awards

1996 Silver Birch Award for *Bringing Up Beauty*

1997 Manitoba Young Reader's Choice Award for *Bringing Up Beauty*

Selected articles about Sylvia McNicoll

Langton, Marg. "Local Authors Tackle Real Life Issues for Kids." *Hamilton Spectator* 27 Aug. 1998: 5.

McNicoll, Sylvia. "Where I Get My Ideas." *Teaching Librarian* 5.1 (1997): 22-4.

Sherman, Gisela. "Profile: Sylvia McNicoll." *Canadian Children's Literature* 90 (1998): 45-50.

For more information about Sylvia McNicoll, visit her Web site at www.netaccess.on.ca/~mcnicoll.

Tololwa M. Mollel
AUTHOR

Born
Arusha, Tanzania, in East Africa

School
"I did my elementary, secondary, high school, and university in Tanzania; I did further studies at the University of Alberta in Edmonton."

Where I live now
Edmonton, Alberta

My favourite book when I was young
"*Treasure Island* by Robert Louis Stevenson, *Robinson Crusoe* by Daniel Defoe, and Greek and Norse myths."

My favourite book now
The Good Earth by Pearl S. Buck

Career
Writer, storyteller

Family
"I am married and I have two sons who are growing like grass. I have no pets — never had any."

The room where I create
"I am banished to the basement of our house where my writing won't harm anyone."

Spare time
"Hiking, playing soccer (in the spring and summer), tennis, and lots of reading."

When I was growing up
"As a kid, I wanted to be many things when I grew up — a pirate and treasure hunter (after I read *Treasure Island*), and possessor of my own island (like *Robinson Crusoe*). I wanted an Aladdin's lamp for Christmas. I wanted to be an inventor, inventing a car that runs on water; a magician; a professional table tennis player. I made my own toys as a kid. I had two homes, my grandparents' home and my parents' home. I did chores in both homes, and I read like mad."

My first book (and how it happened)
"*The Orphan Boy*, published by Oxford University Press in 1990. It is a folktale that was told to me by a Maasai elder. I was so touched by it, I thought people far and wide in other cultures might enjoy it too. So I wrote it in English, making big and small changes to the original story told to me."

Where my ideas come from
"My ideas come from many sources — from old folktales and books; from characters I see around me, especially when I travel, who look like they ought to be in a story. I get other ideas from strange or interesting things people say and how they say them; from things I see that get stuck in my mind; from daydreaming just before I go to bed and when I have just woken up and am not sure whether to get up or not. I also get ideas for other stories when I am working on a particular story."

Who and what influenced me
"I think I was influenced by all the writers whose books have impressed me, and by my language arts teachers. Very far back, I must have been influenced by my grandfather, who liked to tell stories and who demanded stories from me in return; and also my grandmother who liked to tell suppertime stories, mostly folktales."

How I work
"When I get an idea for a story, I write it down in a special notebook I keep as a bank for new ideas. When I think of some more ideas, I write them down in the notebook too. I don't rush to make a story right away. I let the ideas simmer in my brain for a long, long time. I gather thousands of little ideas for the story, the character, the plot, the scenes, dialogue. When I think I have all or most pieces I need to make the first draft, I start on the story in bits and pieces. At this stage, I write anywhere: travelling on a bus or plane, in a restaurant waiting for food,

while watching my son's soccer game. When I have a rough draft of the story, that's when I really begin working. I make countless drafts before I consider the story finished."

Something nobody knew about me (until now)

"I once dreamed of having (longed to have) a pet lizard, who would live in my sleeve and would know when to come out and when to stay put."

My favourite book that I've created

"I don't really want to have a favourite book among the ones I've created. My favourite story is any that I happen to be working on. A new story is like an adventure to me. There are all kinds of discoveries to be made, about the characters, the action, and the setting. A new story is like a maze. What path do I take to make a story satisfactory to me and to the reader? What should a character say? How should he or she say it? What should a character look like? Sound like? How does a character walk? Talk? What are the best words I can use? What kind of sentences should I use? Short? Long? Once I finish the story, the adventure is over, and I look forward to the next new story."

Tips for young creators

"Patience, patience, patience. A story needs time to grow. Be willing to step back from your draft, for a few weeks while you work on another story. Time will allow you to get fresh ideas, find better words and ways of phrasing things, when you do go back to something you have written after being away from it for a few days, weeks, months. Time is an important ingredient in the writing process."

Tololwa M. Mollel

BIBLIOGRAPHY

Mollel, Tololwa. *The Orphan Boy.* Toronto: Oxford/Stoddart Kids, 1990. 1995 Paper 0-7737-5710-4; Cloth 0-19-540783-0. Illustrations by Paul Morin.

—. *Rhinos for Lunch and Elephants for Supper!* Toronto: Oxford/Stoddart Kids 1991. 1994 Paper 0-7737-5716-3. Illustrations by Barbara Spurll.

—. *A Promise to the Sun: A Story of Africa.* Toronto: Little, Brown, 1992. Illustrations by Beatriz Vidal. Out of print.

—. *The Princess Who Lost Her Hair: An Akamba Legend.* Mahwah, NJ: Troll Associates, 1992 Paper 0-8167-2816-X; Cloth 0-8167-2815-1. Illustrations by Charles Reasoner.

—. *The King and the Tortoise.* Toronto: Lester Publishing, 1993 Cloth 1-895555-40-X. Illustrations by Kathy Blankley.

—. *The Flying Tortoise: An Igbo Tale.* Toronto: Stoddart Kids, 1994 Cloth 0-19-540990-6. Illustrations by Barbara Spurll.

—. *Big Boy.* Toronto: Stoddart Kids, 1995 Cloth 0-7737-2851-1. Illustrations by E. B. Lewis.

—. *Dume's Roar.* Toronto: Stoddart Kids, 1997 Cloth 0-7737-30003-6. Illustrations by Kathy Blankley Roman.

—. *Kele's Secret.* Toronto: Stoddart Kids, 1997 Cloth 0-7737-3007-9. Illustrations by Catherine Stock.

—. *Ananse's Feast: An Ashanti Tale.* New York: Clarion Books, 1997 Cloth 0-395-67402-6. Illustrations by Andrew Glass.

—. *Kitoto the Mighty.* Toronto: Stoddart Kids, 1998 Cloth 0-7737-3019-2. Illustrations by Kristi Frost.

—. *Shadow Dance.* New York: Clarion Books, 1998 Cloth 0-395-82909-7. Illustrations by Donna Perrone.

—. *Song Bird.* New York: Clarion Books, 1999 Cloth 0-395-82908-9. Illustrations by Rosanne Litzinger.

—. *My Row and Piles of Coins.* Boston: Houghton Mifflin, 1999 Cloth 0-395-75186-1. Illustrations by E.B. Lewis.

Awards

1993 Florida Reading Association Award for *Rhinos for Lunch and Elephants for Supper!*

1996 R. Ross Annett Award for Children's Literature for *Big Boy*

Selected articles about Tololwa Mollel

Aman, Mary Jo. "An Interview with Tololwa Mollel." *Newsletter of the United States Board on Books for Young People* 21.1 (1996): 3, 7.

Jenkinson, Dave. "Tololwa Mollel: "Eater of Words, Storyteller and Picturebook Author." *Emergency Librarian* 21.3 (1994): 61-4.

Saldanha, Louise. "Bordering on the Mainstream: The Writing of Tololwa Mollel." *Canadian Children's Literature* 81 (1996): 24-30.

"Tololwa Mollel." *Something About the Author.* Detroit: Gale Research, vol. 88 (1997): 138-144.

Robin Muller
AUTHOR/ILLUSTRATOR

Born
October 30, 1953, Toronto, Ontario

School
Toronto, Ontario

His favourite books when he was young
Fairy tales, Greek mythology and history

Career
Writer and illustrator of children's books

The room where he creates
Robin likes to work in a small room that has a window overlooking trees.

Spare time
Robin's hobby is rescuing old or damaged toys from junkstore shelves. He once found a wooden dog with ball joints. It was cracked, its paint was chipped, and one of its paws was missing. "But the toy filled me with such a wonderful sense of it having been loved, that I could almost see a child playing with it."

Months later as he was looking through some old family photographs, he came across a picture of himself when he was five holding the same toy. Its body wasn't cracked, and the paint was still bright, but one of its paws was missing — the same paw that was missing on the dog he had bought!

When he was growing up

When Robin was a child he had very little exposure to children's books. "There were no bookstores or libraries near my home at that time. In fact, the only library that we had was a mobile one (a library on wheels) that came once every two weeks, and even then we were only allowed to withdraw one book at a time."

Because there were so few children's books available, Robin's father would read passages from plays by Shakespeare to him in place of bedtime stories. "I think it was listening to Shakespeare as a child that first sparked my interest in language and history."

When he was in public school, Robin started a little publishing house. He was only eight years old. When he was in high school, Robin started a school newspaper to compete with the existing one. Called *Exodus*, the paper featured short stories, poems, book reviews and even paid advertisements.

His first book (and how it happened)

As a teenager, Robin had a job working in the warehouse of a large children's publishing house. He found the books so exciting, he decided to try his hand at book writing. He wrote and illustrated a story called *Rupert's Star*, about a boy trying and failing to capture a star. The book was turned down by every publisher he sent it to, and he was so disappointed by the experience that it was ten years before he tried to get something published again. His second attempt was successful, and he dedicated a later book, *The Sorcerer's Apprentice*, to *Rupert's Star*.

How he works

Robin likes to use pencils and he prefers to print instead of write his words. When working on a story, he likes to use school work books instead of loose sheets of paper.

Robin both writes and illustrates his own books.

Working between ten and twelve hours a day means it can take roughly a year for Robin to write and illustrate a book. *The Sorcerer's Apprentice* took Robin eight months to illustrate, *The Magic Paintbrush* took a full year, and *The Angel Tree* took two years. When he illustrates a book he works on nothing else.

"There's a great commitment of time involved, and I don't really have the ability to do anything else until I'm finished. I've often thought it would be nice to have a nine to five job."

Where his ideas come from

Memories of stories that excited him as a child, adventures and games he played out in cardboard forts, and castles he and his friends built in a ravine near his house. He also uses collections of stories for his research. For instance, *Mollie Whuppie and the Giant* is a Gaelic story and *Tatterhood* is from Finland. Robin likes to think of folk and fairy tales as a river of stories running through the centuries.

"The stories we hear today are, for the most part, the same stories that people listened to hundreds of years ago, and in all that time they have lost none of their power to delight or move us."

Robin Muller

Bibliography

Muller, Robin. *Mollie Whuppie and the Giant*. Richmond Hill: Scholastic Canada, 1982 Cloth 0-590-71106-7. 1983 Paper 0-590-71170-9. 1993 Paper 0-590-74036-9. Illustrations by the author.

—. *Tatterhood*. Richmond Hill: Scholastic Canada, 1984 Paper 0-590-71446-5; Cloth 0-590-71411-2. Illustrations by the author.

—. *The Sorcerer's Apprentice*. Toronto: Kids Can Press, 1985 Paper 0-919964-84-2. Illustrations by the author.

—. *The Lucky Old Woman*. Toronto: Kids Can Press, 1987. Illustrations by the author. Out of print.

—. *Little Kay*. Richmond Hill: Scholastic Canada, 1988 Cloth 0-590-74887-8. 1989 Paper 0-590-71886-X. 1990 Paper 0-590-73757-0. Illustrations by the author.♣

—. *The Magic Paintbrush*. Toronto: Doubleday Canada, 1989. 1993 Paper 0-385-25373-7. Illustrations by the author.

—. *The Nightwood*. Toronto: Doubleday Canada, 1991 Cloth 0-385-25305-2. 1995 Paper 0-385-25544-6. Illustrations by the author.

—. *Hickory Dickory Dock*. Richmond Hill: Scholastic Canada, 1992 Cloth 0-590-73616-7. 1995 Paper 0-590-73089-4. Illustrations by Suzanne Duranceau.

—. *Row, Row, Row Your Boat*. Richmond Hill: Scholastic Canada, 1993 Cloth 0-590-74584-0. 1996 Paper 0-590-24667-4; Illustrations by the author.

—. *Little Wonder*. Richmond Hill: Scholastic Canada, 1994 Cloth 0-590-24225-3. 1997 Paper 0-590-24988-3. Illustrations by the author.

—. *The Angel Tree*. Toronto: Doubleday Canada, 1997 Cloth 0-385-25560-8. Illustrations by the author.

Awards

1985 IODE Book Award – Toronto Chapter for *The Sorcerer's Apprentice*

1989 Governor General's Literary Award for *The Magic Paintbrush*

Selected articles about Robin Muller

Greenwood, Barbara. "Robin Muller." *Behind the Story*. Ed. Barbara Greenwood. Markham: Pembroke Publishers, 1995: 66-68.

"Hope for Outsiders: Frieda Wishinsky Speaks with Robin Muller." *Books in Canada* May 1998: 36.

Robert Munsch
AUTHOR

Born
June 11, 1945, at St. Margaret's Hospital in Pittsburgh, Pennsylvania; the fourth of nine children.

School
All Saints Elementary School, Etna, Pennsylvania; North Catholic High School, Pittsburgh, Pennsylvania; Fordham University; Boston University, all in the U.S.A.

Where I live now
"I live beside a hill in Guelph, Ontario."

My favourite book when I was young
Angus Lost by Marjorie Flack.

My favourite book now
Five Kingdoms, An Illustrated Guide to the Phyla of Life on Earth by Lynn Margulis.

Career
"I started off studying to be a Catholic priest, worked as a farm worker in France, went into daycare, taught in university for a while, and then, about 15 years ago, just started writing."

Family
"I have a wife named Ann, children named Julie, Tyya and Andrew. Julie is in *David's Father*, Andrew is in *I Have To Go*, and Tyya is in *Something Good*. I have a pet named Cinder. He is a black dog. Cinder is not in any book."

The room where I create
"The room where I write is in the basement of my house. It is all covered with pictures and letters from kids, but I actually create stories by telling them in front of kids and that is wherever I happen to be telling stories."

Spare time
"I like to walk my dog, take bicycle rides and work in my garden."

When I was growing up
"I had lots of brothers and sisters and we lived in a big, white, old farmhouse. Even though there was no farm left around it, there was still a lot of land with apple trees and peach trees and pear trees."

My first book (and how it happened)
"The first story I ever made up was the one called *Mortimer*, but it wasn't my first book. I made *Mortimer* for a nursery school where I was teaching. The first story that became a book was called *Mud Puddle*. I also made it up in a nursery school where I was teaching. The kid in the book, Jule Ann, was a kid who was in the nursery school. She is now married and living in Ontario."

Where my ideas come from
"Sometimes I get my ideas from standing up in front of an audience and saying 'Hey, I'm going to tell a new story.' Someone puts up their hand and I tell a new story about them. Usually it stinks, but every once in awhile it's really good and turns into a book. Most of my ideas aren't any good, but every once in a while, an idea comes along and it is good. Sometimes I get ideas from the letters that kids send me."

Who and what influenced me
"I have never studied how to write. I think I have been most influenced by the audiences of children that I tell stories to."

How I work
"I just keep telling stories and see which ones turn out. The story usually doesn't get good until I have told it about 100 times."

Something nobody knew about me (until now)
"When I go grocery shopping I like to push the grocery cart into the stall in the parking lot very fast and make a very loud crash and have all the carts jump all over the place."

My favourite book that I've created

"My favourite books are the ones that have my own kids in them: *David's Father*, *I Have To Go*, *Something Good* and *Love You Forever*.

Tips for young creators

"Before you write something down, tell it to three of your friends on three different days, then write it down. It will be better."

Robert Munsch

BIBLIOGRAPHY

Munsch, Robert. *The Dark*. Toronto: Annick Press, 1979. 1986 Annikin Paper 0-920303-47-1. Rev. ed. 1997 Paper 1-55037-450-8; Cloth 1-55037-451-6. Illustrations by Sami Suomalainen.

—. *The Paper Bag Princess*. Toronto: Annick Press, 1980 Paper 0-920236-16-2; Cloth 0-920236-82-0; Annikin Paper 0-920236-25-1. Illustrations by Michael Martchenko.

—. *Jonathan Cleaned Up — Then He Heard a Sound, or, Blackberry Subway Jam*. Toronto: Annick Press, 1981 Paper 0-920236-20-0; Cloth 0-920236-22-7; Annikin Paper 0-920236-21-9. Illustrations by Michael Martchenko.

—. *Mud Puddle*. Toronto: Annick Press, 1981 Annikin Paper 0-920236-23-5. 1996 Paper 1-55037-468-0; Cloth 1-55037-469-9. Illustrations by Sami Suomalainen.

—. *Murmel, Murmel, Murmel*. Toronto: Annick Press, 1982 Paper 0-920236-31-6; Cloth 0-920236-29-4. 1988 Annikin Paper 1-55037-011-X. Illustrations by Michael Martchenko. ♣

—. *The Boy in the Drawer*. Toronto: Annick Press, 1982 Paper 0-920236-36-7; Cloth 0-920236-34-0. 1986 Annikin Paper 0-920303-50-1. Illustrations by Michael Martchenko.

—. *David's Father*. Toronto: Annick Press, 1983. Paper 0-920236-64-2; Cloth 0-920236-62-6. 1988 Annikin Paper 1-55037-011-1. Illustrations by Michael Martchenko.

—. *Angela's Airplane*. Toronto: Annick Press, 1983 Annikin Paper 0-920236-75-8. 1988 Paper 1-55037-026-X; Cloth 1-55037-027-8. Illustrations by Michael Martchenko.

—. *The Fire Station*. Toronto: Annick Press, 1983 Annikin Paper 0-920236-77-4. 1991 Paper 1-55037-171-1; Cloth 1-55037-170-3. Illustrations by Michael Martchenko.

—. *Mortimer*. Toronto: Annick Press, 1983 Annikin Paper 0-920236-68-5. Rev. ed. 1985 Paper 0-920303-11-0; Cloth 0-920303-12-9. Illustrations by Michael Martchenko.

—. *Millicent and the Wind*. Toronto: Annick Press, 1984 Paper 0-920236-93-6; Cloth 0-920236-98-7. 1988 Annikin Paper 1-55037-010-3. Illustrations by Suzanne Duranceau.

—. *Thomas' Snowsuit*. Toronto: Annick Press, 1985 Paper 0-920303-33-1; Cloth 0-920303-32-3. Illustrations by Michael Martchenko.

—. *50 Below Zero*. Toronto: Annick Press, 1986 Paper 0-920236-91-X; Cloth 0-920236-86-3. Illustrations by Michael Martchenko.

—. *Love You Forever*. Toronto: Firefly Books, 1986 Paper 0-920668-37-2; Cloth 0-920668-36-4. Illustrations by Sheila McGraw. ♣

—. *I Have to Go!* Toronto: Annick Press, 1986 Annikin Paper 0-920303-51-X. 1987 Paper 0-920303-74-9; Cloth 0-920303-77-3. Illustrations by Michael Martchenko.

—. *Moira's Birthday*. Toronto: Annick Press, 1987 Paper 0-920303-83-8; Cloth 0-920303-85-4. 1995 Annikin Paper 1-55037-389-7. Illustrations by Michael Martchenko.

—. *Giant or Waiting for the Thursday Boat*. Toronto: Annick Press, 1989. Illustrations by Gilles Tibo. Out of print.

—. *Pigs*. Toronto: Annick Press, 1989 Paper 1-55037-038-3; Cloth 1-55037-039-1. 1995 Annikin Paper 1-55037-388-9. Illustrations by Michael Martchenko.

—. *Good Families Don't*. Toronto: Doubleday Canada, 1990 Paper 0-385-25267-6. Illustrations by Alan Daniel.

—. *Something Good*. Toronto: Annick Press, 1990 Paper 1-55037-100-2; Cloth 1-55037-099-5. 1995 Annikin Paper 1-55037-390-0. Illustrations by Michael Martchenko.

—. *Show and Tell*. Toronto: Annick Press, 1991 Paper 1-55037-197-5; Cloth 1-55037-195-9. Illustrations by Michael Martchenko.

—. *Get Me Another One!* Toronto: Doubleday Canada, 1992 Paper 0-385-25337-0. Illustrations by Shawn Steffler.

—. *Purple, Green and Yellow*. Toronto: Annick, 1992 Paper 1-55037-256-4; Cloth 1-55037-255-6. Illustrations by Hélène Desputeaux. ♣

—. *Wait and See*. Toronto: Annick Press, 1993 Paper 1-55037-334-X; Cloth 1-55037-335-8. Illustrations by Michael Martchenko.

—. *Where is Gah-ning?* Toronto: Annick Press, 1994 Paper 1-55037-982-8; Cloth 1-55037-983-6. Illustrations by Hélène Desputeaux. ♣

—. *From Far Away*. Toronto: Annick Press, 1995. Illustrations by Michael Martchenko. Out of print.

—. *Stephanie's Ponytail*. Toronto: Annick Press, 1996 Paper 1-55037-484-2; Cloth 1-55037-485-0. Illustrations by Michael Martchenko.

—. *Alligator Baby*. Richmond Hill: Scholastic Canada, 1997 Paper 0-590-12387-4; Cloth 0-590-12386-6. Illustrations by Michael Martchenko.

—. *Andrew's Loose Tooth*. Richmond Hill: Scholastic Canada, 1997 Paper 0-590-12435-8; Cloth 0-590-12375-0. Illustrations by Michael Martchenko.

continued

—. *Get Out of Bed*. Richmond Hill: Scholastic Canada, 1998 Paper 0-590-12473-0; Cloth 0-590-12472-2. Illustrations by Alan and Lea Daniel.

—. *Ribbon Rescue*. Richmond Hill: Scholastic Canada, 1999 Paper 0-590-03871-0 Cloth 0-590- 03870-2. Illustrations by Eugenie Fernandes.

—. *We Share Everything*. Richmond Hill: Scholastic Canada, 1999 Paper 0-590-51450-4 Cloth 0-590-51449-0. Illustrations by Michael Martchenko.

—. *Mmm, Cookies*. Richmond Hill: Scholastic Canada, 2000 Paper 0-590-51694-9 Cloth 0-590-89603-2. Illustrations by Michael Martchenko.

Munsch, Robert, and Michael Arvaarluk Kusugak. *A Promise is a Promise*. Toronto: Annick Press, 1988 Paper 1-55037-008-1; Cloth 1-55037-009-X. Illustrations by Vladyana Krykorka.

Awards

1986 Ruth Schwartz Children's Book Award for *Thomas' Snowsuit*

1987 Vicky Metcalf Award for a Body of Work

1991 Canadian Booksellers Association Author of the Year Award

Selected articles about Robert Munsch

Kirchhoff, H.J. "Once There Was a Man Who Made Kids Laugh." *The Globe and Mail* [Toronto] 27 Apr. 1991: C16.

Landon, Katelyn. "What About Bob?" *The Reader's Showcase* 2.3 (1994): 6.

Walker, Susan. "Surrealistic Munsch a Superstar Storyteller." *The Toronto Star* 19 Oct. 1995.

For more information about Robert Munsch, visit his Web site at www.robertmunsch.com.

Barbara Nichol
AUTHOR

Born
Vancouver, British Columbia

School
"Westcott Elementary, Crofton House School (Vancouver, British Columbia); Elmwood School (Ottawa, Ontario); Katherine Branson School (Ross, California); St. Clare's College (Oxford, England); University of Toronto, University of British Columbia. I didn't graduate from university."

Where I live now
Toronto, Ontario

My favourite books when I was young
"I don't remember what I preferred. I think I read a lot of *Nancy Drew* books and some Enid Blyton adventures. My mother loved reading us classics: *The Jungle Books*, A. A. Milne. I remember her pleasure at these books more than mine. I loved Pippi Longstocking; she didn't have to take orders from anyone."

My favourite book now
"I can't imagine any serious reader being able to answer such a question. Books, being reflections of the inner landscapes of their authors, are infinitely varied and have such different things to offer. It's always comparing apples to oranges.

"The book I've spent the most time thinking about and that made me most happy while I was reading it was Marcel Proust's *In Search of Lost Time*. I was happy, reading his book, that there was such a person in the world, who thought things through so carefully."

Career
"I've written news programs, documentaries, comedy shows for radio and television, humour for magazines, comedy sketches for theatre, radio and television, a game show, and 'Sesame Street.' This is a partial list. I've done all sorts of things."

The room where I create
"I have an office in my house. I don't think it matters what your office is like, as far as writing goes, at least in my case."

Spare time
"I have dinner with friends every night. I gossip on the phone. I make tapestries. I go to the gym. I read, if my mind is quiet enough."

Who and what influenced me
"Writers were respected in my family. I suppose that had an effect. I was quite rebellious when I was young and was often considered a bad child — at school. Consequently I was given the impression that I wasn't going to amount to much. (A teacher in Grade 6 told me that my 'light of hope had gone out' — a terrible thing to say to a child, no matter how annoying the child might be at that minute.)

"My first real professional encouragement came from boyfriends — two in particular — who were writers already and felt I had something to offer. One was a comedy writer. Another was a magazine writer who wrote for American magazines.

"I mention these people as influences because it's possible to have all the talent in the world (not that I do) but never accomplish a thing, without proper encouragement. Writers have to have enough ego to believe that they have a right to speak up in the world, that they might have something to say. You have to have some particular vision of the world and you have to find a way to get it on to paper. Just as important, however, is your attitude — a conviction that your voice is important and an unwillingness to be put in your place."

My favourite book that I've created
"I don't have a favourite. If I did, I'm not sure I'd own up to it."

Tips for young creators

"Obey your own instincts. Take other people's advice with a grain of salt. Concentrate on discovering the vision that is yours and yours alone, and head off in that direction."

Barbara Nichol

BIBLIOGRAPHY

Nichol, Barbara. *Beethoven Lives Upstairs.* Toronto: Lester Publishing, 1993 Cloth 1- 895555-21-3. Illustrations by Scott Cameron.

—. *Biscuits in the Cupboard.* Toronto: Stoddart Publishing, 1997 Cloth 0-7737-3025-7. Illustrations by Philippe Béha.

—. *Dippers.* Toronto: Tundra Books, 1997 Cloth 0-88776-396-0. Illustrations by Barry Moser.

Barbara Nichol has also written numerous screenplays, television episodes and radio shows.

Awards

1996 Genie Award for Best Short Film for *Home for Blind Women*

1996 Golden Spire Award for Best Short Film Under Fifteen Minutes for *Home for Blind Women*

1998 Mr. Christie's Book Award for *Biscuits in the Cupboard*

Sheldon Oberman
AUTHOR

Born
May 20, 1949

School
Winnipeg, Manitoba

Where I live now
"In a rambling three storey house in a old neighbourhood with lots of outdoor cafes, elm trees and a slow wide river."

My favourite books when I was young
"Brightly illustrated picture books. Later, *Classic Illustrated* comic books, *Superman* and *Batman*. Then came the *Hardy Boys* and an adventure series by Enid Blyton. Soon I was reading the *Reader's Digest*, the encyclopedia, Mark Twain, Jules Verne, Alfred Hitchcock and anything funny. I read everything I could find."

My favourite book now
"I'm reading collections of folktales, quotes, anecdotes and short stories."

Career
"I've been a railway porter, door-to-door salesman, cook, waiter, usher, farm worker, furniture mover, filmmaker, songwriter, actor, journalist. Now I teach, tell stories and write books for adults and children."

Family
"I have three children; Adam Morrison Oberman; Mira Shanti Oberman; and my youngest, Jesse Paul Shoshan Tookoome Dveris-Oberman. (We gave him all the leftover names because he is the last kid.) Adam is studying for his Ph.D in Math. Mira is studying for a journalism degree. Jesse is six. He is studying for Grade 1.

"My wife, Lisa Dveris, is a social worker."

The room where I create
"I have two rooms. I have a basement office where I do the business of writing like answering messages and planning workshops.

"My other room is a writing studio in an old building downtown. It has no telephone, no fridge, no visitors. It has a desk, a chair and a pullout couch. That's where I do my writing (and napping). Both rooms are filled with books, strange things I've collected and odd objects of art that I create."

Spare time
"I write, teach, work and play with family and friends and do my daily chores. I also take time for reading, exercise, garage sales, house projects and art projects."

When I was growing up
"I grew up over my parents' store in an old immigrant neighbourhood. I was an only child with no other kids in the area. I spent a lot of time playing by myself and reading. I didn't talk much — until I turned 14. Then I started talking a lot; I told stories and cracked jokes. I got plenty of attention from the kids in class but I became a major headache to my teachers. I set a school record — 45 detentions from just one of my teachers. My classmates saw me as a great mouthpiece and they elected me class president.

"I kept talking after school and made many friends. I had read so many stories and heard my parents tell so many stories that I became a storyteller. That's still what I do today."

My first book (and how it happened)
"When I started 'growing up' (university, job, marriage, family), I had no more time for stories until my children began asking for them at bedtime. Soon I began making up stories and songs.

"One of their favourites was a rhyming story created to ease their fears about monsters. I showed it to a friend, Fred Penner, who was starting out as a children's entertainer. He asked if he could use my poem. Fred Penner and I went on to create many poems and songs for his albums and later for his national television show. Pretty soon I was writing books for kids and adults."

Where my ideas come from

"Reading. I learn how to write from reading other writers. Also, a good story inspires me to create my own.

"An open mind. I try to have time each day when my mind is relaxed and open to new thoughts. Sometimes it's after a shower, a nap or exercise. It can happen when I'm alone or when I'm with friends.

"Avoid mind traps. When I get upset, angry or worried, my mind gets blocked. I try to keep my mind free. Too much television is also not good. If I watch two or three shows in a row, my mind gets overloaded and I'm not as open to creative ideas."

How I work

"Recently I finished a major project. I caught up on my sleep and my chores, hung out with some friends. All the while I kept looking for my next idea.

"Finally, I went to my studio as early as I could. I made myself a coffee, did some reading, cleared away old business, wrote in my journal, organized my planner and edited some earlier writing. I stuck it out each day till quitting time, 5:45 pm. After a few days I was spending more and more time staring out the window, doing serious day-dreaming. Then I got an idea — I'd write an article for the paper on how I get ideas. I wrote and rewrote it a few times and sent it in.

"However, a children's book of the same length can take 20 or 30 rewrites spread over a couple of years. Other people read it and give me an opinion. I even test out the story by telling it to an audience."

Who and what influenced me

"Everybody whom I ever cared about has shaped me and that has shaped my writing. I have also been shaped by some wonderful teachers and by wonderful writers whom I have met in person or through their books. Now, the people who influence me the most are those who read my work. Their appreciation and encouragement keeps me writing."

Something not many people know about me

"My mother is a professional psychic. My father was a champion weightlifter. My dad ran a cafe on Main Street that was a hangout for a motorcycle gang. My job was to wash the dishes and watch that no one stole anything or walked out without paying.

"I grew up pretty poor. I shared my room with a boarder who helped pay the rent. However, even though my home was cramped, when I opened up a book, limitless worlds opened up to me."

My favourite book that I've created

"I give each book everything I can. I could not love one more than another. Of course, other people can. Many people favour *The Always Prayer Shawl*. It's a story about how my grandfather came to this country as a boy and what happened to him and to his prayer shawl."

Tips for young creators

"Live intensely. Read extensively. Write with everything you've got."

Sheldon Oberman

BIBLIOGRAPHY

Oberman, Sheldon. *The Lion in the Lake Alphabet Book*. Winnipeg: Peguis Press, 1988 Cloth 0-920541-36-4. Illustrations by Scott Barham.

—. *TV Sal and the Game Show From Outer Space*. Red Deer: Red Deer College Press, 1993 Cloth 0-88995-093-8. Illustrated by Craig Terlson.

—. *The Always Prayer Shawl*. Honesdale Penn.: Boyds Mills Press, 1994 Cloth 1-878093-22-3. Illustrations by Ted Lewin.

—. *The White Stone in the Castle Wall*. Toronto: Tundra Press, 1994 Paper 0-88776-379-0; Cloth 88776-333-2. Illustrations by Les Tait.

—. *By the Hanukkah Light*. Honesdale Penn.: Boyds Mills Press, 1997 Cloth 1-56397-658-7. Illustrations by Neil Waldman.

—. *The Shaman's Nephew: A Life in the Far North*. Toronto: Stoddart Kids, 1999. Cloth 0-773-73200-4. Illustrations by Simon Tookoome

—. *Solomon Sheeba and the Hoopoe: A Jewish and African Tale*. Honesdale, Penn.: Boyds Mills Press, 1999. Illustrations by Neal Waldman.

Penner, Fred, and Sheldon Oberman. *Julie Gerond and the Polka Dot Pony*. Winnipeg: Hyperion Press, 1988. Illustrated by Alan Pakarnyk. Out of print.

Awards

1991 Leipzig Germany International Book Fair Silver Medal for *The Lion in the Lake*

1994 American Jewish Book Award for *The Always Prayer Shawl*

1994 Sydney Taylor American Librarians Award for *The Always Prayer Shawl*

1997 McNally Robinson Book for Young People Award for *By the Hanukkah Light*

Selected articles about Sheldon Oberman

D'Anna, Lynnette. "Sheldon Oberman." *Interchange* Dec. 1993.

Jenkinson, David. "Profiles: Sheldon Oberman." *Resource Links* 1.6 (1996): 248-251.

For more information on Sheldon Oberman, visit his Web site: www.merlin.mb.ca/~soberman

Kenneth Oppel
AUTHOR

Born
August 31, 1967, Port Alberni, British Columbia

School
University of Toronto, Toronto, Ontario

Where I live now
Toronto, Ontario

My favourite book when I was young
Danny, Champion of the World by Roald Dahl

My favourite book now
Bliss by Peter Carey

Career
Writer

Family
Wife, Philippa Sheppard; daughter, Sophia; new baby, Nathanial

The room where I create
"My study on the third floor of my house."

Spare time
"Read, watch films, spend time with my friends, long walks, travel, swimming."

When I was growing up
"I always wrote when I was a kid. When I was 11, I started writing a science-fiction epic which, as I went on, became increasingly similar to *Star Wars*. So I gave that up, and later started on another saga which began shaping up dangerously close to something from Tolkien, so that had to go too. By Grade 7, I'd made my mind up that I wanted to be a writer. Earlier career goals had included a scientist (but only if I could do things with test tubes) and an architect (I loved copying out house plans and drawing buildings).

"When I was in my very early teens, I was writing swords-and-sorcery stories, inspired by my fascination with Dungeons and Dragons. What appealed to me so much about D&D was that it was always more of a story than game. After the D&D stage (12 to 14) came the video game stage (14 to 16) which involved compulsively stock-piling quarters and cycling off to video arcades regardless of the distance.

"During high school, I cleared up my video game addiction, and then devoted all my energy to teenage angst. I'd read *The Catcher in the Rye* when I was in Grade 9, and was devastated by it. For the next two years, I decided Holden Caulfield and I had a lot in common, dislocated from life, constantly dismayed by the world. I think what this really meant was that I couldn't get a girlfriend. The short stories I wrote at this time tended to be largely autobiographical, about the trials of adolescence: broken friendships, girl troubles, first love."

My first book (and how it happened)
"I got the idea for my first book, *Colin's Fantastic Video Adventure*, during my video game stage. Writing it was actually good therapy, a withdrawal technique if you will, as it enabled me to experience video games vicariously without spending huge amounts of money. I wrote the first draft during the summer holidays when I was 14, rewrote it the following summer, and then had my lucky break. A family friend who knew the late Roald Dahl offered to show him my story. Roald Dahl read and liked the story well enough to pass it on to his own literary agent, who took me on, and shortly thereafter sold the book to Puffin in London and E.P. Dutton in New York. It was published in 1985, just as I was finishing high school."

Where my ideas come from
"I often get inspired by places, and my books are frequently kick-started by an idea for a fabulous setting, like a museum, or a shantytown built in the harbour of a huge city. I also sometimes get inspired by a

really good title, and work from there, meditating on it — a mood, or an incident, or a character starts to develop from that."

Who and what influenced me

"My parents were always incredibly supportive of my writing, reading everything I did, making comments. I remember making a vow to my father when I was 13, that I wanted to have something published before I'd turned 14. Now, Philippa is always the first to read a new story, and her comments are crucial for me. She always has good editing suggestions, and has given me great ideas for stories from time to time."

How I work

"I treat my writing like a full-time, nine-to-five job. I work on a computer (I can't imagine working without one) and I try to write 1000 words a day. Sometimes I go way over, sometimes I fall short, but that's the daily goal. The ratio of actual typing to thinking/daydreaming/looking out the window, is about 1:10. But you have to do it, sit down in front of the screen everyday, if only to get in the right frame of mind.

"I need to write my novels at least twice before I really know the story, ideally with a number of weeks or months between drafts. With each rewriting, it's like superimposing another layer. The story gets deeper and deeper. Three drafts to reach the finished book is average for me. The first run-through tends to be concerned with plot, quite mechanical, then later, the characters get more fully developed and the themes and motifs that were embryonic, are worked out and developed too. By the end, it should be an organic whole, everything linked."

Something nobody knew about me (until now)

"When Philippa and I got married, we moved immediately to Oxford, where she was starting her doctorate in Renaissance Drama. We were very poor and I think it was fear of total destitution which made me as productive as I was during the next 18 months. I finished a novel, as well as six other books, including a picture book and a series of five junior novels."

My favourite book that I've created

Silverwing

Tips for young creators

"Have the discipline not just to write, but to rewrite. Good writing never comes easily."

Kenneth Oppel

BIBLIOGRAPHY

Oppel, Kenneth. *Colin's Fantastic Video Adventure*. Toronto: Penguin Books Canada, 1985. Out of print.

—. *The Live-Forever Machine*. Toronto: Kids Can Press, 1990 Paper 1-55074-010-5.

—. *Cosimo Cat*. Richmond Hill: Scholastic Canada, 1991 Paper 0-590-73651-5; Cloth 0-590-73649-3. 1992 Paper 0-590-73650-7. Illustrations by Regolo Ricci.

—. *Dead Water Zone*. Toronto: Kids Can Press, 1992 Paper 1-55074-092-X; Cloth 1-55074-112-8.

—. *Galactic Snapshots*. Toronto: Penguin Books Canada, 1993. Out of print.

—. *A Bad Case of Ghosts*. Toronto: Penguin Books Canada, 1994. Out of print.

—. *A Bad Case of Magic*. Toronto: Penguin Books Canada, 1994. Out of print.

—. *A Bad Case of Robots*. Toronto: Penguin Books Canada, 1994. Out of print.

—. *A Bad Case of Dinosaurs*. Toronto: Penguin Books Canada, 1994 0-14-036734-9.

—. *Cosmic Snapshots*. Toronto: Penguin Books Canada, 1994. Out of print.

—. *Follow That Star*. Toronto: Kids Can Press, 1994 Cloth 1-55074-134-9. Illustrations by Kim LaFave. ✦

—. *Emma's Emu*. Toronto: Penguin Books Canada, 1995. Markham: Fitzhenry & Whiteside, 1999 Paper 0-590-1458-X. Illustrated by Kim LaFave.

—. *A Bad Case of Super Goo*. Toronto: Penguin Books Canada, 1996 0-14-038085-X.

—. *Silverwing*. Toronto: HarperCollins, 1997 Paper 0-00-648179-5.

—. *Sunwing*. Toronto: HarperCollins, 1999 Paper 0-00-648166-3.

Awards

1995 Air Canada Literary Award (for a writer under 30)

1998 Blue Heron Award for *Silverwing*

1998 Silver Birch Award for *Silverwing*

1998 Canadian Library Association Book of the Year for Children Award for *Silverwing*

1998 Mr. Christie's Book Award for *Silverwing*

Selected articles about Kenneth Oppel

Feliciter. July/August 1998: 50-51.

Jenkinson, Dave. "Profile: Kenneth Oppel." *Resource Links* 2.5 (1997): 199-202.

Pyper, Andrew. "Taking Flight." *Quill and Quire* Oct. 1998: 41-42.

Roger Paré
AUTHOR/ILLUSTRATOR

Born
November 25, 1929, Ville-Marie, Quebec

Where I live now
Montreal, Quebec

Career
Illustrator

Family
Three grown-up children

The room where he creates
Studio in his house

Spare time
One of Roger's favorite "sports" is to walk in Montreal searching for new faces and new expressions. He also enjoys cross-country and downhill skiing, birdwatching and fishing.

When he was growing up
Roger received formal education only until the end of Grade 10 in the Quebec community of Ville-Marie. His teachers encouraged him to paint and draw. As a result of developing his talents as an artist at an early age, he enjoyed a 25-year career with Radio Canada as a graphic artist for children's television programs.

His first book
His career as a children's book illustrator began in 1979 with *Une Fenêtre dans ma Tête*. Since that time he has built an enviable reputation in both French and English Canada publishing worlds.

Where his ideas come from
Roger spends a good deal of time thinking about the kind of children's books he wants to produce. He checks libraries and bookstores, noting what is not available. "For me, books begin through surveying existing children's books, then asking mothers, teachers, and publishers about the real needs of children. This is very important. I also try to observe personally what books kids prefer. My intention is to have fun making a book, so that the kid will also have fun looking at it."

How he works
"I walk a lot and I do my thinking while I walk. Then I try to apply those thoughts when I sit down in the morning to work."

Roger's way of mixing text and illustration varies with each book. "With the books I am working on now, I am doing the text and the art at the same time. With other books I've done in the past, I would do the drawing first and the writing after."

Each book or series begins with a concept. "For instance, in my recent series in French, each book begins with one image. Then I add something with each (succeeding) page. So the children can explore it in both directions, forwards and backwards."

Illustrating for children
It is evident that, even though his illustrations emphasize humour, Roger is very serious about what he wants to accomplish with his children's books. He has a great deal of respect for children's capacity to appreciate good art in a picture book. "What I want for children's books are illustrations that will have the quality of a painting. I think that children are sensitive and can feel what an artist can tell with images. When an illustration is so explicit, there needs to be little writing — the image must reach the reader above all."

Roger Paré

BIBLIOGRAPHY
Inglehart, Anne. *Radio Dog.* New York: Elsevier Dutton, 1979. Illustrations by Roger Paré. Out of print.

Paré, Roger. *A, B, C... Read with Me.* Montreal: la courte échelle, 1985. Illustrations by the author. Out of print.

—. *123...Count with Me.* Trans. by David Homel. Toronto: Annick Press, 1986. Out of print. (Title available in French)

—. *The Annick ABC*. Trans. by David Homel. Toronto: Annick Press, 1987 Annikin Paper 1-55037-059-X. Illustrations by the author.♣

—. *A Friend Like You*. Trans. by David Homel. Toronto: Annick Press, 1988 Paper 0-920303-05-6; Annikin Paper 0-920303-80-3. Illustrations by the author.♣

—. *L'Alphabet: A Child's Introduction to the Letters and Sounds of French*. Lincolnwood, IL: NTC Publishing, 1990 Cloth 0-8442-1395-0. Illustrations by the author.

—. *Un elephant*. Montreal: la courte échelle, 1993 1-89021-199-1. Illustrations by the author.

—. *Un chat*. Montreal: la courte échelle, 1993 1-89021-198-3. Illustrations by the author.

—. *Plaisirs de vacances*. Montreal: la courte échelle, 1995 2-89021-253-X. Illustrations by the author.

—. *Les contraires*. Montreal: la courte échelle, 1996 2-89021-272-6. Illustrations by the author.

—. *Le Gout de Savoir*. Montreal: la courte échelle, 1999 Cloth 2-890-21-368-4.

—. *Plaisirs*. Montreal: la courte échelle, 1999 Cloth 2-89021-369-2.

—. *Plaisirs de Musique*. Montreal: la courte échelle, 1999 Cloth 2-89021-394-3.

—. *Les couleurs*. Montreal: la courte échelle, 1997 2-890021-304-8. Illustrations by the author.

Paré, Roger, and Bertrand Gauthier. *Summer Days*. Trans. by David Homel. Toronto: Annick Press, 1989 Paper 1-55037-044-8; Cloth 1-55037-043-X. Illustrations by Roger Paré.♣

—. *Circus Days*. Trans. by David Homel. Toronto: Annick Press, 1990 Paper 1-55037-020-0; Cloth 1-55037-021-9. Illustrations by Roger Paré.♣

—. *Play Time*. Trans. by David Homel. Toronto: Annick Press, 1990 Paper 1-55037-086-3; Cloth 1-55037-087-1. Illustrations by Roger Paré.♣

—. *Winter Games*. Trans. by David Homel. Toronto: Annick Press, 1991 Paper 1-55037-184-3; Cloth 1-55037-187-8. Illustrations by Roger Paré.♣

—. *Animal Capers*. Trans. by David Homel. Toronto: Annick Press, 1992 Paper 1-55037-244-0; Cloth 1-55037-243-2. Illustrations by Roger Paré.♣

Awards
1979 Canada Council Children's Literature Prize for *Une Fenêtre dans ma Tête*

1985 Canada Council Children's Literature Prize for *L'Alphabet (ABC)*

Kit Pearson
AUTHOR

Born
April 30, 1947, Edmonton, Alberta

School
Crofton House School (Vancouver); University of Alberta, B.A., University of British Columbia, Master of Library Science, Simmons College Centre for the Study of Children's Literature

Where I live now
Vancouver, British Columbia

My favourite book when I was young
Swallows and Amazons

My favourite book now
The Once and Future King

Career
Writer; children's librarian and reference librarian at St. Catharines, North York, and Burnaby Public Libraries, 1976-1990.

Family
"My parents, Kay and Sandy; my brother and sister-in-law, Ron and Betty Anne; their children, Joe, Anne and Will; my other brother, Ian; my Cairn terrier, Flora, and my border terrier, Poppy.

The room where I create
"A sunny room in my house."

Spare time
"Read, walk, birdwatch, garden, play the piano, cross-country ski, go to films, travel."

When I was growing up
"I was a shy child who spent much of her time reading or playing outside — exploring a lake outside of Edmonton (the setting for *A Handful of Time*) and an abandoned Vancouver golf course with various family dogs. I liked piano lessons, climbing trees, and making up imaginary games with my two best friends in Vancouver. When we were 12 we vowed we would never grow up, but of course we had to. I like being a grown-up much more than I expected."

My first book (and how it happened)
"In my thirties I read an adult novel called *Frost In May* by Antonia Fraser, about a girl who attends a convent school at the turn of the century in England. When I finished it I thought 'Why don't I write a story about my school?' *The Daring Game* is based on my experiences attending a girls' boarding school in Vancouver for Grades 10 to 12. Boarding school is such an enclosed, eccentric world; I thought it would be a good setting for kids living in their own society, without adults, which was my favourite kind of story when I was young. It's a very autobiographical novel. The setting, the school events, and even the food are the same as at the real school; but I fictionalized it by writing about girls in Grade 7 instead of high school, and by making up most of the dares. It took me a year to write and another year to find a publisher."

Where my ideas come from
"Because I write about being young, many of my ideas, especially for my first two books, came from my own childhood and adolescence. But they also come from history — such as in the World War II trilogy — from stories I've heard from family and friends, and from being incurably curious. I'm always staring at people and eavesdropping on their conversations. Sometimes it gets me into trouble, but I can't help it!"

Who and what influenced me
"The greatest influences in my life have been books. Some of my favourite authors as a child — Arthur Ransome, P. L. Travers, Edward Eager, Frances Hodgson Burnett, C.S. Lewis, E. Nesbit, Noel Streatfield, and many others, have inspired the kinds of stories and characters I create.

"When I finished L. M. Montgomery's *Emily of New Moon*, at age 12, I decided that I, like Emily, would become a writer. It took me 23 years to finally do it! That's when I took two writing courses in Boston which gave me the courage to start my first book."

How I work

"An idea usually grows in my mind for months — sometimes years — and I gradually begin to make notes on it, usually scraps about characters and setting and situation.

"If the book takes place in the past I have to do lots of research. I write all my drafts on a computer. I don't make an outline and I don't know what's going to happen in each chapter until I write it.

"The first draft, which goes very quickly, is very short and sloppily written — what some people call 'pre-writing.' Then I make an outline, trying to get the plot and characters to work together.

"I do a much longer second draft. Then I print it out and go over it with a pencil, playing with the words and polishing and tightening it — this is my favourite stage. I do several more versions until it's ready for my editor to see. He makes suggestions and I do one final draft before the book is printed. I write best in the mornings — usually for about four hours, until my dogs insist on a walk. I take breaks between drafts to let them 'cook' and to get some perspective on them."

Something nobody knew about me (until now)

"I like to play old Rolling Stones records really loud and dance around the house to them."

My favourite book that I've created

"This is tricky, because it varies so much. Sometimes it's the one I'm working on and sometimes it's one I haven't read for a while; it depends on my mood.

"I'd rather pick my favourite characters — Eliza, from *The Daring Game* because she's so brave and kind; and Gavin from *The Lights Go On Again* because he's so vulnerable — I feel like his mother!"

Tips for young creators

"The best way to learn how to write is to read — to try many different kinds of books, like trying different kinds of food. That's the only way you'll find out what you like. What you like is what you'll be best at writing about.

"You don't have to write when you're young if you don't want to — I didn't. Maybe you're not ready yet. If you're not ready to write stories but you want to practise, try keeping a diary — a secret journal with blank pages that you write in when you feel like it.

"Lots of people — teachers, authors of writing books, writers — will tell you how to write. You might find it good advice, but if you disagree remember that everyone writes differently and that you have to find the way that's truest to *you*.

"This means that, if you really want to be a writer when you grow up, you have to be patient and let your talent grow."

Kit Pearson

BIBLIOGRAPHY

Pearson, Kit. *The Daring Game.* Toronto: Penguin Books Canada, 1986 Cloth 0-670-80751-6. 1987 Paper 0-14-031932-8.

—. *A Handful of Time.* Toronto: Penguin Books Canada, 1987 Paper 0-14-032268-X; Cloth 0-670-81532-2.

—. *The Sky is Falling.* Toronto: Penguin Books Canada, 1989. 1991 Paper 0-14-034189-7.

—. *The Singing Basket.* Toronto: Penguin Books Canada, 1990 Cloth 0-88899-104-5. Illustrations by Anne Blades.

—. *Looking at the Moon.* Toronto: Penguin Books Canada, 1991 Cloth 0-670-84097-1. 1993 Paper 0-14-034852-2.

——. *The Lights Go On Again.* Toronto: Penguin Books Canada, 1993 Cloth 0-670-84919-7.

—. *Awake and Dreaming.* Toronto: Penguin Books Canada, 1996 0-670-86954-6.1999 Paper 0-14-038166-X.

—, ed. *This Land: A Cross Country Anthology of Canadian Fiction for Young Readers.* Toronto: Viking, 1998 Cloth 0-670-87896-0.

Awards

1988 Canadian Library Association Book of the Year for Children Award for *A Handful of Time*

1989 Mr. Christie's Book Award for *The Sky is Falling*

1990 Canadian Library Association Book of the Year for Children Award for *The Sky is Falling*

1990 Geoffrey Bilson Award for Historical Fiction for Young People for *The Sky is Falling*

1994 Manitoba Young Reader's Choice Award for *Looking at the Moon*

1994 IODE Violet Downey Book Award for *The Lights Go On Again*

1997 Ruth Schwartz Children's Book Award for *Awake and Dreaming*

1997 Governor General's Award for *Awake and Dreaming*

1998 Vicky Metcalf Award for a Body of Work

Selected articles about Kit Pearson

Flick, Jane. "'Writing is the Deepest Pleasure I Know': an Interview with Kit Pearson." *Canadian Children's Literature* 74 (1994): 16-28.

"Kit Pearson." *Something about the Author: Autobiography Series.* Detroit: Gale Research, vol. 25 (1997).

"Kit Pearson." *Twentieth Century Young Adult Writers.* Detroit: St. James Press, 1994: 522-523.

Margriet Ruurs
AUTHOR

Born
December 2, 1952

School
Elementary and high school in The Netherlands; M.A. in Education, Simon Fraser University, Vancouver, British Columbia

Where I live now
Okanagan Valley in British Columbia

My favourite books when I was young
Pippi Longstocking, fairytales.

My favourite book now
"Any book that makes me laugh or cry. I read several YA novels and about 12 picture books a week."

Career
"I teach writing enrichment workshops in schools, conduct teachers' professional development and college workshops on children's literature and try to spend the rest of my time writing and researching new books. I also present at many International Reading Association conferences throughout the States."

Family
"I am happily married to my best friend Kees and have two sons, Alexander and Arnout."

The room where I create
"I have a wonderful room full of books. My computer desk is under the window from which I have a view of rolling farmland and snowcapped hills. I am surrounded by books, book posters and teddy bears. Behind me is a couch on which my dog and two cats all sleep together while I write. I try out my stories on them."

Spare time
"I like to spend any spare time with my husband. We like to putter in the garden or go on hikes. I read all the time and knit sweaters that usually don't fit anyone."

When I was growing up
"I loved reading. All I did was read. Sometimes my library books were due and my dad would drive me to the public library at 8 o'clock at night… in my pajamas! When I was in Grade 8 my teachers told me that I should be a writer and I went to meet a very famous Dutch author. But he was a big man who smoked cigars, and recited strange poetry in a dark room full of dark books. If that was an author, I didn't want to be one!

"Thank goodness I kept on reading and writing and discovered that writing can be the most fun thing to do."

My first book (and how it happened)
"I worked in a primate centre, raising baby chimpanzees. Everyone always wanted to hear the stories and see the pictures of those fun chimps. I wrote it all down, showed it to a big publisher (in Holland) and *voilà…* they published it!"

Where my ideas come from
"My ideas pop into my head for many different reasons. Sometimes it's something interesting I learn about, or something funny someone says. I mix those first ideas with imagination and let the idea 'compost' in my head until a story sprouts up.

"When I was very young my father told me lots of stories. On weekend mornings I'd crawl in his bed and he would make up wonderful stories full of mischief. My dad was also a talented painter.

"Undoubtedly, all the books I read as a child influenced me. I grew up on the fun, humorous, often rhyming texts of Annie M.G. Schmidt, Holland's most famous author and winner of the Hans Christian Andersen Award."

How I work
"I find each book is different. Sometimes that idea that has been fermenting in my brain will pop out and I'll write for hours.

Other times I write a bit, I research, I rewrite, I read it out loud. I do spend a lot of time on editing and rewriting because it always makes the story better."

Something nobody knew about me (until now)

"Sometimes I hide chocolate and eat it when I'm home alone."

My favourite book I've created

"I really don't have a favourite. They're all so different. I love the illustrations in *A Mountain Alphabet*, I like that silly chicken Emma and *Big Little Dog* makes me cry. Maybe my next book will be my favourite…"

Tips for young creators

"Read! Read picture books, read novels, read Canadian authors, read old fairy tales, read magazines, and then read some more. And when you start to try to get your writing published, never give up. Learn from others, don't be satisfied too easily and keep writing."

Margriet Ruurs

BIBLIOGRAPHY

Ruurs, Margriet. *Apenkinderen.* Amsterdam: Leopold Publishing, 1982.

—. *Spectacular Spiders.* Gabriola Island: Pacific Edge Publishing, 1995. 1-895110-20-3.

—. *Fireweed.* Whitehorse: Burns and Morton, 1986. Out of print.

—. *Big Little Dog.* Manotick: Penumbra Press, 1992 Paper 0-921254-46-6. Illustrations by Marc Houde.

—. *A Mountain Alphabet.* Toronto: Tundra Books, 1996 Paper 0-88776-384-7; Cloth 0-88776-374- X. Illustrations by Andrew Kiss.

—. *Emma's Eggs.* Toronto: Stoddart Kids, 1996 Cloth 0-7737-2972-0. 1997 Paper 0-7737-5090-4. Illustrations by Barbara Spurll.

—. *Emma and the Coyote.* Toronto: Stoddart Kids, 1999 0-7737-3140-7. Illustrations by Barbara Spurll.

Awards

1997 Storytelling World Award for *Emma's Eggs*

Barbara Claassen Smucker
AUTHOR

Born
September 1, 1915, Newton, Kansas, U.S.A.

School
Bethel College and Kansas State University, both in Kansas; Rosary College Library School, Illinois, U.S.A.

My favourite books when I was young
Anne of Green Gables by L.M. Montgomery, *The Wizard of Oz* by Frank Baum.

Career
Writer, children's librarian.

Family
Husband, Donovan; three children, Rebecca, Timothy and Thomas; four grandchildren, Tamara, Amy, Sarah and Aaron

When I was growing up
"I decided to become a writer in Grade 7, primarily because my English teacher in my hometown of Newton, Kansas, encouraged me. When I confided my aspiration to a young minister who was writing a novel, he organized the Potential Writer's Club in our town. It included an elderly Mexican man who wrote poetry, a farm boy, and my best friend, the cemetery sexton's daughter. We met weekly. It was in this club that I wrote my first novel with my friend. We considered it a treasure that should never be destroyed, so we buried it in a wheat field. Over 50 years later, a tall apartment building stands on guard on top of it."

Beginning to write
"My first job was newspaper reporting. My most exciting assignments were to meet the train at the railway station when it stopped for refuelling. There were often famous people on board and I was sometimes granted interviews. I caught fleeting glimpses of Mary Pickford and Clara Bow.

"The interview that changed my life was with a young Mennonite minister and university professor, Donovan Smucker, who shortly became my husband. We travelled widely, lived in many places, and in 1969 moved to Canada, where he became a professor at the University of Waterloo and I became a children's librarian at the Kitchener Public Library. I had prepared for this job at an accredited library school, where my interest in children's books became an obsession."

My first book (and how it happened)
"I published my first book for boys and girls, *Henry's Red Sea*, in 1955. It's the fictionalized account of the escape of 1,000 Mennonite refugees from Russia to Paraguay after World War II. The story was told one evening in our home by a man who took part in the event. Our three small children didn't move for two hours during the telling. I thought, 'This is a story that should be recorded for children.' But I didn't want to reduce it to dry historical facts; I wanted to retain the drama and make history come alive. The book is still in print."

Writing historical fiction
"Most of my books have been based on dramatic historical events that involve tests of courage by both real and fictional characters. I try to imagine myself as a boy or girl taking part in the story. My book *Underground to Canada* is based on such a period in Canada's history. The story was planted in my mind in the 1960s when my husband became president of an all-black, church-related college in Mississippi and I was a librarian and teacher there. It was at the height of the black civil rights movement and many black students were hostile toward the white faculty. When tension at the college threatened to erupt into violence after the death of Martin Luther King, we decided to move to Ontario.

"As a librarian in Kitchener, the tragic history of slavery and black prejudice reappeared when young people doing projects on the subject came to me for books. I could find no material on the drama of the 40,000 black slaves who escaped to freedom in Canada around 1850. I visited Dresden, Ontario, where a cabin, a chapel, a school, and a sawmill built by escaped slaves still stand. I dug through old books in the library archives and discovered Alexander Ross, a Canadian ornithologist who risked his life to travel to southern plantations and inform slaves about the underground railway that led from the South to the Canadian border. Both blacks and whites cooperated in this adventure, proving to me that people need not be separated by skin colour."

Barbara Claassen Smucker

BIBLIOGRAPHY

Smucker, Barbara. *Henry's Red Sea.* Scottsdale: Herald Press, 1955 Paper 0-8361-1372-1.

—. *Wigwam in the City.* New York: Dutton, 1966. Rpt. as *Susan.* New York: Scholastic, 1972. Out of print.

—. *Underground to Canada.* Toronto: Penguin Books Canada, 1978 Paper 0-14-031122-X. Rpt. in U.S.A. as *Runaway to Freedom.* New York: HarperCollins, 1979 Paper 0-06-440106-5. New edition Toronto: Penguin Books Canada, 1999 Paper 0-14-130686-6. Introduction by Lawrence Hill.

—. *Days of Terror.* Toronto: Penguin Books Canada, 1979. 1991 Paper 0-14-031306-0.

—. *Amish Adventure.* Toronto: Penguin Books Canada, 1984 Paper 0-14-031702-3.

—. *White Mist.* Toronto: Penguin Books Canada, 1987 Paper 0-14-032144-6.

—. *Jacob's Little Giant.* Toronto: Penguin Books Canada, 1987 Paper 0-14-032326-0.

—. *Incredible Jumbo.* Toronto: Penguin Books Canada, 1990 Paper 0-14-034235-4.

—. *Garth and the Mermaid.* Toronto: Penguin Books Canada, 1994 Paper 0-14-031702-3.

—. *Selina and the Bear Paw Quilt.* Toronto: Lester Publishing, 1995 Cloth 1-895555-90-6. Toronto: Stoddart Kids, 1996 Paper 0-7737-5837-2 Cloth 0-7737-2992-5. Illustrations by Janet Wilson.

—. *Selina and the Shoo-Fly Pie.* Toronto: Stoddart Kids, 1998 Cloth 0-7737-3018-4. Illustrated by Janet Wilson.

Awards

1979 Canada Council Children's Literature Prize for *Days of Terror*

1980 Ruth Schwartz Children's Book Award for *Days of Terror*

1988 Vicky Metcalf Award for a Body of Work

1991 IODE Violet Downey Book Award for *Incredible Jumbo*

Selected articles about Barbara Smucker

"Barbara Claassen Smucker." *Something About the Author: Autobiography Series.* ed. Joyce Nakamura. Detroit: Gale Research, vol. 11 (1991): 321-335.

Gertridge, Allison. *Meet Canadian Authors and Illustrators.* Richmond Hill: Scholastic Canada, 1994: 92-3.

Salata, Estelle. *Behind the Story.* Ed. Barbara Greenwood. Markham: Pembroke Publishers, 1995: 72-4.

Ted Staunton
AUTHOR

Born
"I was born on March 29, 1956 at Toronto Western Hospital. I was late."

School
"I went to Park Lawn Public School and Royal York Collegiate, both in Etobicoke, Ontario, and later to the University of Toronto."

Where I live now
"In Port Hope, Ontario — a place I like a whole lot."

My favourite book when I was young
"There were a bunch: *Babar* by Jean de Brunhoff, *Farmer Boy* by Laura Ingalls Wilder, *The Wind in the Willows* by Kenneth Grahame, *Swallows and Amazons* by Arthur Ransome, and *Charlotte's Web* by E.B. White."

My favourite book now
"*The Adventures of Huckleberry Finn* by Mark Twain, *Lake Wobegon Days* by Garrison Keillor, *Collected Stories of Frank O'Connor*, and the *Ramona* books by Beverly Cleary, to name a few."

Career
Writer, storyteller

Family
"Wife, Melanie; son, Will; cat, Archie (even though she's a girl)."

The room where I create
"... is upstairs. It's the smallest room in the house. In fact, when we moved in we discussed whether or not it was a closet. Sometimes I also write at the cottage."

Spare time
"I like to run, read, sing and play guitar and banjo music with my friends, watch movies and have fun with my family."

When I was growing up
"I was a lot shorter than I am now. Also younger. I liked to read and pretend a lot and sometime in high school I started thinking about becoming an author. Before that, I was planning on being a cowboy. Does anyone know Roy Rogers anymore? Gene Autry? Trigger? The Lone Ranger? Those were the days, boy."

My first book (and how it happened)
"My first book was called *Puddleman*. I wrote it as an assignment when I went to teacher's college and the professor I wrote it for encouraged me to send it to a publisher. I did, and the very first publisher I tried, Kids Can Press, accepted it. I was so lucky, I didn't even know I was lucky!"

Where my ideas come from
"My ideas usually come from real life incidents I see or hear about. Usually though, these incidents are only one situation and not a complete story, so next you have to imagine how your characters got into such a mess and how to get them out.

"For the *Maggie and Cyril* stories, I occasionally worked backwards. I'd read fact books about science or Hallowe'en or world records that I thought Maggie might read. Then I would look for things that might come in handy as problem solvers. For instance how to hold water in a sieve, or how to turn your mouth green. Then, I'd come up with a problem to suit the solution."

Who and what influenced me
"Lots of people have influenced me in very different ways. My mom, dad, family, friends and teachers have all given me help, encouragement, ideas, examples, meals, songs and laundry assistance. Helpful in other ways were the books I mentioned in my list of favourites. Also really important to me are books by John Holt and Robert Coles, people who spend lots of time with real-life kids, thinking about what they say and do."

How I work
"Usually I'll get some odds and ends of ideas from things in real life, all unconnected, and start thinking about how they might go together. Then I'll make a

plan of the whole story and show it to my wife. She'll tell me it stinks. I'll sulk, then realize she's right and make it better. When it's good enough, I'll start writing and show each chapter to my wife as I finish it. She'll tell me it stinks. I'll sulk, then realize...but you've probably got the idea by now."

My favourite book that I've created

"My favourite book is always the one I'm writing right now. By the time I've finished it, I'll be tired of it. Later, I'll see more clearly that there are parts of it that I'll like a lot and other parts that aren't so hot, but by then I'll be all excited about the next one."

Tips for young creators

"Read anything that interests you. Reading widely is more important than writing when you are young. It helps give you the equipment you'll need to be a writer. Don't worry if you don't have many ideas; no one has many good ones. Try to write stories like the ones you enjoy reading. Imitate your favourites. Your own style comes later, when you get bored with sounding like someone else, or you can't make your brain work like theirs."

Ted Staunton

BIBLIOGRAPHY

Staunton, Ted. *Puddleman* (Little Kids Series). Toronto: Kids Can Press, 1983. Red Deer: Red Deer Press, 1999 0-88995-190-X. Illustrations by Brenda Clark.

—. *Taking Care of Crumley*. Toronto: Kids Can Press, 1984. Illustrations by Tina Holdcroft. Out of print.

—. *Maggie and Me* (Maggie and Cyril Series). Toronto: Kids Can Press, 1986. Port Hope: Staunton, 1995 Paper 0-9699926-0-2.

—. *Greenapple Street Blues* (Maggie and Cyril Series). Toronto: Kids Can Press, 1987. Port Hope: Staunton, 1995.

—. *Mushmouth and the Marvel* (Maggie and Cyril Series). Toronto: Kids Can Press, 1988. Port Hope: Staunton, 1995 Paper 0-9699926-2-9.

—. *Great Minds Think Alike* (Maggie and Cyril Series). Toronto: Kids Can Press, 1989. Port Hope: Staunton, 1995 Paper 0-9699926-1-0.

—. *Miss Fishley Afloat*. Toronto: Kids Can Press, 1990. Illustrations by Eric Parker. Out of print.

—. *Taking the Long Way Home* (Maggie and Cyril Series). Toronto: Kids Can Press, 1992. Port Hope: Staunton, 1995.

—. *Anna Takes Charge*. Toronto: Yorkdale Shopping Centre; Scarborough: Scarborough Town Centre; Brampton: Bramalea City Centre, 1993. Illustrations by Michael Martchenko. Out of print.

—. *Simon's Surprise*. Toronto: Kids Can Press, 1986. Illustrations by Sylvie Daigneault. Out of print. ♣ (French title still in print.)

—. *Morgan Makes Magic*. Halifax: Formac, 1997 Paper 0-88780-390-3; Cloth 0-88780-391-1. Illustrations by Bill Slavin.

—. *Hope Springs A Leak*. Red Deer: Red Deer Press, 1998 Paper 0-88995-174-8.

—. *Morgan and the Money*. Halifax: Formac, 1998 Paper 0-88780-456-X; Cloth 0-88780-457-8. Illustrations by Bill Slavin.

—. *Two False Moves* (Monkey Mountain series). Red Deer: Red Deer Press, 2000. Paper 0-88995-205-1.

—. *The Monkey Mountain Monster* (Monkey Mountain series). Red Deer: Red Deer Press, 2000. Paper 0-88995-206-X.

—. *Forgive Us Our Travises* (Monkey Mountain series). Red Deer: Red Deer Press, 2000. Paper 0-88995-207-8.

Kathy Stinson
AUTHOR

Born
April 22, 1952, Toronto, Ontario

School
Douglas Park Public School, Bloordale Sr. Public School, Vincent Massey C.I., all in Etobicoke, Ontario; Lakeshore Teachers College, University of Toronto (part-time), Toronto, Ontario

Where I live now
Near Rockwood, Ontario, in a hamlet (Everton) between Guelph and Erin.

My favourite book when I was young
"Books by Beverly Cleary, Laura Ingalls Wilder, Eleanor Estes, Arthur Ransome. The only Canadian book I remember reading as a child was *The Bells on Finland Street* by Lyn Cook."

Career
Mail sorter, teacher, parent, waitress, pre-school program instructor, writer.

Family
Kathy lives with Peter Carver in a big house in the country, enjoying visits from her grown-up kids Matt and Kelly, stepdaughters Kate and Stephanie, and grandson Michael.

The room where I create
"My computer is in a cozy yellow room in the basement, but my brain seems to like creating when I'm biking alone up the 7th Line, too, or walking in the woods near my home."

Spare time
"Read, do jigsaw puzzles, read, visit friends, read, go for walks, read."

When I was growing up
"I loved to read; I could read before I started school, and I visited the public library often and took out as many books as were allowed. I read in bed before going to sleep, often by the streetlight shining in the window after my mom made me turn out my light. At school I got in trouble for talking and giggling too much with my friends."

My first book (and how it happened)
"After losing an argument with my then three-year-old daughter over which stockings she would wear to visit her Gramma, I wrote *Red is Best*. I contacted the Children's Book Centre ('Canadian' wasn't yet part of its name) to find out how to go about submitting it to publishers."

Where my ideas come from
"They're everywhere. My earliest books were inspired by things my own two kids said or did — like Kelly's insistence on the red stockings, like Matthew's struggle over whether he was big or little. As Matthew and Kelly have grown older, I've depended more on things happening in other people's families. Hearing about a friend's musical beds kind of night reminded me of nights I'd had trouble sleeping at different times in my life. I combined my friend's experience and my own, gave it more of a structure than real life actually has, and wrote *Who is Sleeping in Aunty's Bed?*

"The idea for *Fish House Secrets* came from the place on the south shore of Nova Scotia where the story is set. As I began to write about that place, characters appeared on the scene. I followed them around and soon began to discover their stories.

"I get ideas from my childhood, and from things happening around me as I go about day-to-day living. After hearing about a girl forced by a court order to choose between her parents, I wrote *one year commencing*. I didn't know the 'real' girl, didn't even know her name, but I dedicated the book to her anyway.

"Occasionally someone will suggest an idea that intrigues me in some way. For example, Heather Collins' husband encouraged Heather and me to do *The Dressed Up Book* as a kind of sequel to *The Bare Naked Book*. And there's a deaf character in *The Great Pebble Creek Bike Race*, because of a suggestion someone made once when I was touring."

Who and what influenced me

"My *Pebble Creek* novels are dedicated to two of the most important influences in my life. Without the love of books my mom instilled in me and the example of my dad's willingness to take chances in life, I could not have become the writer I am. And I think the cumulative effect of all the books I read — as a child and as an adult, as a teacher and as a parent — made it almost inevitable that I would one day decide I wanted to write books myself. I'm inspired by writers whose work shows delight in and respect for language and offers insights into the lives of ordinary and extraordinary people."

How I work

"I always have a number of projects on the go, of various kinds and at various stages. That way, if work on one isn't going well, or is awaiting a publisher's attention, there's something else to turn to. I do most of my work on computer, but at our cottage, which doesn't have electricity, I write longhand. Morning is my best writing time, so I try to keep the business aspects of being a writer to the afternoon."

Something nobody knew about me (until now)

"The first time I fell in love was in Grade 2. The boy's name was Terry Campbell."

Tips for young creators

"Read lots. Write about what's important to you, something you care about. Have fun with your writing, even when it's hard work. For a whole book full of more specific tips, read my book *Writing Your Best Picture Book Ever*."

Kathy Stinson

BIBLIOGRAPHY

Stinson, Kathy. *Red is Best* (Annick Toddler Series). Toronto: Annick Press, 1982 Paper 0-920236-26-X; Cloth 0-920236-24-3; Annikin Paper 1-55037-252-1. Illustrations by Robin Baird Lewis. ♣

—. *Big or Little?* Toronto: Annick Press, 1983 Paper 0-920236-32-4; Cloth 0-92023-630-8. 1985 Annikin Paper 0-920303-19-6. Illustrations by Robin Baird Lewis. ♣

—. *Mom and Dad Don't Live Together Anymore*. Toronto: Annick Press, 1984 Paper 0-920236-87-1; Cloth 0-920236-92-8. Illustrations by Nancy Lou Reynolds.

—. *The Bare Naked Book*. Toronto: Annick Press, 1986 Paper 0-920303-53-6; Cloth 0-920303-52-8. Illustrations by Heather Collins. ♣

—. *Seven Clues in Pebble Creek* (Blue Kite Series). Toronto: James Lorimer & Co., 1987 Paper 1-55028-036-8; Cloth 1-55028-038-4.

—. *Teddy Rabbit*. Toronto: Annick Press, 1988. Illustrations by Stéphane Poulin. Out of print. ♣ (Title in print in French)

—. *The Dressed Up Book*. Toronto: Annick Press, 1990 Paper 1-55037-104-5; Cloth 1-55037-103-7. Illustrations by Heather Collins.

—. *Who is Sleeping in Aunty's Bed?* Toronto: Stoddart/Oxford University Press, 1991. 1992 Paper 0-19-540852-7. Illustrations by Robin Baird Lewis.

—. *Writing Picture Books: What Works and What Doesn't*. Markham: Pembroke Publishers, 1991 Paper 0-921217-72-2.

—. *Fish House Secrets*. Saskatoon: Thistledown Press, 1992. Paper 1-895449-10-3.

—. *Steven's Baseball Mitt: A Book About Being Adopted*. Toronto: Annick Press, 1992. Out of print. (U.S. edition available: *I Feel Different: A Book About Being Adopted*. Los Angeles: Western Psychological Services, 1998 Paper 0-87424-355-6.) Illustrations by Robin Baird Lewis.

—. *The Fabulous Ball Book*. Don Mills: Stoddart/Oxford University Press, 1993 Paper 0-19-540913-2. Illustrations by Heather Collins.

—. *Writing Your Best Picture Book Ever*. Markham: Pembroke Publishers, 1994 Paper 1-55138-028-5. Illustrations by Alan and Lea Daniel.

—. *The Great Pebble Creek Bike Race* (Blue Kite Series). Toronto: James Lorimer & Co., 1994 Paper 1-55028-442-8; Cloth 1-55028-443-6.

—. *Those Green Things*. Toronto: Annick Press, 1985. Rev. ed. 1995 Paper 1-55037-376-5; Cloth 1-55037-377-3. Illustrations by Deirdre Betteridge.

—. "Babysitting Helen." *Takes: Stories For Young Adults*. Ed. R.P. MacIntyre. Saskatoon: Thistletown Press, 1996 Paper 1-895449-54-5.

—. *one year commencing*. Saskatoon: Thistledown Press, 1997 Paper 1-895449-65-0.

Awards

1982 IODE Book Award - Municipal Chapter of Toronto for *Red is Best*

Selected articles about Kathy Stinson

Jenkinson, Dave. "Portraits: Kathy Stinson." *Emergency Librarian* (May-June 1987).

Wagner, Dale. "Kathy Stinson." *CANSCAIP News* 12.4 (1990).

Stinson, Kathy. *Canadian Children's Literature* 68 (1992): 136-7.

Shelley Tanaka
AUTHOR

Born
June 28, 1950, Toronto, Ontario

Schools
Three Valleys Drive Public School and George S. Henry S.S. in Don Mills, Ontario; Queen's University (B.A. Hons.); University of Toronto (M.A.)

Where I live now
Kingston, Ontario

My favourite books when I was young
"I was a big fan of series — the Narnia books, the *Anne* books, the *Pooh* books, Enid Blyton's *Adventure* books, Trixie Belden."

My favourite books right now
The Man by Raymond Briggs

Career
Camp counsellor, receptionist, translator, book editor, writer.

Family
"I live with my partner and our daughters, Claire and Jessica. Also Fergie, a black Lab; Puddles, a calico cat; several goldfish."

The room where I create
"I have just moved from the country, where I had a big office with huge windows on three sides, to the city, where I have a tiny office with one small window. Everything in my new office has been arranged so that my desk can face the window. In the country I could look out and see birds at the feeder, my dog sitting on top of the septic tank and occasionally a fox trotting down the road. Now I watch people walking their dogs, or cars trying to parallel park. I've decided that windows are important to me, though not necessarily good for my work!"

Spare time
"When I have spare time, I am very lazy. I like to sleep in and play cards and cook and eat good food with friends. Actually, I manage to do all these things even when I don't have time to spare."

When I was growing up
"When I was 12, I made up a story about a little sparkle of light that lived in the chrome of the bathtub faucet. I thought it was a wonderful story, but when I wrote it out and showed it to my teacher, it wasn't so great. Some stories are better not written down."

My first book (and how it happened)
"Through my work as an editor, I knew Mary Alice Downie, and she asked me to write a story for a series of historical picture books that she was editing. I wrote about a little Japanese girl moving to Vancouver at the turn of the century. The story was based on my grandmother's experiences. It was called *Michi's New Year* and was illustrated by Ron Berg. It has made me a better editor to have my own work critiqued by others. It's certainly made me a nicer one."

Where my ideas come from
"Most of the books I write are not my own ideas. A publisher or book packager usually suggests a topic, or teams me up with a co-writer or expert, and then I do whatever we all agree on. This means I can write books quite quickly, because it's the thinking and creating that take up so much time. Maybe when people stop approaching me with good ideas, I will have to think of one on my own."

Who and what influenced me
"I have been lucky enough to work as an editor with many of the very best children's writers in Canada, including Martha Brooks, Sarah Ellis, Sheree Fitch, Jean Little, Kevin Major, Diana Wieler and Tim Wynne-Jones. They are a constant reminder of what really good writing is, and this keeps me pretty humble."

How I work

"I spend a fair bit of time doing 'busy' work – making notes and lists, revising and retyping notes and lists, sorting and resorting things into specific piles. I like to think all this helps me stay organized and on track, but I would probably be better off doing less fussing and more real work."

Something nobody knew about me (until now)

"When I play Solitaire, as soon as I see that I'm not going to get out, I scrap the hand and start over. Is that cheating?"

My favourite book that I've created

"My favourite book is usually the one I've just finished writing. After you've handed it in to the publisher but before anyone has read it — that's the best time. That's when your work seems perfect."

Tips for young creators

"Date and keep your old stories and journals — give them to your mum to put away. You'll want to go back and reread them one day."

Shelley Tanaka

BIBLIOGRAPHY

Tanaka, Shelley. *Michi's New Year*. Toronto: PMA Books, 1980. Illustrations by Ron Berg. Out of print.

—. *The Cat Lover's Diary*. Toronto: Madison Press/McClelland and Stewart, 1984. Out of print.

—. *The Ann of Green Gables Diary*. Toronto: Bantam, 1987. Out of print.

—. *The Secrets of Vesuvius*. Madison Press/Random House Canada, 1990. Out of print.

—. *The Heat is On: Facing Our Energy Problem*. Toronto: Douglas & McIntyre, 1991 Paper 1- 55054-200-1. Illustrations by Steve Beinicke.

—. *A Great Round Wonder: My Book of the World*. Toronto: Douglas & McIntyre, 1993 Cloth 0-55054-213-3. Illustrated by Debi Perna.

—. *The Disaster of the Hindenburg*. Madison Press/Scholastic Canada, 1993 Cloth 0-590-45750-0.

—. *The Illustrated Father Goose*. Toronto: Little Brown, 1995 Cloth 0-316-52709-2. Illustrated by Laurie McGraw.

—. *On Board the Titanic*. Toronto: Madison Press/Scholastic Canada, 1996 Cloth 0-590-24894-4. 1997 Paper 0-590-24895-2. Illustrations by Ken Marschall.

—. *Discovering the Iceman*. Toronto: Madison Press/Scholastic Canada 1996 Paper 0-590-24951-7. Illustrations by Laurie McGraw.

—. *The Buried City of Pompeii*. Toronto: Madison Press/Scholastic Canada, 1997 Cloth 0-590- 12377-7. Illustrations by Greg Ruhl.

—, adapt. *Anne of Green Gables*. By L.M. Montgomery. Toronto: Seal Books, 1998 Paper 0-7704- 2744-8.

—. *Graveyards of the Dinosaurs*. Toronto: Madison Press/Scholastic Canada, 1998 Paper 0-590- 12447-1; Cloth 0-590-12446-3.

—. *Lost Temple of the Aztecs*. Toronto: Madison Press/Scholastic Canada, 1998 Paper 0-590-12479-X; Cloth 0-590-12478-1. Illustrations by Greg Ruhl.

—. *Secrets of the Mummies: Uncovering the Bodies of Ancient Egyptians*. Toronto: Madison Press/Scholastic Canada, 1999 Cloth 0-590-51494-6. Illustrations by Greg Ruhl. ✱

Tanaka, Shelley, and Ernie Coombs. *Mr. Dressup's Book of Things to Make and Do*. Toronto: CBC Enterprises, 1982. Toronto: Stoddart Books, 1991 Paper 0-7737-5459-8.

—. *Mr. Dressup's 50 More Things to Make and Do*. Toronto: Stoddart Books, 1991 Paper 0-7737- 5460-1.

—. *Mr. Dressup's Birthday Party Book: Painless Parties for Young Children — and their Parents*. Toronto: Douglas & McIntyre, 1988. Out of print.

Tanaka, Shelley, and William Kaplan. *One More Border*. Toronto: Groundwood Books, 1998 Cloth 0-88899-332-3.

Awards

German Academy for Children's and Young People's Literature Book of the Month for *Secrets of Vesuvius*

1997 Silver Birch Award for *On Board the Titanic*

1997 Information Book Award for *On Board the Titanic*

1997 Mr. Christie's Book Award for *Discovering the Iceman*

1998 Information Book Award for *The Buried City of Pompeii*

Selected articles about Shelley Tanaka

Barrett, Sylvia. "Tanaka's Pastoral Idyll." *Quill and Quire* Oct. 1991.

O'Reilly, Gillian. "The Two Hats (and Many Books) of Shelley Tanaka." *Children's Book News*, Spring 1998.

C.J. (Carrie) Taylor
AUTHOR/ILLUSTRATOR

Born
August 31, 1952, Montreal, Quebec

Life
Self-taught

Where she lives now
Chateauguay, Quebec

Lifestyle
Artist

Family
Husband, Norman Keene; three children, Matthew, Kristy and Joseph. Two grandsons, Andrew (six years old) and Morise (eight months old)

Spare time
"Since January 1992, I have been the host of a weekly radio program called 'Earthsongs' on CKRK FM, Mohawk Radio in Kahnawake, Quebec. Books are reviewed, songs by and about natives are played, stories are told, and ecological concerns are aired."

When she was growing up
"I started painting when I was 16 years old with an old set of oil paints that belonged to my mother. I sold my first painting for five dollars. My talent comes from my mother. My subject matter comes from my father.

My father's mother was a Mohawk, who lost her status when her first husband died and she married a non-native. She was a sad woman, and her sadness intrigued me."

Discovering her native roots when she was six years old, Carrie has been fascinated with legends ever since. "We lived in the country in the middle of nowhere and I was always by myself. It gave me a chance to think things through to find out who I was."

Her first book (and how it happened)
May Cutler, president of Tundra Books admired Carrie's work and asked if she wanted to write and illustrate native legends for children. Tundra launched her first book, *How Two-Feather was saved from loneliness*, which is based on an Abenaki tale of a lonely man who becomes enchanted with a mystical woman. "The book takes in three origins — how corn, communal living and fire came into the world," Carrie says.

Where her ideas come from
Carrie's interest in native legends peaked when she began to investigate her own native heritage. "I've been on a lifelong search to find my heritage and

personality. My art and books are an extension of that."

How she works
The legends Carrie chooses to illustrate are the ones she sees most vividly in her imagination. "In all my books I'm looking for the qualities of a hero and whether the legend is a good story with good morals for children."

Research is also an important part of Carrie's work. "When I'm researching a story I have to make sure that the environment is authentic, that the style of dress the natives wear is authentic and the type of spirituality I'm portraying is authentic. This is important because I want to dispel the stereotypes about natives." Carrie works in acrylic, pencil, watercolour and oils.

C. J. Taylor

BIBLIOGRAPHY
Taylor, C. J. *How Two-Feather was saved from loneliness: An Abenaki Legend.* Montreal: Tundra Books, 1990 Cloth 0-88776-254-9. 1992 Paper 0-88776-282-4. Illustrations by the author. ✱

—. *The Ghost and Lone Warrior: An Arapaho Legend.* Montreal: Tundra Books, 1991 Cloth 0-88776-263-8. 1993 Paper 0-88776-308-1. Illustrations by the author. ✱

—. *Little Water and the gift of the animals: A Seneca Legend.* Montreal: Tundra Books, 1992 Cloth 0-88776-285-9. 1997 Paper 0-88776-400-2. Illustrations by the author. ♣

—. *How we saw the world: Nine Native stories of the way things began.* Montreal: Tundra Books, 1993 Cloth 0-88776-302-2. 1996 Paper 0-88776-373-1. Illustrations by the author.

—. *The secret of the white buffalo: An Oglala Sioux Legend.* Montreal: Tundra Books, 1993 Cloth 0-88776-321-9. 1997 Paper 0-88776-399-5. Illustrations by the author. ♣

—. *Bones in the basket: Native stories of the origin of people.* Montreal: Tundra Books, 1994 Cloth 0-88776-327-8. Illustrations by the author. ♣

—. *Monster from the swamp: Native legends about demons, monsters and other creatures.* Toronto: Tundra Books, 1995 Cloth 0-88776-361-8. Illustrations by the author.

—. *Messenger of Spring.* Toronto: Tundra Books, 1997 Cloth 0-88776-361-8. Illustrations by the author.

Selected articles about C. J. Taylor

Clemence, Verne. "Books Express Native Spirituality and Identity." *The Star Phoenix* [Saskatoon] 21 Mar. 1992.

Tousley, Nancy. "Native Author Brings Legends to Life." *Calgary Herald* 24 Mar. 1992 A10-11.

Van Luven, Lynne. "Network Needed for Communication among Natives, Metis Author Says." *The Edmonton Journal* 23 Mar. 1992.

Varcoe, Chris. "Art and Words Capture Traditional Indian Legends." *The Leader-Post* [Regina] 4 Apr. 1992.

Cora Taylor
AUTHOR

Born
"January 14, 1936, Fort Qu'Appelle, Saskatchewan. I was born in a sanatorium — my mother had tuberculosis and wasn't allowed to hold me until I was five months old."

School
"I grew up on my grandmother's farm near Fort Carlton, Saskatchewan and attended the same one-room school that my mother had. I took Grade 9 by correspondence and then went to Stobart High School in Duck Lake, Saskatchewan."

Where I live now
"I presently live in Edmonton, Alberta but I travel a lot and often spend two or three months in a hideaway, writing."

My favourite book when I was young
"Lots of favourites — *Huckleberry Finn*, *The Call of the Wild*, *Anne of Green Gables*, *My Friend Flicka*, *Wild Animals I Have Known*, and the younger Thornton Burgess books. As you can see there were a lot of animal books."

My favourite book now
"William Mayne's *The Jersey Shore*, Diana Wynne Jones's *Time of the Ghost*, Joan Aiken's *Midnight is a Place* and anything by Patricia Wrightson. Top Canadian favourites would be Welwyn Katz's *Whalesinger*, Brian Doyle's *Angel Square*, Martha Brooks's *Paradise Cafe* and Tim Wynne-Jones's *Some of the Kinder Planets*."

Career
"I always wanted to be a writer but it was not a practical career choice. I worked as a secretary until I was 34, then managed to get to the University of Alberta and then taught school. Although I always wrote (and published some things) I didn't become a full-time writer until I was 50 years old. The moral is: don't give up your dream."

Family
"I have four children, four step-children, and 18 terrific grandchildren. For 22 years I lived on a small farm in the Winterburn district raising donkeys, goats, chickens, a goose named Henrietta and an assortment of dogs, cats and rabbits."

The room where I create
"...has to have a view. The desk at my office in Edmonton overlooks the beautiful Saskatchewan River valley. In California (I like to spend two or three winter months there) I'm on a cliff overlooking the ocean."

Spare time
"Reading tops the list, but I consider it part of my 'job' — wonderful to have a job where what you have to do is what you like best. I spend most of my free time being with my grandchildren. I love to travel, which includes visiting museums and learning about the history of the place."

When I was growing up
"Being an only child on a farm is probably the best thing that can happen to a person. You have to create your own cast of characters for company. The world I created consisted of three countries. I named them, peopled them and moved from one country to another changing personalities as I went.

"In Grassland I was Loretta Monteray — fiery, exotic and unconfined. When I rode horseback I was always Loretta. Grassland was the sheep pasture and the sheep barn, but it also included the big cattle and horse barn and the fields going back to the banks of the North Saskatchewan River. Loretta did a lot of running, riding and sneaking around with important messages for help. My dog Pal was renamed 'Fang of the North' for these occasions.

"In Dreamland, which consisted of the garden and the house, I was Coral van Traube — aristocratic and brilliantly intellectual. We had wonderful gardens: there were acres of landscaped paths, flower beds, arbours, trellises, lily ponds, rock gardens and bog gardens with fruit trees and flowering bushes all around. It was my Versailles. Coral was eventually persuaded to run for Prime Minister (making campaign speeches on the veranda roof to a throng of tiger lilies). Naturally she won hands down. I did all my reading as Coral.

"The other country was called Slurr. It was not pleasant. It consisted of the machine sheds, the pig pens and other unsavoury areas. Naturally it was inhabited by a lot of nasty criminal types. Luckily for law and order they had me — Wondergirl! Wondergirl was usually in costume — a bathing suit and my aunt's old red skirt ripped down the side and tied around the neck. Wondergirl did a lot of crawling along roofs, hanging from rafters and her specialty was leaping from small buildings, cape billowing."

My first book (and how it happened)
"*Julie* began as a short story I wrote during a writing class at university. The trouble with *Julie* was that I found the character so interesting that I kept writing more and the story got longer and longer. Until then I hadn't thought that I could write a novel; it had always seemed to be an enormous task. The character of Julie still fascinates me, which is why I did a sequel and will probably do another book about her."

Where my ideas come from
"They come from dreams, grandchildren, family history, news stories, Canadian history and stories people have told me. They are all interspersed with memories of childhood."

Who and what influenced me
"The books I've read all my life. My grandmother, mother and aunts who allowed me to develop my imagination during that wonderful childhood. The King James version of *The Bible* and *The Book of Common Prayer*, which contains the most beautiful writing ever done. Shakespeare and all the poets my mother quoted to me as a child. And the man who helped me find my writing voice — W.O. Mitchell."

How I work
"I'm incredibly lazy, so I have to write to a very rigid schedule. No sleeping in, no missing a day when I'm working on a first draft. I'm a morning person, so I write every morning, seven days a week and don't quit until I've produced a certain number of pages. I do incredible amounts of rewriting but I'm less structured about that and usually there are deadlines involved to keep me in line."

Something nobody knew about me (until now)
"I cannot resist the urge to collect things. It's a curse because I don't have the big farm house any more. I'm trying to limit myself to chess sets, china-head dolls, crosses (from different countries), angels (all kinds but especially glass and brass ones) and original Canadian picture book art."

Tips for young creators
"Write from inside. Imagine you are the character. That way you can make your writing more realistic. It's better to write a vivid scene or event than to write a short story when you haven't developed your style. Writing takes practice — doing certain parts over and over until you are in control and confident. So, do a few paragraphs or a page trying to convey a feeling, a smell, a room. Keep it short; that way you won't get so tired when you're polishing it. I think haiku is great practice. Everybody can rewrite three lines without getting too fed up with rewriting."

Cora Taylor

BIBLIOGRAPHY

Taylor, Cora. *Julie*. Vancouver: Douglas & McIntyre, 1985. 1992 Paper 1-55054-122-6. 1995 Paper 1-55054-459-4.

—. *Julie's Secret*. Vancouver: Douglas & McIntyre, 1991 Paper 1-55054-124-2. 1995 Paper 1-55054-460-8.

—. *The Doll*. Vancouver: Douglas & McIntyre, 1992 Paper 1-55054-218-4.

—. *Ghost Voyages*. Richmond Hill: Scholastic Canada, 1992. Out of print.

—. *Summer of the Mad Monk*. Toronto: Groundwood Books, 1994 Cloth 1-55054-174-9. 1995 Paper 1-55054-457-8.

. *Vanishing Act*. Red Deer: Red Deer Press, 1997 Paper 0-88995-165-9.

Awards
1985 Canada Council Children's Literature Prize for *Julie*

1985 R. Ross Annett Award for Children's Literature for *Julie*

1986 Canadian Library Association Book of the Year Award for Children for *Julie*

1988 Ruth Schwartz Children's Book Award for *The Doll*

1991 Austrian Youth Book Prize for *Julie* (in translation)

1992 White Ravens Selection of the International Youth Library, Munich for *Julie's Secret*

1995 Canadian Library Association Book of the Year for Children Award for *Summer of the Mad Monk*

Selected articles about Cora Taylor
Gertridge, Allison. "Cora Taylor." *Meet Canadian Authors and Illustrators*. Richmond Hill, Scholastic Canada, 1994.

Ryan-Fisher, Bonnie. "The Accidental but Fortuitous Career: Cora Taylor, Children's Writer." *CCL* 88 (1997): 31-5.

Jan Thornhill
AUTHOR/ILLUSTRATOR

Born

1955, Sudbury, Ontario

School

Elementary and high school in Richmond Hill and Thornhill, Ontario; Ontario College of Art, Toronto, Ontario

Where I live now

"In the woods near Havelock, Ontario in a house my husband and I built."

My favourite book when I was young

The Bad Child's Book of Beasts by Hilaire Belloc.

My favourite book now

Precious Bane by Mary Webb.

Career

"Illustrator and writer (I write adult fiction, too), although I once spent six months sewing beads and sequins on Dolly Parton's dresses."

Family

"Husband, Fred Gottschalk. We have a dog called Betty Boots and a bunch of goldfish in a rain barrel."

The room where I create

"I have a little studio where I write, and, until recently, I did all my illustrations on the dining room table. Lately I've been experimenting with illustration on the computer."

Spare time

"Gardening, seed-saving, mushroom-hunting, swimming, travelling, reading, making a mess."

When I was growing up

"I've made pictures since I could hold a crayon, partly because my mother, an artist, always encouraged me. I've always read a lot and kept a journal for years.

"My family went on regular weekend walks in the country which gave me an early and long-lasting appreciation of nature, particularly because my father is a walking encyclopedia of the sciences. By the time I was 10, I'd collected so many birds' nests and animal skulls, fossils and shells, feathers and leaves, that I turned our basement into a museum and charged five cents to get in. My mother was the only one who paid."

My first book (and how it happened)

"*The Wildlife ABC* was the result of three things: I was bored with drawing hands, money and unattractive businessmen for newspapers and magazines; I'd become involved in environmental issues; and I thought if I made a kids' book, I'd make wheelbarrows full of money (ha).

"I came up with the concept of an ABC using Canadian wildlife because I couldn't find anything similar in the library. I did four sample illustrations, wrote four sample 'nature notes', wrote the rhyming text, researched Canadian publishers at the library, and then sat on the whole thing for two years. My husband finally forced me to send it to a publisher. I chose Greey de Pencier, now Owl Books, because of their nature and science interest. They called me immediately and accepted my proposal. Much later I found out how rarely things happen this way in children's book publishing."

Where my ideas come from

"Ideas come from different places. The tree book developed after I'd spent a few weeks making maple syrup in the open woods, staring for hours at the leafless trees. After noticing all the scars and broken limbs and woodpeckers looking for nesting holes, it occurred to me that each tree had a separate and unique story to tell. The book evolved from that point.

"I often come up with what seems like a simple concept, and then the project gets more complicated as I progress. The idea of linking retold animal folk tales in *Crow and Fox* seemed simple, but ended up being an almost endless task of searching for, listing, categorizing, and juggling two-animal tales until my head was spinning."

Who and what influenced me
"The wonders of the natural world. My parents and a couple of extraordinary teachers in school. Countless writers. Artists from all cultures, both ancient and modern. My husband, Fred, who with one cutting remark, made me rethink my illustration style and loosen up so that I could do something that was all my own. That was in 1982 and I've been happy ever since."

How I work
"Except for the noise of birds outside, I write in silence. I write everything over and over again, constantly changing a word here, a comma there, reading it aloud until it sounds right to me. This can be a slow process — it took 20 complete rewrites of *Wild in the City* from beginning to end before I was happy with it, 25 for *A Tree in a Forest*. The final editing happens while I'm working on the illustrations. That way I can drop unnecessary word descriptions of things that I've made obvious in the illustrations themselves."

Something nobody knew about me (until now)
"Whenever I start a final illustration, after the rough pencil drawing is done, I'm always afraid that it's going to be awful when it's finished. I feel that way until almost the minute that it's done, which is sometimes two or three weeks later. It's a scary process, but I think it keeps me from being bored while I work."

Tips for young creators
"If you want to write, you have to read. So read, read, and read some more. If you like drawing, draw. Draw anything. Draw your hand in different positions. Look at other people's drawings and paintings and try to figure out what they did to create different effects. Don't be impatient. I spend up to three weeks working on one illustration, sometimes 14 hours a day. Don't give up. I've been drawing almost every day for more than 35 years and I'm still not always sure of myself or happy with what I've done, but that doesn't stop me from trying."

Jan Thornhill

BIBLIOGRAPHY

Crease, Skid. *In the Great Meadow*. Willowdale: Annick Press, 1994 Paper 1-55037-998-4; Cloth 1-55037-999-2. Illustrations by Jan Thornhill.

Thornhill, Jan. *The Wildlife ABC: A Nature Alphabet*. Toronto: Owl Books, 1988 Cloth 0-920775-29-2. 1994 Paper 1-895688-13-2. Illustrations by the author.

—. *The Wildlife 123: A Nature Counting Book*. Toronto: Owl Books, 1989 Cloth 0-920775-39-X. 1994 Paper 1-895688-14-0. Illustrations by the author.

—. *A Tree in the Forest*. Toronto: Owl Books, 1991 Paper 1-895688-18-3; Cloth 0-920775-64-0. Illustrations by the author.

—. *Crow and Fox and Other Animal Legends*. Toronto: Owl Books, 1993 Cloth 1-895688-11-6. Illustrations by the author.

—. *Wild in the City*. Toronto: Owl Books, 1995 Cloth 1-895688-33-7. Paper 1-895688-72-8. Illustrations by the author.

—. *Before and After: A Book of Nature Timescapes*. Toronto: Owl Books, 1997 Cloth 1-895688-61-2. Illustrations by the author.

Awards
1990 UNICEF - Ezra Jack Keats International Award for Excellence in Children's Book Illustration for *The Wildlife 123*

1992 Information Book Award for *A Tree in the Forest*

Selected articles about Jan Thornhill
Siamon, Sharon. "Introducing Jan Thornhill." *CANSCAIP News* 19.3 (1997):1-4.

Rhea Tregebov
AUTHOR

Born
August 15, 1953, Saskatoon, Saskatchewan

Schools
University of Manitoba, Cornell University, Boston University

Where I live now
Toronto, Ontario

My favourite books when I was young
Anne of Green Gables, Girl of the Limberlost, Alice in Wonderland

My favourite book now
Cherries and Cherry Pits by Vera B. Williams

Career
Children's book author, poet, creative writing instructor, editor

Family
Son Sasha, born 1985

The room where I create
"...feels like a tree house in summer. We're on the third floor of a triplex and my desk looks out the window onto a big old honey locust tree. The building is at the top of a hill, so in winter, when the leaves are gone, I can see all the way to Lake Ontario. I have a wall full of books (lots of poetry and reference books) and two computers to write with."

Spare time
"I enjoy gardening and jogging, and am re-learning how to play piano."

When I was growing up
"I had to miss a lot of school because I had asthma. So I spent a lot of time reading and had to rely on my imagination to keep me amused. I enjoyed all sorts of crafts and drawing as well as reading, and used to make little villages out of cardboard, as well as clothes for my doll. My parents also loved books, and they always seemed interested in my ideas. We were a family who talked to each other a lot. Because my younger sister was more than five years younger than me, I think I got to stay a child longer. I would babysit her and be able to play games that I would otherwise have felt too grown up for."

My first book (and how it happened)
"My first book, *The Extraordinary Ordinary Everything Room*, began as a bedtime story that I told to my son, Sasha. At about two or three years old, Sasha insisted that we 'make-up' stories rather than read him books. Of all the stories I told him, two became picture books: *The Extraordinary Ordinary Everything Room* and *The Big Storm*. I had worked on a number of projects as an editor with Second Story Press, who have published all the *Sasha* books, and they had been encouraging me for years to try my hand at picture books. So they were very happy when I offered them *The Extraordinary Ordinary Everything Room*, and helped me revise and rewrite to get it right."

Where my ideas come from
"All the *Sasha* books were inspired by my own son's experiences. *The Big Storm* is based on my mother's childhood in Winnipeg and the bedtime stories that she told me, and which I in turn told Sasha. However, I don't think the stories would have been successful if I hadn't felt a very strong and deep connection between the experiences I observed in my son's early childhood and my own experiences as a child. In many ways, I am writing from my own childhood as much as my son's or my mother's."

Who and what influenced me
"I began my writing career as a poet for grown-ups, and I still am writing poetry. In some ways, I find picture books similar to poetry: they're written to be read aloud and they're brief, so every word counts. My goal is that

every picture book be as powerful and meaningful as a poem."

How I work

"I usually spend a lot of time just thinking about the idea for a book, making sure that the heart of the book is a good one, that it connects to something I care about a lot. Once I get to the writing stage, I rewrite and rewrite and rewrite. I read different versions to classes of students and to my son and see how the children respond. Then I rewrite and rewrite and rewrite some more. I enjoy writing; for me it's like making mudpies. I'll fiddle and fiddle and fiddle with a single sentence until it feels just right, and I'm very happy while I'm doing it. I also share some of the revisions with my editor. I've been very lucky to have the same wonderful editor for three of the four books I've published, and she's a really big help."

Something nobody knew about me (until now)

"I make terrific chocolate chip cookies!"

My favourite book that I've created

"All of them!"

Tips for young creators

"Make sure that what you're writing is something that you really care about, something that means a lot to you. And don't be afraid to work hard: the more work you put into your writing, the more your readers will get out of it."

Rhea Tregebov

BIBLIOGRAPHY

Tregebov, Rhea. *The Extraordinary Ordinary Everything Room*. Toronto: Second Story Press, 1991 Paper 0-929005-24-4. Illustrations by Hélène Desputeaux. ♣

—. *The Big Storm*. Toronto: Kids Can Press, 1992 Cloth 1-55074-081-4. 1993 Paper 1-55074-117-9. Illustrations by Maryann Kovalski. ♣

—. *Sasha and the Wiggly Tooth*. Toronto: Second Story Press, 1993 Paper 0-929005-50-3; Cloth 0-929005-51-1. Illustrations by Hélène Desputeaux. ♣

—. *Sasha and the Wind*. Toronto: Second Story Press, 1996 Paper 0-929005-83-X; Cloth 0- 9290005-84-8. Illustrations by Hélène Desputeaux. ♣

—. *What-If Sara*. Toronto: Second Story Press, 1999 Paper 1-896764-20-7; Cloth 1-896764-22- 3. Illustrations by Leanne Franson.

Awards

1994 CNIB Tiny Torgi Award for *The Big Storm*

Rhea Tregebov has also won numerous awards for her adult poetry.

Don Trembath
AUTHOR

Born
1963, Winnipeg, Manitoba

School
University of Alberta, Edmonton

Where I live now
Morinville, Alberta

My favourite books when I was young
The Hardy Boys, Alfred Hitchcock's *Mystery* magazines

My favourite book now
The Catcher in the Rye

Career
"I am currently a writer and a stay-at-home dad. Other positions include: visiting instructor, freelance writer, newspaper reporter/editor, heavy equipment operator, labourer and copywriter."

Family
Wife, Lisa; son, Riley; daughters, Walker and Bebe

The room where I create
"I write in the living room. I have a tall computer cabinet that stands between the couch on one side and a rocking chair and large living room window on the other. I work in the early, early morning, when everything else in the house is still quiet. I use to work in my own little room that I called my office, but our house is small, our family is growing and the room was needed for other things. The cabinet I work at is made of wood, and is lined with several shelves and spaces that are crammed with paper, books and of course, my computer."

Spare time
"We have no television in our house. We put it in a box and put the box in the basement. So, in my spare time I hang out with the kids. We go skating in the winter and camping in the summer. We go to libraries and both the older kids are in music and drama. I enjoy going to the movies, but really, I don't see too many, because spare time is not something I have a lot of."

When I was growing up
"As a kid, I was into sports: hockey, football, soccer and baseball. At night, when I was alone in my room, I would read books and magazines. None of my friends ever knew I was into reading or, later, when I was around 12 or 13, writing, because I never told them. My family always knew though.

"I have a mom and a dad and three brothers — two older and one younger. They have always been tremendously supportive of me and my writing. I remember telling Lisa when we started going out (we were about 16) that I wanted to be a writer and write books, and she responded as if I had told her I wanted to be a teacher or a plumber, which is exactly what I wanted, and probably needed. I did not want special status. I did not want her saying 'what makes you think...?' All I wanted was acceptance of my dreams and that's exactly what I got."

My first book (and how it happened)
"My first book was called *The Tuesday Café*. I was out playing hockey with my brother and a few friends over the lunch hour of a Friday afternoon. When we came home, the phone rang. It was Bob Tyrrell, the publisher at Orca, phoning to offer me a contract. I hung up the phone and walked into the room where Lisa and my brother were playing with Riley and Walker. I said, 'You'll never guess what happened.' Lisa said, 'You just got a publisher for your book.' I said, 'How did you know?' She said, 'Because I've never seen that look on your face before.'"

Where my ideas come from
"I get my ideas from inside my life. *The Tuesday Café* involves characters based on people I have met at some of the writing classes I have taught. *A Fly Named Alfred* revolves around a column Harper writes that is very similar to a column that I

used to write at the University of Alberta. *A Beautiful Place on Yonge Street* is a love story, and I have some experience with that. My next book, *Lefty Carmichael Has A Fit* is about a young boy with epilepsy, which is a condition my son Riley has. But even more so, each book is a slice of life of a young man (Harper Winslow and, coming soon, Lefty) moving somewhat awkwardly, but in an interesting way, through adolescence, which is something I also did, with moderate success."

Who and what influenced me

"Writers, as a whole, have influenced me. For a long, long time, I have loved the idea of sitting down at a desk and creating someone or something. The one writer who rises above the rest, as far as I'm concerned is J.D. Salinger. I have read his novels and his short stories, and I really do not know if I have ever, or will ever, come across anyone who pours as much into his characters as he does. I love the way he creates his people, and cares for his people. That is the way in which I aspire to write."

How I work

"First, I think of an idea, then I think of a character to tell the story. This process can take a while, and I rarely write anything down until I feel I have something of note to say, and someone who is interesting, captivating, and readable enough to say it. Starting the book is the hardest part because the main character, who in each of my novels has also been the narrator, has to be virtually complete in my head in terms of personality, background, mannerisms, style of speech, sense of humour, interests, friends, family, etc., before I can write a successful beginning."

Something nobody knew about me (until now)

"As I said earlier, I never told any of my friends, aside from Lisa, who was more than just a friend, that I wanted to be a writer. That's why, when I see someone today with whom I went to school, they cannot believe what I'm doing. But, writing was not cool when I was a kid. I wanted to be cool, so I hung out and learned to smoke and drink, but I never told anyone about my writing."

My favourite book that I've created

"My favourite book has always been the one I'm working on, be it *Alfred* or *Yonge Street* or, at present, *Lefty Carmichael*."

Tips for young creators

"Don't get caught up in the urgency to 'get published.' Write for the fun of it. Write to express yourself. Write to tell stories."

Don Trembath

BIBLIOGRAPHY

Trembath, Don. *The Tuesday Café*. Victoria: Orca Book Publishers, 1996 Paper 1-55143-074-6.

—. *A Fly Named Alfred*. Victoria: Orca Book Publishers, 1997 Paper 1-55143-083-5.

—. *A Beautiful Place on Yonge Street*. Victoria: Orca Book Publishers, 1998 Paper 1-55143-121-1.

—. *Lefty Carmichael Has a Fit*. Victoria: Orca Book Publishers, 1999 Paper 1-55143-166-1.

Awards

1997 R. Ross Annett Award for Children's Literature for *The Tuesday Café*

Selected articles about Don Trembath

Jenkinson, Dave. "Profiles: Don Trembath." *Resource Links* 3.2 (1997): 55-8.

Maxine Trottier
AUTHOR

Born
May 3, 1950, Grosse Pointe Farms, Michigan, U.S.A.

School
University of Western Ontario, London, Ontario; B.A. in English

Where I live now
Port Stanley, Ontario

My favourite books when I was young
"*Treasure Island, Through the Looking Glass* and *Alice in Wonderland, Anne of Green Gables, The Eagle of the Ninth.* I could go on, but anything romantic drew me. It still does."

My favourite book now
"I have many favourites; anything historical has a place in my heart. Often, the book that I am currently reading is my favourite."

Career
"I have taught elementary school for 29 years. I still teach Grade 2 as well as write."

Family
Husband William Doig and two Yorkies, Ceilidh and Moon.

The room where I create
"I have a large, sunny studio. One big window looks past a huge magnolia tree to Lake Erie. My computer sits in an alcove facing another window set with stained glass. It makes the ash trees outside look purple and blue. Books and file folders are piled here and there; nylon dog bones and doggy toys litter the floor. Art from my picture books hangs on the walls."

Spare time
"I read. I sail. I take long walks and listen to music. In a way I do not really have any spare time. I use every minute to think and plan and dream. I have even been known to write in my sleep."

When I was growing up
"When I wasn't reading, drawing or writing stories, I wandered in the fields around my home. We built tree forts and played baseball. In the winter we skated on frozen ponds. It was always pretend; we were never ourselves. Sometimes I was Maid Marion or Jane but just as often I was Robin Hood or Tarzan or Superman. A wet towel over a bathing suit on a hot summer day makes a wonderful cape."

My first book (and how it happened)
"It was at a staff party for the principal who was leaving to work in another school. Someone had given him a helium-filled balloon. He loosely wrapped the string around a lawn chair. When the wind caught it and blew it away, he chased it through the neighbourhood, leaping over hedges and flower beds. 'That balloon will come down and make some child's day,' I said, and the idea for *The Big Heart* was conceived."

Where my ideas come from
"I cannot really say from where the ideas come because I never try to think of something about which to write; I let the idea come to me. I write around ideas. If your mind is always open to possibilities, ideas will sneak into your head. The story that emerges is a small image connected with a much larger picture. I write about the things in which I am interested and the things about which I care."

Who and what influenced me
"Who? Every person I ever met and every writer who has put ideas on paper in a wonderful way. What? Sailing has for many years been a part of my life. We live on a sailboat in the summers and I write there; so many stories have taken shape on the water. It has been the romantic force behind many of my books."

How I work
"Since I'm still teaching elementary school at this point, during the week the days are devoted to my Grade 2 students. But I still write. Every morning I rise very

early and go for a long walk along the lake. While I walk, I think about what I am writing. I listen to music that suits the story's time period. I plan out the plot, all the sentences and phrases and write the story in my head. When I sit down to type at my computer on the weekend, the story is there waiting to appear on the pages."

Something nobody knew about me (until now)

"I always ask each illustrator to put a dragonfly somewhere in the book. Dragonflies and damselflies are beautiful insects. I love to watch them flitting past or hovering over the water when I am writing outside on the deck of our boat in the summers. My studio and home are filled with dragonfly art, models and pins."

My favourite book that I've created

"There is something about each of my books that is special to me. As well, there are the unpublished books, waiting in the distance to be read and to make someone laugh or cry. I sometimes say that my favourite book is the one that has just been published."

Tips for young creators

"Never stop pretending. You can never be too old to dream. If you want to be a writer you must work very hard writing every day to shape those dreams into good stories. It is a very difficult thing to become published. So many writers are trying to do just that. More than anything else you must write for the joy of it, for the pure pleasure of seeing a fine story come to life from beginning to end."

Maxine Trottier

BIBLIOGRAPHY

Trottier, Maxine. *Alison's House.* Oxford University Press, 1993 Paper 0-19-540968-X. Illustrations by Michael Martchenko.

—. *The Tiny Kite of Eddie Wing.* Toronto: Stoddart Kids, 1995 Cloth 0-7737-2865-1. Illustrations by Al Van Mil.

—. *The Voyage of Wood Duck.* Sydney: UCCB Press, 1995 Paper 0-920336-70-1. Illustrations by Patsy MacAuley-MacKinnon.

—. *Loon Rock.* Sydney: UCCB Press, 1996 Paper 0-920336-84-1. Illustrations by Dozay Christmas.

—. *Pavlova's Gift.* Toronto: Stoddart Kids, 1996 Cloth 0-7737-2969-0. Illustrations by Victoria Berdichevsky.

—. *A Safe Place.* Morton Grove IL: Albert Whitman, 1997 Cloth 0-8075-7212-8. Illustrations by Judith Friedman.

—. *Heartsong.* Sydney: UCCB Press, 1997 Paper 0-920336-90-6. Illustrations by Patsy MacAuley-MacKinnon.

—. *Prairie Willow.* Toronto: Stoddart Kids, 1998 Cloth 0-7737-3067-2. Illustrations by Laura Fernandez and Rick Jacobson.

—. *The Walking Stick.* Toronto: Stoddart Kids, 1998 Cloth 0-7737-31016. Illustrations by Annouchka Gravel Galouchko.

—. *One is Canada.* Toronto: HarperCollins, 1999 Cloth 0-00-224556-6. Illustrations by Bill Slavin.

—. *Flags.* Toronto: Stoddart Kids, 1999 Cloth 7737-3136-9. Illustrations by Paul Morin.

—. *Claire's Gift.* Richmond Hill: Scholastic Canada, 1999 Cloth 0-590-51461-X. Illustrations by Rajka Kupesic.

—. *Dreamstones.* Toronto: Stoddart Kids, 1999 Cloth 0-7737-3191-1. Illustrations by Stella East.

—. *A Circle of Silver.* Toronto: Stoddart Kids, 1999 Paper 0-7737-6055-5.

—. *Native Crafts: Inspired by North America's First People.* Toronto: Kids Can Press, 2000 Paper 1-55074-549-2. Illustrated by Esperança Melo.

Trottier, Maxine, and Margaret A. McDowell. *The Big Heart.* Toronto: Annick Press, 1991. Illustrations by Maxine Trottier. Out of print.

Awards

1995 Federation of Women Teachers Associations of Ontario Writers Award for *The Tiny Kite of Eddie Wing*

1996 Federation of Women Teachers Associations of Ontario Writers Award for *The Voyage of Wood Duck*

1996 Canadian Library Association Book of the Year for Children Award for *The Tiny Kite of Eddie Wing*

1998 Marianna Dempster Memorial Award for *Heartsong*

For more information about Maxine Trottier, visit her Web site at www.execulink.com/~maxitrot/maxine.htm.

W.D. Valgardson
AUTHOR

Born
1939

School
Gimli Public School, Gimli, Manitoba

Where I live now
Victoria, British Columbia

My favourite books when I was young
Three Billy Goats Gruff, Treasure Island and *Robin Hood*

My favourite book now
Pride and Prejudice

Career
High school teacher, university professor

The room where I create
"Large upstairs study, fireplace, built-in bookshelves, patio. The room is blue. Large desk, computer, printer, fax. Couch, table, television, stationary bicycle (for when I'm watching television)."

Spare time
Reading, walking, visiting.

When I was growing up
"I spent time riding my bike, swimming in the lake, ice skating, and visiting my father's fishing camp. One day, a small airplane landed on the lake ice. My father knew the pilot and he arranged for us to go on a ride in the plane.

"When I was in Grade 3 I got to go with my parents to live in their fishing camp. We had to travel overnight on a freight boat. I woke up in the dark. The boat was stuck on a sand bar and had to be pulled loose. We had a wonderful time exploring the wilderness. We found the skull and the antlers of a moose."

My first book (and how it happened)
"When I started writing, I made a common mistake. I thought my life was boring so I wrote about faraway things. Unfortunately, I didn't know anything about these places. When I finally started to write about what I knew about (fishing, farming, going to school, small town life) I got published."

Where my ideas come from
"From dreams, experiences, reading."

Who and what influenced me
"My grandmother teaching me to read when I was five. Parents who bought books. Good teachers who showed me how to understand and write stories."

How I work
"I see an image or a character. By the time I've figured where the image is or who the character is (age, name, family, motive, friends, favourite music, favourite food etc.) I usually have a story. I don't usually start with an idea that I want to dramatize."

Something nobody knew about me (until now)
"When I was little my mother used to put me on the bus and send me 60 miles to Winnipeg. My grandmother would meet me. One time my grandmother didn't turn up and I took a city bus, then transferred to another bus and got safely to my grandparents' house. I felt very pleased with myself."

My favourite book that I've created
"*Sarah and the People of Sand River.*"

Tips for young creators
"The stories you have to tell are unique because you are unique. Write about things you know and things you care about. Try to understand the characters around you because then you'll be able to create interesting fictional characters. Keep a journal."

W.D. Valgardson

BIBLIOGRAPHY

Valgardson, W.D. *Thor.* Toronto: Groundwood Books, 1994 0-88899-209-2. Illustrations by Ange Zhang.

—. *Sarah and the People of Sand River.* Toronto: Groundwood Books, 1996 0-88899-255-6.

—. *Garbage Creek and Other Stories.* Toronto: Groundwood Books, 1997 Paper 0-88899-308-0; Cloth 0-88899-297-1.

—. *The Divorced Kids Club and Other Stories.* Toronto: Groundwood Books 1999. Paper 0-88899-370-6, Cloth 0-88899-369-2.

—. *Frances.* Toronto, Groundwood Books, 2000 Cloth 0-88899-386-2; Paper 0-88899-397-8.

W.D. Valgardson has also written many award winning books for adults.

Awards

1994 Mr. Christie's Book Award for *Thor*

1995 Honorary Doctorate, University of Winnipeg

1998 Vicky Metcalf Short Story Award for "The Chicken Lady" in *Garbage Creek and Other Stories*

Selected articles about W.D. Valgardson

"All it Takes is Attitude, Writing Crusader Says." *Times Colonist* 25 June, 1995.

"Ceremony and Success: an Interview with Dr. W. Valgardson." *Logberg-Heimskringla* 10 May 1996.

"Reverse Paranoia and the Creative Process." *Western People* 25 Jan. 1996.

Eric Walters
AUTHOR

Born
March 3, 1957, Toronto, Ontario

School
"General Mercer (K-6). I went to high school at York Memorial Collegiate Institute in Toronto. My B.A.(hons.), B.S.W., and M.S.W. are all from York University and my B.Ed. is from University of Toronto."

Where I live now
Mississauga, Ontario

My favourite books when I was young
Animal stories, *Owls in the Family*

My favourite book now
Danny the Champion of the World

Career
Elementary school teacher at the Peel Board of Education (on leave); social worker on the crisis team of the Credit Valley Hospital (presently half-time); Peel Children's Aid Society.

Family
"Wife Anita (married 15 years); children: Christina (13), Nicholas (10), Julia (6)."

The room where I create
"Everywhere! Lying on the living room floor, Wendy's restaurants, sitting in my car, sometimes even in my office."

Spare time
"Coaching and playing basketball and soccer."

When I was growing up
"I loved playing sports and having pets. I always played soccer, basketball and road hockey. I was the City of Toronto champion in triple jump and long jump in Grades 5 and 6.

"Animals were a big part of my life. At one time I had a dog, three cats, six squirrels, an alligator, a boa constrictor and two dozen turtles. My room smelled very . . . interesting."

My first book (and how it happened)
"My first book was *Stand Your Ground*. It was written for my class of Grade 5 students. They were a wonderfully creative group who loved storytelling. We were doing a unit on local studies and I wanted to create a book that reflected our community. I set it in Streetsville at our school (Vista Heights) and featured local sights."

Where my ideas come from
"Family history, newspaper articles, history books, career encounters, and out of the blue."

Who and what influenced me
"My Grade 5 teacher Chris Gay; other writers (Mordecai Richler, Kurt Vonnegut Jr., Robertson Davies, Martyn Godfrey, William Bell); my wife Anna."

How I work
"I start with an idea which is at least part way mapped out. But I respect the opinions of my characters and often allow them to decide where the story should go (that may sound crazy — and if it doesn't, you're probably a writer)."

Something nobody knew about me (until now)
"I still play basketball and soccer. I recently played one-on-one basketball with a player 7'3" tall. I won 21-9!"

My favourite book that I've created
"The one I'm writing this moment — at least until it is finished — and then the next one is my favourite."

Tips for young creators
"Do research. Add detail and description from all five senses. Tell or show not just what's happening but how people feel about it."

Eric Walters

BIBLIOGRAPHY

Walters, Eric. *Stand Your Ground.* Toronto: Stoddart Kids, 1994 0-7736-7421-7.

—. *Stars.* Toronto: Stoddart Kids, 1996 Paper 0-7736-7447-0.

—. *Trapped in Ice.* Toronto: Penguin, 1997 Cloth 0-670-87542-2.

—. *Diamonds in the Rough.* Toronto: Stoddart Kids, 1998 Paper 0-7736-7470-5.

—. *Stranded.* Toronto: HarperCollins, 1998 Paper 0-00-648110-8.

—. *War of the Eagles.* Vancouver: Orca Book Publishers, 1998 Paper 1-55143-099-1.

—. *Three on Three.* Vancouver: Orca Book Publishers, 1999 Paper 1-55143-170-X.

—. *The Hydrofoil Mystery.* Toronto: Penguin Books Canada, 1999 Cloth 0-670-88186-4; 2000 Paper 0-14-130220-8.

—. *Caged Eagles.* Vancouver: Orca Book Publishers, 2000 Paper 1-55143-139-4; Cloth 1-55143-182-3.

—. *The Bully Boys.* Toronto: Penguin Books Canada, 2000 Cloth 0-670-88885-0.

Awards

1997 Blue Heron Award for *Stars*

1997 Silver Birch Award for *Stars*

For more information about Eric Walters, visit his Web site at www.interlog.com/~ewalters.

Betty Waterton
AUTHOR

Born
Oshawa, Ontario

School
West Vancouver High School, attended Vancouver School of Art, both in Vancouver, British Columbia

Where I live now
Sidney, British Columbia (on Vancouver Island)

My favourite books when I was young
Little Women, Treasure Island, King Solomon's Mines, Donovan Pasha (by Gilbert Parker)

My favourite book now
The Letters of J.R.R. Tolkien

Career
"Art-related jobs on a newspaper and for a television studio, also commission portrait painting. All in the past."

Family
One son, one daughter (grown); nine grandchildren.

The room where I create
"A room lined with bookshelves, one desk, a word processor, and a sofa bed. From the window I can see the top of Saltspring Island and the Malahat, and at the corner is a lovely little church with a silver steeple."

Spare time
Volunteer work, walking, painting.

When I was growing up
"I did not have any brothers or sisters, but there were books. My parents, who had begun their courtship in a small-town library in Ontario, both loved reading, and every birthday and Christmas I knew I would get books from them and from aunts and uncles. One of the highlights of my early teen years was discovering in a neighbour's attic a complete set of books by H. Rider Haggard. Oh, what joy! I hadn't quite finished reading them all when the neighbours moved away, taking the books with them. But there was still the library, and the 4th Avenue Branch in Vancouver was only 10 blocks away."

My first book (and how it happened)
"My background was in the art field, and I wrote *A Salmon for Simon* with the intention of illustrating it. This didn't happen, of course. The story went out to nine different publishers before it was accepted by Douglas & McIntyre. Since then it has been printed in several languages and has sales of more than 100,000, I understand."

Where my ideas come from
"From snippets of conversation overheard or situations observed. Sometimes I am intrigued by certain people I meet and I can visualize them in a story. I find the world full of wonderful characters for stories; finding the right plot is harder."

Who and what influenced me
"A loving family — both the one I grew up in and the one I have now — and a strong Christian faith."

How I work
"Starting with a character, I mull over in my mind some situations. I generally make some rough notes in pencil and paper, just to get started, then go to the word processor, where the story evolves slowly. It may be necessary to do some research along the way, and I can usually count on doing five or six drafts before I'm finished."

Something nobody knew about me (until now)
"My dog once ate the cover of a library book."

My favourite book that I've created
Petranella

Tips for young creators
"Don't expect your first copy to be your finished copy."

Betty Waterton

BIBLIOGRAPHY

Waterton, Betty. *A Salmon for Simon.* Toronto: Douglas & McIntyre, 1978. 1996 Paper 0-88899-265-3; Rev. ed. 0-88899-276-9. Illustrations by Ann Blades. ♣

—. *Petranella.* Toronto: Douglas & McIntyre, 1980. 1990 Paper 0-88899-108-8. Illustrations by Ann Blades. ♣

—. *Mustard.* Markham: Scholastic, 1983. Out of print.

—. *The White Moose.* Toronto: Ginn Publishing, 1984. Out of print.

—. *Orff, 27 Dragons (and a Snarkel!).* Toronto: Annick Press, 1984. Illustrations by Karen Kulyk. Out of print.

—. *Quincy Rumpel.* Toronto: Douglas & McIntyre, 1984 Paper 0-88899-036-7. Toronto: Groundwood Books, 2000 Paper 0-88899-393-5.

—. "The Cat of Quinty." *Timespinners.* Toronto: Nelson Canada, 1984. Out of print.

—. *The Dog Who Stopped the War* (adapt). Toronto: Douglas & McIntyre, 1985 Paper 0-88899-040-5.

—. *Starring Quincy Rumpel.* Toronto: Groundwood Books, 1986 Paper 0-88899-048-0. Toronto: Groundwood Books, 2000 Paper 0-88899-394-3.

—. *Quincy Rumpel, P.I.* Toronto: Groundwood Books, 1988 Paper 0-88899-081-2.

—. *Plain Noodles.* Toronto: Groundwood Books, 1989. 1997 Paper 0-88899-132-0. Illustrations by Joanne Fitzgerald.

—. *Morris Rumpel and the Wings of Icarus.* Toronto: Groundwood Books, 1989 0-88899-099-5.

—. *Quincy Rumpel and the Sasquatch of Phantom Cove.* Toronto: Groundwood Books, 1990 Paper 0-88899-129-0.

—. *Quincy Rumpel and the Woolly Chaps.* Toronto: Groundwood Books, 1992 Paper 0-88899-160-6.

—. *Quincy Rumpel and the Mystifying Experience.* Toronto: Groundwood Books, 1994 Paper 0-88899-199-1.

—. *Quincy Rumpel and the All-Day Breakfast.* Toronto: Groundwood Books, 1996 Paper 0-88899- 225-4.

—. *The Lighthouse Dog.* Victoria: Orca Book Publishers, 1997 Cloth 1-55143-073-8. 2000 Paper 1-55143-075-4. Illustrations by Dean Griffiths.

Awards
1978 Canada Council Children's Literature Prize for *A Salmon for Simon*

Selected articles about Betty Waterton
Mitik, Trudy. *Canadian Author* July 1996.

Andrea Wayne von Königslöw
AUTHOR/ILLUSTRATOR

Born
1958, Toronto, Ontario

School
Marymount School, Cuernavaca, Mexico; Thornton School for the Arts, Toronto, Ontario; Queen's University, Kingston, Ontario

Where I live now
Toronto, Ontario

My favourite books when I was young
"Dr. Seuss books, *Nancy Drew* and all fairy tales."

My favourite book now
"Authors I enjoy are John Irving, Barbara Gowdy, Margaret Atwood, Timothy Findley and a lot of Canadian children's writers. I still love a good picture book."

Career
Writer and illustrator of children's books

Family
Husband, Rainer von Königslöw; three children, Alexis, Tai and Keir; three cats, Nishy, Whoopi and Grizzabela

The room where I create
"I have a studio in my house where I write and illustrate. It overlooks my garden. I work there almost every day. When my kids come in, I give them paints and they paint at the table beside me."

Spare time
"I exercise, cook and garden. I love plays and movies. I love to spend time with my husband and children most. There is so much to do in Toronto."

When I was growing up
"I was born in Toronto, but when I was eight years old, we moved to Mexico. While we lived there, I learned to speak Spanish and eat raw chili peppers.

"When we returned to Canada, I spent summers at the family cottage on Mary Lake in Ontario's Muskoka area. I stayed in the water so long that my mother was sure I had gills. I loved playing with my friends, and going for long walks and I always drew and painted. I loved painting Muskoka landscapes and animals. I was always a storyteller and told a lot of fibs."

My first book (and how it happened)
"I wrote my first children's book when I was still in university. I sent it to Annick Press. They liked my concepts but it took years to get a good book together. Annick was very patient and they were wonderful to me. I think I'm very lucky. Now I write and illustrate for many publishers."

Where my ideas come from
"I get my ideas from anyone and anything. Sometimes I am just out driving in my car and an idea for a story comes to me. Sometimes I get a story together and sometimes I just write down the idea for a time when a story happens. A story idea may sit in my brain for years until I can write it. Sometimes the stories are good, and sometimes they are not great. My children are also a great source of inspiration."

Who and what influenced me
"I think that Dr. Seuss was my greatest inspiration. I loved his humour. I am writing more poems now because of him. Robert Munsch, Maurice Sendak, Mercer Mayer, Judith Viorst and Stephen Kellogg are also influences. I always loved Michael Martchenko's art; even his pencil lines have action and a life of their own. I love the art of Mireille Levert, and Stéphane Poulin, and would love to paint like them. I also love Barbara Reid's work."

How I work
"I write anytime I can. I always have a few stories on the computer that I work on. Sometimes I will think of a new story in the middle of the night and I have to start it right then. Painting is more difficult. I need a few hours

of uninterrupted time all together. If I mix up just the right colour and the phone rings... the paint dries. I try not to answer but with three children there are always distractions."

Something nobody knew about me (until now)

"It is very hard for me to think of something that no one knows about me. I am a very open person. I tell people almost anything that's on my mind. I love to talk and I especially like to talk about myself."

My favourite book that I've created

"It is so hard to say which of my books is my favourite. I think that my favourite is always the one that I am working on now. If I start a new book, it becomes my favourite."

Tips for young creators

"Keep creating and don't let anyone tell you to stop. If something interesting happens to you, write about it. It may make a good story. Take lots of art classes, especially life drawing. Save all your art and stories and reread them every few years. Keep your imagination open."

Andrea Wayne von Königslöw

BIBLIOGRAPHY

Dunn, Sonja. *Rapunzel's Rap*. Goderich: Moonstone Press, 1992 Paper 0-92025-939-1. Illustrations by Andrea Wayne von Königslöw.

Wayne von Königslöw, Andrea. *Toilet Tales* (Annick Toddler Series). Toronto: Annick Press, 1985 Paper 0-92030313-7; Cloth 0-920303-14-5. 1987 Annikin Paper 0-920303-81-1. Illustrations by the author.

—. *A Tail Between Two Cities*. Toronto: Annick Press, 1987. Illustrations by the author. Out of print.

—. *Peas, Please!* Windsor: Black Moss Press, 1987 Paper 0-88753-191-1. Illustrations by the author. Out of print.

—. *Catching Problems*. Toronto: Annick Press, 1990. Illustrations by the author. Out of print.

—. *That's My Baby?* (Annick Toddler Series). Toronto: Annick Press, 1986. Rev. ed. 1990 Paper 0-92303-57-9. Illustrations by the author.

—. *Frogs*. Toronto: HarperCollins, 1993 Cloth 0-00-223895-0. 1996 Paper 0-00-648057-8. Illustrations by Michael Martchenko.

—. *Would You Love Me?* Toronto: Annick Press, 1997 Paper 1-55037-430-3; Cloth 1-55037-431-1. Illustrations by the author.

—. *Bing and Chutney*. Toronto: Annick Press, 1999. Paper 1-55037-608-X; Cloth 1-55037-609-8. Illustrations by the author.

Wayne von Königslöw, Andrea, and Linda Granfield. *The Make-Your-Own-Button Book*. Toronto: Somerville House, 1993 Paper (with button kit) 0-921051-89-1. Illustrations by Andrea Wayne von Königslöw.

Diana Wieler
AUTHOR

Born
October 14, 1961, Winnipeg, Manitoba

School
Winnipeg, Manitoba; Calgary, Alberta

Where I live now
Winnipeg, Manitoba

My favourite book when I was young
The Blue Castle by L.M. Montgomery

My favourite book now
The World According to Garp by John Irving

Career
Full-time author

Family
Husband, Larry; son, Ben.

The room where I create
"It's in the basement . . . we jokingly call it 'the pit of despair' or just 'the pit'."

Spare time
"I love to do artistic things and have begun to draw and paint. My favourite subject? People of course!"

When I was growing up
"I didn't know that any authors lived in my country, or that any books were written here. I think that's why *The Blue Castle* made such an impression on me. I

thought, 'Well, if the writer doesn't live here, at least she must have visited once!'

"Ours was a low-income, single-parent home, and I was very conscious of being different from other kids. I felt as if I was the only kid in the world without a father. When I visited my friends' houses, I watched their fathers as though they were alien creatures.

"Because I didn't have a brother, boys in school also fascinated me. They seemed so different. What would it be like, I wondered, to have a boy living in the same house? Later I created those boys to live in my mental 'house'. All my young-adult novels are written from the male perspective. I guess I'm still watching and wondering."

My first book (and how it happened)
"My first novel, *Last Chance Summer*, grew out of the experiences I had as a volunteer on a crisis line. As volunteers, we accompanied victims of assault to the police station, or to the hospital. Often we were just sympathetic listeners for someone who needed to talk.

"Many of the people we worked with were young — 15 and under. The experiences seemed to soak into my skin. Even after I had finished volunteering, there were

a lot of memories and emotions left over. *Last Chance Summer* was my way of thinking about them."

Where my ideas come from
"I believe I write from 'the outside in', meaning that I'm greatly affected by things I see and hear. I'm fascinated by lives and experiences of others, particularly if they are different from mine. I'm an avid listener and love to 'absorb' people — whether it's my doctor, my mechanic, or a neighbour down the street. The whole world is full of stories in motion."

Who and what influenced me
"Writing for radio and newspapers was the best training I could have received... my first job was writing commercials for CKXL, a radio station in Calgary. What a terrifying challenge that was — a 19-year-old kid thrown in with 40-year-old veteran copywriters. But what superb training! Instead of writing long, rambling essays — the kind of thing they assign in high school and college — I had to learn to get a message across in 30 seconds. And there was absolutely no room for a writer's fragile ego. If what you'd written didn't meet the station's high standards, it landed back on your desk with two words: 'Fix

it.' These days I am meeting people in film, theatre and music as well as writing, and their talents and devotion to what they do inspire me a lot."

How I work

"Once my son leaves for school in the morning, I go promptly to 'the pit,' which is really a nice, little office I have in the basement. With frequent trips upstairs for coffee, I'll work until about 2:00 in the afternoon — when I finally get dressed! After my son is in bed for the night, around 9:00, I'll work again until midnight. I write on my computer but usually spend half-an-hour before I fall asleep with a notepad on my knees in bed. This schedule can be broken up by meetings, 'craft breaks' (the sudden, wild urge to make something), or sudden shopping trips with my neighbour."

Something nobody knew about me (until now)

"I am a lousy cook and a passionate doll collector. Right now I have more than twenty dolls... antique dolls, cultural dolls, even Barbie dolls. Each one is fascinating to me, whether it's old or new, and I love reading about them."

My favourite book that I've created

"I always love the book that's in my computer at the moment. For me, writing a novel takes a long time — usually around two years. To face it day after day, I have to love the story and characters a lot. I have to live with them, and believe in them."

Tips for young creators

"Be curious. Ask questions. Take things apart. Watch people... and then write the story you would love to read — not the one everyone else wants you to write."

Diana Wieler

BIBLIOGRAPHY

Wieler, Diana. *A Dog On His Own.* Winnipeg: Prairie Publishing, 1983. Out of print.

—. *Last Chance Summer.* Toronto: Groundwood Books, 1986. 1992 Paper 1-55054-225-7.

—. *Bad Boy.* Toronto: Groundwood Books, 1989. 1997 Paper 0-88899-083-9.

—. *Ran Van the Defender.* Toronto: Groundwood Books, 1993. 1997 Paper 0-88899-184-3; Cloth 0-88899-270-X.

—. *To the Mountains by Morning.* Toronto: Groundwood Books, 1995 Cloth 0-88899-227-0. Illustrations by Ange Zhang.

—. *Ran Van: a Worthy Opponent.* Toronto: Groundwood Books, 1995. 1997 Paper 0 88899 219 X; Cloth 0 88899-271-8.

—. *Ran Van: Magic Nation.* Toronto: Groundwood Books, 1997 Paper 0-88899-316-1; Cloth 0- 88899-317-1.

—. *Drive.* Toronto: Groundwood Books, 1998 Paper 0-88899-348-X.

Awards

1984 CBC Literary Competition (Children's Literature) winner for *To the Mountains by Morning*

1986 Vicky Metcalf Short Story Award for "The Boy Who Walked Backwards" in *Prairie Jungle*

1987 Max and Greta Ebel Memorial Award for Children's Writing for *Last Chance Summer*

1989 Governor General's Literary Award for *Bad Boy*

1990 Canadian Library Association Young Adult Book Award for *Bad Boy*

1990 Ruth Schwartz Children's Book Award for *Bad Boy*

1993 Mr. Christie's Book Award for *Ran Van the Defender*

1997 McNally Robinson Book of the Year (Young Adults) for *Ran Van: Magic Nation*

Selected articles about Diana Wieler

"Diana Wieler's Angry Young Men." *Quill and Quire* September 1998: 63-64.

For more information about Diana Wieler, visit her Web site at www.makersgallery.com/wieler/

Budge Wilson
AUTHOR

Born
1927, Halifax, Nova Scotia

School
Dalhousie University, Halifax, Nova Scotia

Where I live now
Near Hubbards, Nova Scotia

My favourite books when I was young
"*The House at Pooh Corner* and later, *The Secret Garden*."

My favourite books now
Various Miracles by Carol Shields; *Bird by Bird* by Anne Lamott; *Othello* by Shakespeare; *The Book of Psalms*; *The House at Pooh Corner* (still).

Career
"Teacher, mother, commercial artist, photographer, fitness instructor (for over 20 years), finally — writer."

Family
"Husband, Alan; two daughters, Glynis and Andrea; one cat, Victor."

The room where I create
"My husband has built me a tiny house in the woods on the edge of a small cliff, with a wonderful view of the sea. That's where I work in the summer — and sometimes even in the winter. I have a little ship's stove that keeps me warm (almost). If it gets to be colder than 14°C inside, I move into the main house, where I have a study. But I work much better when I'm away from people and things that can distract me."

Spare time
"I love to read, write letters, walk on beaches, watch winter storms, dance."

When I was growing up
"I was born in Halifax, Nova Scotia and lived there almost non-stop for the next 26 years of my life. When I was little – in fact when I was big too — I liked drawing better than any other activity. I liked it better than dolls or reading or games, although I loved softball and skipping and hopscotch, and later on I loved basketball.

"In the summers my family had a cottage beside the sea. We did what everyone does: we swam, made sand castles, buried each other in the sand, played games of tag with the waves on incoming tides. The sights, sounds and smells of the sea and beaches have become a large part of my storehouse of memories. Although there were always lots of kids around, I liked to be alone with the sea sometimes — listening, watching."

My first book (and how it happened)
"My first book was *The Best Worst Christmas Present Ever*, published in 1984. I was 56 years old. It was after that that I began to write full-time. I'd always enjoyed writing but put off doing it seriously. In my forties, I worked as a photographer. When my eyes became less sharp, I started taking poor pictures, so I had to give up photography. I thought, 'Well, I always wanted to write, so I'll be a writer.' And that's what I did."

Where my ideas come from
"From memories of my past and the childhoods of my children and their friends. From watching and listening and being very nosy about peoples' lives. From thinking hard until a character or a plot appears in my mind."

Who and what influenced me
"I've been influenced by wonderful teachers in elementary and high school, and by one particular English professor who believed in me. I've also been inspired to write by reading many books by talented and exciting writers, but perhaps I am most influenced by my own desire to write down how I feel about life and people."

How I work
"I work with almost no plan or out-line, and write the first draft very quickly, letting it just come out onto the page with very little organization or even conscious thought. I love this part. Then comes the time for very careful

reading and rereading of the text — changing words, improving sentences, establishing a rhythm, checking the 'sound' of the dialogue. I love this part too. The first part is wild and intense. The second part is slow and careful and peaceful. I write with a pen."

Something nobody knew about me (until now)

"I love to chew bubble gum when I work, snapping and cracking it and making a terrible racket. But I'm always alone when I write, so there's nobody there to mind the noise. I love ferocious storms with high winds and huge waves on the sea. I would rather dance than do anything else. I also like junk food."

My favourite book that I've created

"This is a hard question to answer. I like *A House Far From Home* because it shows how difficult and rewarding relationships can be. I enjoyed writing *Breakdown* because I've known people who have had nervous breakdowns, and I've seen the way they've sometimes become wiser and more peaceful when they've recovered. There is a lot of me and my own experiences in *Thirteen Never Changes* and in *Oliver's Wars*, so they're two of my favourites. But perhaps I like *The Leaving* best of all, because it seems to reach both young people and old people."

Tips for young creators

"Write lots of letters. Keep a diary. Sometimes, try not to think too hard when you write. Let the story or poem or description just arrive all on its own. Try to believe that this will happen if you let it. Get a library card and read many, many stories and poems and novels. Watch people. Listen to the way they talk and to what they are saying. Try not to be busy every minute of the day. Take some time out for sitting and thinking."

Budge Wilson

SELECT BIBLIOGRAPHY

Wilson, Budge. *The Best Worst Christmas Present Ever* (Blue Harbour Series). Richmond Hill: Scholastic Canada, 1984 Paper 0-590-71430-9.

—. *A House Far From Home* (Blue Harbour Series). Richmond Hill: Scholastic Canada, 1986 Paper 0-590-71679-4.

—. *Mystery Lights at Blue Harbour* (Blue Harbour Series). Richmond Hill: Scholastic Canada, 1987 Paper 0-590-71389-2.

—. *Breakdown*. Richmond Hill: Scholastic Canada, 1988 Paper 0-590-71843-6.

—. *Thirteen Never Changes*. Richmond Hill: Scholastic Canada, 1989 Paper 0-590-43488-8.

—. *The Leaving*. Concord: House of Anansi, 1990 Paper 0-88784-503-7 Toronto: General Publishing, 1992 Paper 0-7736-7363-6.

—. *Madame Belzile and Ramsay Hitherton-Hobbs*. Halifax: Nimbus Publishing, 1990 Paper 0-921054-38-6. Illustrations by Etta Moffat.

—. *Lorinda's Diary* (Gemini Series). Toronto: General Publishing, 1991 Paper 0-7736-7348-2.

—. *Cassandra's Driftwood*. Porter's Lake: Pottersfield Press, 1994 Paper 0-919001-85-8. Illustrations by Terry Roscoe.

—. *Cordelia Clark*. Toronto: Stoddart Kids, 1994 Paper 0-7736-7423-3.

—. *The Courtship*. Concord: House of Anansi, 1994 Paper 0-88784-550-9.

—. *Oliver's Wars* (Junior Gemini Series). Toronto: Stoddart Kids, 1992. 1994 Paper 0-7736- 7416-0.

—. *The Dandelion Garden*. New York: Putnam/Philomel, 1995. Out of print.

—. *Harold and Harold*. Lawrencetown Beach: Pottersfield Press, 1995 Paper 0-919001-94-7. Illustrations by Terry Roscoe.

—. *Mothers and Other Strangers*. New York: Harcourt Brace, 1996 Cloth 0-15-200312-6.

—. *Duff the Giant Killer*. Halifax: Formac, 1997 Paper 0-88780-383-2;

Cloth 0-88780-383-0. Illustrations by Kim LaFave.

—. *The Long Wait*. Toronto: Stoddart Kids, 1997 Cloth 0-7737-3021-4. Illustrations by Eugenie Fernandes.

—. *Sharla*. Toronto: Stoddart Kids, 1997 Paper 0-7736-7467-5.

—. "Dreams." *This Land: A Cross-Country Anthology of Canadian Fiction for Young Readers*. Ed. Kit Pearson. Toronto: Viking, 1998 Cloth 0-670-87896-0.

—. *The Cat That Barked*. Lawrencetown Beach: Pottersfield Press, 1998 Paper 1-895900-17-4. Illustrations by Terry Roscoe.

—. *The Fear of Angelina Domino*. Toronto: Stoddart Kids, 2000 Paper 0-7737-6120-9; Cloth 0-7737-3217-9. Illustrations by Eugenie Fernandes.

—. *Duff's Monkey Business*. Halifax: Formac, 2000 Paper 0-88780-498-5; Cloth 0-88780-499-3. Illustrations by Kim LaFave.

Awards

1983 CBC Literary Competition First Prize for Short Fiction for *The Leaving*

1986 Atlantic Writing Competition First Prize for Short Fiction for "My Cousin Clarette"

1991 City of Dartmouth Book Award for *The Leaving*

1991 Canadian Library Association Young Adult Book Award for *The Leaving*

1992 Marianna Dempster Award, Canadian Authors Association for *Lorinda's Diary*

1993 Ann Connor Brimer Award for *Oliver's Wars*

Selected articles about Budge Wilson

Jenkinson, Dave. "Portraits: Budge Wilson." *Emergency Librarian* 23.2 (1995): 61-4.

Kulyk-Keefer, Janice. "'Brightly, Aggressively Golden:' Verbal Agency in Budge Wilson's *The Leaving*." *Atlantis* 20.1 (1995): 195-201.

Sandeki, Claudette. "Budge Wilson — The Pleasure of Making Something Out of Nothing." *Canadian Author* Winter 1996: 17-19.

Frieda Wishinsky
AUTHOR

Born
July 14, 1948, Munich, Germany

School
Elementary and high school in New York City; B.A., City University of New York; Master of Science, Ferkauf Yeshiva University (Special Education)

Where I live now
Toronto, Ontario

My favourite books when I was young
"Time travel books, fantasy, history, biographies."

My favourite book now
"I like a wide range of books — especially autobiographies. I like books by Helene Hanff and biographies by Doris Kearns Goodwin."

Career
"I taught special education to all ages for 23 years. Now, I write almost full-time. I also help out in my husband's medical office."

Family
Husband and best friend: Dr. Bill Wishinsky; kids: David and Suzie.

The room where I create
"I write either at the kitchen table near the food or in my library/office near the computer. I also love writing in coffee shops. I'm good at tuning out the noise."

Spare time
"Travel, gardening, talking with friends, reading, walking."

When I was growing up
"I loved the library as a child — I went every Friday and took out the six book maximum. The library also became a social place in Grade 8. In New York City, where I grew up, we'd often congregate there on Friday afternoons to chat and check out books."

My first book (and how it happened)
"My first book was *Oonga Boonga*, published by Little Brown in 1990. I'd met the editor at a conference. She'd rejected (but with wonderfully encouraging letters) eight books before saying yes. It was a great moment. There's nothing like that first acceptance."

Where my ideas come from
"Life, memories, listening to conversations, observing people and events, reading… If you're looking for ideas, they come!"

Who and what influenced me
"Being encouraged by teachers as a child. Reading. The support of editors, my wonderful husband and friends. Travelling. Meeting people."

How I work
"I always keep paper nearby to jot down ideas. Each book is a different experience. Some I outline, some I just write and see where it goes. I do a lot of revising. I like to get feedback."

Something nobody knew about me (until now)
"I feel that you never know what new and exciting experience or person is just around the corner. Just walking down the street can be wonderful and new!"

My favourite book that I've created
"Each one is special in a different way. Each reflects a different aspect of my life, a different memory, a different perspective."

Tips for young creators
"Be persistent. Do what you love. Read and write, write, write."

Frieda Wishinsky

BIBLIOGRAPHY

Wishinsky, Frieda. *Oonga Boonga.* Toronto: Little Brown & Company, 1990. Toronto: Scholastic Canada, 1998 Paper 0-590-12460-9. Illustrations by Suçie Stevenson.

—. *Why Can't You Fold Your Pants Like David Levine?* Toronto: HarperCollins, 1993 Paper 0-00-223994-9. Illustrations by Jackie Snider.

—. *Jennifer Jones Won't Leave Me Alone.* Toronto: HarperCollins, 1995 Cloth 0-00-224403-9. 1996 Paper 0-00-648072-1. Illustrations by Linda Hendry.

—. *Crazy for Chocolate.* Toronto: Scholastic Canada, 1998 Paper 0-590-12397-1.

—. *Each One Special.* Victoria: Orca Book Publishers, 1998 Cloth 1-55143-122-X. Illustrations by Werner Zimmermann.

—. *The Man Who Made Parks: The Story of Parkbuilder Frederick Law Olmsted.* Toronto: Tundra Books, 1999 Cloth 0-88776-435-5. Illustrations by Song Nan Zhang.

—. *So Long, Stinky Queen.* Toronto: Fitzhenry & Whiteside, 2000 Paper 1-55041-529-8. Illlustrations by Linda Hendry.

Mary A. Woodbury
AUTHOR

Born
May 29, 1935, Toronto, Ontario

School
St. George's (London, Ontario); London Teacher's College; writing courses at several universities.

Where I live now
"The river valley in Edmonton, Alberta. I spend summers in the Athabasca Woods."

My favourite books when I was young
Alice in Wonderland, The Secret Garden, Winnie the Pooh, Nancy Drew mysteries, *A Child's Garden of Verses.*

My favourite book now
"For adults, anything by Alice Munro. For kids, Jean Little (*Mama's Going to Buy You a Mockingbird*) and Lois Simmie (*Mr. Got to Go*)."

Career
"Elementary school teacher, journalist, public relations writer. Now, I teach writing to kids, grownups and seniors; and write poetry and books."

Family
"Husband Clair (we met in Grade 11). Four sons: David, Robert, Ian and Peter. Six granddaughters: Sara, Carys, Paige, Miranda, Haley, Merron."

The room where I create
"I write in our second-floor study, by the window that overlooks the street, a giant elm and a family of magpies. I am surrounded by books and manuscripts. Usually my computer is on and my printer ready. A bag with books, hats and stuffed toys is open by the closet — I'm unpacking it from my last school visit. My wire-haired terrier Rosie is curled under the desk trying to sleep — CBC Radio Two is playing classical music."

Spare time
"I love to read and go for long walks with my husband and my dog. I like movies, plays and musical performances. I like cooking and spending time with my grandchildren. I go to meetings with other writers and storytellers, I watch PBS mystery theatre and CBC comedy shows on television."

When I was growing up
"I grew up in a family of storytellers and readers. My mother read me the classics — *Alice in Wonderland, Peter Rabbit.* My dad told funny stories about everything that happened on his road trips and read me *Uncle Wiggly*; my Uncle Jack told me scary fairy tales like *Bluebeard* and recited Robert Service poems very loud. My grandma was best of all with her ghost stories from our Scottish ancestors. We listened to radio programs like *The Shadow Knows* and the *Green Hornet.*

"Mom said that when I went to kindergarten at Brock Avenue School in Toronto a little girl was crying because she didn't want to leave her mother. I put my arm around her shoulder and tried to make her feel better. 'If you'll stop crying I will tell you a story,' I said. She stopped and I told her the story of *Little Red Riding Hood.*

"I guess I've been telling stories ever since — only now they are my own."

My first book (and how it happened)
"My second published book was my first book and my first published book was my second. This is how it happened. I wrote a book about a girl and her grandma. It was based in Toronto on Toronto Island where I spent many happy summers when I was growing up. I sent it to many publishers. I received many nice rejections. My good writing friends made suggestions and I took another summer course in writing. I rewrote the novel and sent it away again. Then I sat down and wrote another novel called *Where in the World is*

Jenny Parker? based on my memories of living in Italy with my family. I made it a mystery and had a great time writing it from a 12-year-old girl's point of view.

"One day Shelley Tanaka called (she was working at Groundwood Books at the time). She liked my Toronto Island story a lot but thought it needed work. Did I have anything else? I sent *Jenny Parker* to her and took my Toronto story back.

"A few months later Diane Kerner at Scholastic phoned to say she loved my Toronto story. Shortly after *Jenny Parker* came out in 1989 I sold *Letting Go* to Scholastic. I haven't looked back since."

Where my ideas come from

"I have always paid attention to people and how they act and how they handle themselves in difficult situations. So characters are really important. I love places — Toronto and London where I grew up, Edmonton and the prairies where I have lived for 20 years, and Italy and the U.S. where I have lived in the past. So setting is very important. I wanted to write about those places and those people.

"For *Brad's Universe* I knew a couple of close friends and relatives (sons, even) who were like Brad in their early teens. I had also met men like Brad's father. The plot came partly from memories, partly from people I know and partly from imagination. I have never been a 14-year-old boy who is big for his age, smart and awkward with people but while I was writing I imagined my way into it.

"I clip newspaper stories that intrigue me — the idea for *Jess and the Runaway Grandpa* came from that. My next *Polly McDoodle* mystery is based on a bratty kid who gets in the road all the time — like many nine-year-olds I've met. My next YA has a ghost and a Volkswagen —maybe because of my Grandma's ghost stories and my son's love of VWs."

"I sniff out stories everywhere. I won't live long enough to write them all. You'll have to write some."

Who and what influenced me

"Margaret Laurence, especially her book *A Bird in the House*. I had a really good Language Arts teacher who encouraged me to write. I studied writing under Sandy Frances Duncan. Many good books have inspired me, like *Who Has Seen the Wind* by W.O Mitchell."

How I work

"I keep a journal with ideas, poems and reflections in it. When an idea or a character won't go away that's when I take it to the next step. I have a big hardcover book where I doodle, write character sketches and life histories of prospective characters.

"Finally I sit down at the computer and write a scene. I work all morning, print a copy and go on with my daily tasks — walking the dog, talking to friends, making food. I go to sleep thinking about the next scene; when I get up, I write it. So it goes for as many months as it takes. I write about four drafts before I show friends — more before I send it to my publisher."

Something nobody knew about me (until now)

"I'm really afraid of birds or bats loose in the house. Last summer I woke up to six bats flying around my room when I was visiting a friend in B.C. My friend let the bats out but I wouldn't sleep in that room for two nights."

Tips for young creators

"Don't be in too much of a hurry when you are writing an exciting scene. The more details, senses and feelings you put down the more powerful the scene will be. A minute of action could take several pages of story."

Mary Woodbury

BIBLIOGRAPHY

Woodbury, Mary. *Where in the World is Jenny Parker?* Toronto: Groundwood Books, 1989 Paper 0-88899-085-5.

—. *The Midwife's Tale*. Winfield: Woodlake Books, 1990. Out of print.

—. *Letting Go*. Richmond Hill: Scholastic Canada, 1992 Paper 0-590-74047-4.

—. *The Invisible Polly McDoodle*. Regina: Coteau, 1994 Paper 1-55050-062-7.

—. *A Gift for Johnny-Know-It-All*. Edmonton: River Books, 1996. Out of print.

—. *Fruitbodies*. Edmonton: Books Collective, 1996 Paper 1-895836-17-4.

—. *Jess and the Runaway Grandpa*. Regina: Coteau, 1997 1-55050-113-5.

—. *Brad's Universe*. Victoria: Orca Book Publishers, 1998 Paper 1-55143-120-3.

—. *The Intrepid Polly McDoodle*. Regina: Coteau, 1998 Paper 1-55050-133-X.

Selected articles about Mary Woodbury

Chander, Tim. "Persistence Pays Off for Edmonton Writer." *City Life* [Edmonton] 9 March 1994: 10.

King, Randy. *The Regina Free Press* 7 June 1997: 7.

Thompson, William. "Alzheimer's Voice Bridges Gap with Kids." *The Edmonton Journal* Fall 1997.

Tim Wynne-Jones
AUTHOR

Born
August 12, 1948, Cheshire, England

Where I live now
"In the pine woods of eastern Ontario."

My favourite books when I was young
"I loved Jules Verne's *Journey to the Centre of the Earth*; A.C. Doyle's *The Lost World*; H.G. Wells; *The Hardy Boys; Tom Swift;* Enid Blyton's *Adventure* novels, especially *The Mountain of Adventure; The House at Pooh Corner* by A.A. Milne."

My favourite books now
"Of the last two years: *Notes from a Small Place*, Bill Bryson; *Let it Bleed*, Ian Rankin; *The Day of the Triffids*, John Wyndham; *The Golden Compass*, Phillip Pullman; *About a Boy*, Nick Hornby."

Career
Writer, editor, teacher

Family
Wife, Amanda Lewis; children, Xan, Maddy, Lewis; cats, Milo, Maisie and Razz.

The room where I create
"My office in the attic."

Spare time
"Walking, cooking, reading."

When I was growing up
"I ran away from home with a tea cozy on my head; built twig houses in the woods in northern British Columbia; went out on a tug boat everyday and one day boarded a naval destroyer just back from the war in Korea; and I had a rock all my own in West Vancouver. It was my island, my ship. All the neighbours had rocks too. Our ships stayed put. I was goalie for my church-league hockey team, I sang in a boy's choir as the soloist. I won best singer in Ottawa three years in a row."

My first book (and how it happened)
"*Odd's End* is a mystery novel for adults. I had just finished getting my Masters degree from York University and I was tired of school work, so I took the summer off to write a book. I wrote it in five weeks. I got up early and wrote whenever I felt like it. I ate a lot of olives. I scared myself silly. My wife was away in California. I wanted to finish the book before she got back. I did."

Where my ideas come from
"The Ideas Store, but I can't remember the address right now. Try to imagine where it is. Try to imagine who runs it. Try to imagine how much ideas cost."

Who and what influenced me
"The books of Graham Greene, Richard Brautigan, Kurt Vonnegut! And music! Especially Stephen Sondheim and The Beatles."

How I work
"Early in the morning, six o'clock, before anyone is up. Working as fast as I can and then going back again and again to find better and better words and phrases. Waiting. (There's a lot of waiting.) But not for inspiration. Really, I'm just waiting for my silent partner (my unconscious mind) to help me out."

Something nobody knew about me (until now)
"No, I can't tell you. Okay, okay. You've got me. I'll tell. Until this very minute nobody knew that I was the kind of person who wouldn't tell somebody something nobody knew about me. Can you believe it?"

My favourite book that I've created
"*Odd's End* for the break-neck speed of it. *Zoom at Sea* for the hidden beauty of it that just came out without me knowing it. *Some of the Kinder Planet*s in which I learned, finally, that I loved the way I wrote and must just keep trying to write like me, since I can't be anyone else anyway."

Tips for young creators

"Just do it! Write a lot. Write what you want, write until you don't like what you're writing and then stop. Finishing only counts in school assignments. There are no child prodigies in the field of writing, so don't be in a hurry. Write the way you play tag or ball or skip — just for the fun of it. All the time you do that you're developing a writing muscle. So when you get a truly great idea you'll have the strength to run with it."

Tim Wynne-Jones

BIBLIOGRAPHY

Wynne-Jones, Tim. *Madelaine & Ermadillo*. Toronto: Now We Are Six Press, 1976. Illustrations by Lindsey Hallam. Out of print.

—. *Zoom at Sea*. Toronto: Groundwood Books, 1983. 1993 Cloth 0-88899-172-X. 1997 Paper 88899-106-1. Illustrations by Eric Beddows.

—. *Zoom Away*. Toronto: Groundwood Books, 1985. 1993 Cloth 0-88899-173-8. 1997 Paper 0-88899-151-7. Illustrations by Eric Beddows.

—. *I'll Make You Small*. Toronto: Groundwood Books, 1986. 1990 Paper 0-88899-105-3. Illustrations by Maryann Kovalski.

—. *Mischief City*. Toronto: Groundwood Books, 1986 Cloth 0-88899-049-9. Illustrations by Victor Gad.

—. *Architect of the Moon*. Toronto: Groundwood Books, 1988. 1991 Paper 0-88899-150-9. Illustrations by Ian Wallace.

—. *The Hour of the Frog*. Toronto: Groundwood Books, 1989 Cloth 0-88899-096-0. Illustrations by Catharine O'Neill.

—. *Zoom Upstream*. Toronto: Groundwood Books, 1992 Cloth 0-88899-109-6. 1993 (Meadow Mouse Paperback) 0-88899-188-6. Illustrations by Eric Beddows.

—. *Mouse in the Manger*. Toronto: Penguin Books Canada, 1993 Cloth 0-670-85027-6. Illustrations by Elaine Blier.

—. *The Last Piece of Sky*. Toronto: Groundwood Books, 1993 Cloth 0-88899-181-9. Illustrations by Marie-Louise Gay. ❖

—. *Some of the Kinder Planets*. Toronto: Groundwood Books, 1993 Paper 0-88899-207-6.

—. *The Book of Changes*. Toronto: Groundwood Books, 1994 Paper 0-88899-223-8.

—. *The Maestro*. Toronto: Groundwood Books, 1995 Paper 0-88899-242-4. 1996 Paper 0-88899-263-7.

—, adapt. *The Hunchback of Notre Dame*. By Victor Hugo. Toronto: Key Porter Books, 1996 Cloth 1-55013-773-5. 1997 Paper 1-55013-872-3. Illustrations by Bill Slavin.

—, adapt. *Dracula*. By Bram Stoker. Toronto: Key Porter Books, 1997 Paper 1-55013-900-2. Illustrations by Laszlo Gal.

—. "Gloria." *This Land: A Cross-Country Anthology of Canadian Fiction for Young Readers*. Ed. Kit Pearson. Toronto: Viking, 1998 Cloth 0-670-87896-0.

—. *Stephen Fair*. Toronto: Groundwood Books, 1998 Paper 0-88899-295-5.

—. *On Tumbledown Hill*. Red Deer: Red Deer Press, 1998 Cloth 0-88995-186-1. Illustrations by Dušan Petričić.

—. *Lord of the Fries*. Toronto: Groundwood Books, 1999 Paper 0-88899-274-2.

Lewis, Amanda, and Tim Wynne-Jones. *Rosie Backstage*. Toronto: Kids Can Press, 1994 Paper 1-55074-148-9; Cloth 1-55074-209-4. Illustrations by Bill Slavin.

Awards

1983 IODE Book Award - Municipal Chapter of Toronto for *Zoom at Sea*

1984 Ruth Schwartz Children's Book Award for *Zoom at Sea*

1993 Governor General's Literary Award for *Some of the Kinder Planets*

1994 Canadian Library Association Book of the Year for Children Award for *Some of the Kinder Planets*

1994 Vicky Metcalf Short Story Award for "The Hope Bakery" in *Some of the Kinder Planets*

1995 Boston Globe/Horn Book Award for *Some of the Kinder Planets*

1995 Governor General's Literary Award for *The Maestro*

1997 Vicky Metcalf Award for a Body of Work

Selected articles about Tim Wynne-Jones

Beaty, Mary. "On the Line." *Quill and Quire* Nov. 1992.

MacPhee, Joyce. "Profile: Tim Wynne-Jones." *CM* 22.1 (1994): 4.

Something about the Author. Detroit: Gale Research, vol. 67 (1992): 214-215.

Paul Yee
AUTHOR

Born
October 1, 1956, Spalding, Saskatchewan

School
Vancouver, British Columbia

Where I live now
Toronto, Ontario

My favourite book when I was young
A Wrinkle in Time by Madeline L'Engle

My favourite book now
A Prayer for Owen Meany by John Irving

Career
"I worked at the Vancouver City Archives and the Archives of Ontario for a total of 15 years before becoming a policy analyst with the provincial government. In February 1997, I started writing full-time."

Family
"I live with someone but we have no pets."

The room where I create
"I don't have a particular room where I create. When I start writing, I write in longhand, and I will write in the kitchen, out in the backyard, in the living room, in bed, in the dining room — wherever I feel comfortable. I have a study where my computer sits, and that's where I do the word processing and editing. But the actual writing occurs all over the house."

Spare time
"Write, read, see movies, swim, cycle."

When I was growing up
"I was shy and afraid to speak up. I came from a family where there wasn't much money, and so the clothes I wore were sometimes patched or unfashionable. My Aunt Lillian, who raised me, loved to knit. She made me a sweater, but she ran out of yarn, so she finished it off with a different-coloured yarn. It was a strange-looking sweater, but I still had to wear it. I was ashamed of the house we lived in, so I never invited friends over. If it rained, I had to wear galoshes. But none of the other children ever wore galoshes, so I felt stupid. On top of all that, I wasn't very good at sports: I couldn't swing hard enough at baseball and I couldn't catch a football. I used to dread physical education classes, especially gymnastics."

My first book (and how it happened)
"My first book was *Teach Me to Fly, Skyfighter!* In 1980, James Lorimer, a Canadian publisher, was putting out a series of books called *Adventure in Canada*, with stories set in different neighbourhoods across Canada. Lorimer wanted one book to come from Vancouver's Chinatown, and they wanted someone who came from the community to write it. At that time, I had done a lot of volunteer work in Chinatown and I had written some short stories that had been published. So they asked me if I wanted to write a book about children in the Chinatown/Strathcona neighbourhood. I had grown up there myself, so of course I was interested."

Where my ideas come from
"My ideas come from my community. Chinese people have lived in Canada since before Confederation. In British Columbia, they worked in all the frontier industries: gold and coal mines, salmon canneries, logging camps, shingle mills. Thriving communities called Chinatowns were formed where early Chinese-Canadian families started. Much of this history has been forgotten or lost. In my writing, I try to tell stories about the earlier generations of Chinese-Canadians because they lived through very difficult times, and helped smooth the way for later generations to enjoy life in Canada."

Who and what influenced me

"Feeling that I belong to a community is important to me. Often Chinese-Canadians who are born or grow up here do not feel connected to a Chinese community because they don't speak Chinese or they live far away from Chinatown or they're too busy with other things. For me, I learned a lot about myself from doing volunteer work in Chinatown and I became more knowledgeable about the issues affecting the Chinese community.

"My Aunt Lillian has been the major influence in my writing because she was a very strong woman. She was born in Vancouver in 1895 and lived through some very dark times in Canadian history. However, she was always very proud to be Chinese."

How I work

"For my writing, I do outlines, as detailed as possible, whether for fiction or non-fiction. For fiction, this means drawing up characters and preparing chapter-by-chapter descriptions of the action in the story. The description for each chapter will be about three or four paragraphs. This means that by the time I really start to write, I already know what the ending will be. For non-fiction, this means identifying the key ideas that I want to convey in each chapter. Since my non-fiction is based on historical research, those key ideas come out of the notes I have taken at libraries and archives. I make sure that I have enough data to support the key ideas."

Something nobody knew about me (until now)

"I really miss Vancouver, my hometown."

My favourite book that I've created

Tales from Gold Mountain.

Tips for young creators

"So you want to write too? The most important things are to know why you want to write and to figure out what you have to say that is unique. From there on, I think it's all technical learning and determination."

Paul Yee

BIBLIOGRAPHY

Yee, Paul. *Teach me to Fly, Skyfighter! and Other Stories.* Toronto: James Lorimer & Co., 1983 Paper 0-88862-645-2; Cloth 0-88862-646-0. Illustrations by Sky Lee.

—. *The Curses of Third Uncle.* Toronto: James Lorimer & Co., 1986 Paper 0-88862-909-5; Cloth 0-88862-910-9.

—. *Saltwater City: The Chinese in Vancouver.* Vancouver: Douglas & McIntyre, 1988. 1997 Cloth 0-88894-616-3.

—. *Tales from Gold Mountain: The Chinese in the New World.* Toronto: Groundwood Books, 1989 Cloth 0-88899-098-7. Illustrations by Simon Ng.

—. *Roses Sing on New Snow.* Toronto: Groundwood Books, 1991 Cloth 0-88899-144-4. 1994 Paper 0-88899-217-3. Illustrations by Harvey Chan.

—. *Breakaway.* Toronto: Groundwood Books, 1994. 1997 Paper 0-88899-201-7; Cloth 0-88899-289-0.

—. *Ghost Train.* Toronto: Groundwood Books, 1996 Cloth 0-88899-257-2. Illustrations by Harvey Chan.

—. *Struggle and Hope: The Story of Chinese Canadians.* Toronto: Umbrella Press, 1996 Cloth 1-895642-14-0.

—. "Spirits of the Railway." *This Land: A Cross-Country Anthology of Canadian Fiction for Young Readers.* Ed. Kit Pearson. Toronto: Viking, 1998 Cloth 0-670-87896-0.

—. *The Boy in the Attic.* Toronto: Groundwood Books, 1998 Cloth 0-88899-330-7. Illustrations by Gu Xiong.

Awards

1990 IODE Violet Downey Book Award for *Tales from Gold Mountain*

1990 Sheila A. Egoff Children's Book Prize for *Tales from Gold Mountain*

1992 Ruth Schwartz Children's Book Award for *Roses Sing on New Snow*

1996 Governor General's Literary Award for *Ghost Train*

1997 Ruth Schwartz Children's Book Award for *Ghost Train*

1998 Prix Enfantasie (Switzerland) for *le train fantome*

Selected articles about Paul Yee

Davis, Marie C. "'A Backward Way of Thanking People': Paul Yee on his Historical Fiction." *Canadian Children's Literature* 83 (1996): 50-68.

Jenkinson, Dave. "Portraits: Paul Yee." *Emergency Librarian* 22.5 (1995): 61-64.

Ludmila Zeman
AUTHOR/ILLUSTRATOR

Born
Czech Republic, April 23, 1947

School
Czech College of Art in Uh. Hradiste

Where I live now
Montreal, Quebec

My favourite books when I was young
"Since I was very young, I have loved all fairy tales and legends. Some of my favourites were: *Arabian Nights*, Hans Christian Andersen's fairy tales, *The Iliad, The Odyssey, Beowulf, Ivanhoe, Treasure Island, Robinson Crusoe, Tom Sawyer* and *Huckleberry Finn*."

Career
Filmmaker, writer and illustrator

Family
My husband, Eugene Spaleny, and two daughters Linda and Malvina

The room where I create
"I work on my pictures in a small room in my house. This small studio has a large table with many wooden boxes filled with pencils, paint brushes and other tools that I use for my pictures. I also have a large window and a wall-sized bookshelf that is filled with my favourite books and magazines. I have many pictures and paintings on my walls. Some are from my previous books and others are from my films."

Spare time
"I like to see movies in the theatre and read books. In the summer, I play tennis with my friends and in the winter I ski with my family."

When I was growing up
"I grew up in a filmmaker's family, five minutes away from a major studio where my father, Karel Zeman, a renowned film director, worked. My father made films mostly for children and I spent all my free time by his side. I admired the way he could sketch, plan the storyboards and direct his crew. The film studio was like a real kingdom for me. I was usually helping to make puppets, painting backgrounds for different films and most importantly, I was sitting in the projection room watching movies. Today when I work, I still think of everything that I learned in the studio and from my father."

My first book (and how it happened)
"My husband and I had finished working on our film *Lord of the Sky*, and in order to start the next film, we needed to raise some money. It was nearly impossible, and in desperation I took a few screenplays and sketches to Tundra Books in Montreal. The publisher, May Cutler, liked my pictures and storyboards very much and gave me the opportunity, support and freedom to make the *Gilgamesh* trilogy."

Where my ideas come from
"My ideas come from the many books that I read during my childhood. They gave me a lot of knowledge and understanding about life."

Who and what influenced me
"My greatest influences and inspiration come from my father, Karel Zeman, as well as illustrators such as Arthur Rackham, Gustave Doré, Maurice Sendak and Ralph Steadman and writers such as Edgar Allan Poe, Leo Tolstoy, Franz Kafka and Ernest Hemingway."

How I work
"When creating a picture book or animated film, I must first have a simple idea, a story I can tell in a few sentences. Then, I draw the story in a series of sequences and each is accompanied by a text (identical to the storyboards for an animated film). For the picture books, I draw about 24 to 30 sequences depending on the number of pages in the book. I try as much as possible to tell the whole story by picture. The skills I have gained from filmmaking

are helpful in making the images full of movement, space and action.

"When I feel that the preliminary drawings are telling the story well, I start to look for an appropriate style of design. Each illustration must also be created with space for the text. I come back to the text only when I have finished all the illustrations in colour. The illustrations show me exactly what the words must say to balance the picture. I work long hours for eight or nine months on each picture book to make the story attractive and fresh."

My favourite book that I've created

"*Gilgamesh the King*. It is still my favourite book because it was the first one that I created in Canada. It is also one of the most unique and incredible epics ever written. It is the oldest story of mankind, unravelling the beginning of human civilization. When I started to retell the *Epic of Gilgamesh* I fell in love with this beautiful, old poem and during my research I realized how important the wisdom and examples of human experience are for children's intellectual and cultural development.

"Creating the *Gilgamesh* trilogy was quite a difficult task since not many visual references related to this story exist. I spent over two years researching and collecting information concerning artifacts from Mesopotamia that exist in museums around the world. To take a jewel of human history, and revive it in a new form which has never been done before, was a big challenge and a great source of inspiration."

Ludmila Zeman

BIBLIOGRAPHY

Zeman, Ludmila. adapt. *Gilgamesh the King*. Montreal: Tundra Books, 1992 Cloth 0-88776-283-2. Illustrations by the author.

—. adapt. *The Revenge of Ishtar*. Montreal: Tundra Books, 1994 Cloth 0-88776-315-4. Illustrations by the author.

—. adapt. *The Last Quest of Gilgamesh*. Montreal: Tundra Books, 1994 Cloth 0-88776-328-6. Illustrations by the author.

—. *The First Red Maple Leaf*. Montreal: Tundra Books, 1997 Cloth 0-88776-372-3. Illustrations by the author.

—. *Sindbad: From the Tales of The Thousand and One Nights*. Toronto: Tundra Books, 1999 Cloth 88776-460 6. Illustrations by the author.

Awards

1995 Governor General's Literary Award for *The Last Quest of Gilgamesh*

Selected articles about Ludmila Zeman

"Between the Lines, Stories Live." *Canadian Children's Literature* 73 (1994)

Song Nan Zhang
AUTHOR/ILLUSTRATOR

Born
June 22, 1942, Shanghai, China

School
Central Institute of Fine Arts, Beijing, China

Where I live now
Montreal, Quebec

My favourite books when I was young
The children's stories of Hans Christian Andersen

My favourite book now
Paintings in the Musée d'Orsay

Career
Artist (oil painter); children's book illustrator

Family
Wife, Sheng Li Wang; sons Hao Yu Zhang and Hao Yong Zhang

The room where I create
"I usually work at home, at my dining room/studio. I like the two big north windows there; they let in plenty of natural light, just perfect for oil painting."

When I was growing up
"I was fond of drawing cartoons. I often copied down good cartoon drawings from newspapers on bigger pieces of paper and posted them on walls near school. Later on, I volunteered as the fine arts editor for the wall bulletins of the Shanghai Youth Centre. When I started my academic studies of art, I spent most of my time studying Chinese-style painting. I changed my mind later on, after seeing a retrospective Russian oil exhibit in Beijing. I knew from then on that oil would be my painting medium."

My first book (and how it happened)
"My first book is titled *A Little Tiger in the Chinese Night*. It is an illustrated autobiography of my 50 years in China. May Cutler, the former president of Tundra Books, was the one who first encouraged me to do an illustrated children's book of my own story. I was humbled and surprised at first. I consider the story of myself rather ordinary; I wondered if children of the Americas would be interested in it. After a lot of sweat and hard work, the book was published in 1993. *The Little Tiger*, my first book ever, won a Mr. Christie's Book Award in 1993."

Where my ideas come from
"I think book ideas come from life. Pay attention to the things that happen around us every day. When you go on a trip, observe things that are interesting and take notes. Of course, when you finally decide to write a book, observation alone is not enough. On subjects that you are not so sure about, research will always help."

Who and what influenced me
"I made up my mind when I was 15 that I wanted to become an artist, an oil painter. During the past four decades or so, many artists and many paintings have influenced me. A Chinese saying (on how to achieve success) perhaps best describes my experience: "journey 10 thousand miles, and read 10 thousand books." One has to keep learning new things every step of the way. In my case, I can probably add 'study 10 thousand paintings.'"

How I work
"My works can be divided into two categories. One is based on real life stories, like *A Little Tiger in the Chinese Night*. The other is more of an informative and reference book, like *Five Heavenly Emperors* or *The Children of China*.

"When working with true stories, I like to choose stories that have really touched me. It is easier to come up with text and good illustrations when things are close to your heart.

"When working with books mainly aimed at providing information, the rough research is the key. It is not uncommon for me to have to check with dozens and dozens of books and sources before I begin to write the text and compose the pictures for a book. Only with adequate research will I be able to explain a complex subject in simple language with appropriate illustrations."

Something nobody knew about me (until now)

"My books, so far, are all published in English. But only people close to me know that I speak very little English. When I write a book, I write in Chinese first. My son then translates them into English. In 1997, when Canada's annual Governor General's Literary Awards organization committee sent me a boxful of books and asked me to become a selection committee member, I had to return the books."

My favourite book that I've created

The Children of China.

Tips for young creators

"Success is achieved with determination, creativity, and above all — hard work."

Song Nan Zhang

BIBLIOGRAPHY

Granfield, Linda. *The Legend of the Panda.* Toronto: Tundra Books, 1998 Cloth 0-88776-421-5. Illustrations by Song Nan Zhang.

Zhang, Song Nan. *A Little Tiger in the Chinese Night.* Toronto: Tundra Books, 1993 Cloth 0-88776-320-0. 1995 Paper 0-88776-356-1. Illustrations by the author.

—. *Five Heavenly Emperors: Chinese Myths of Creation.* Toronto: Tundra Books, 1994 Cloth 0-88776-338-3. Illustrations by the author.

—. *The Children of China: A Painter's Journey.* Toronto: Tundra Books, 1995 Paper 0-88776-448-7; Cloth 0-88776-363-4. Illustrations by the author.

—. *Cowboy on the Steppes.* Toronto: McClelland and Stewart, 1997 Cloth 0-88776-410-X. Illustrations by the author.

The Ballad of Mulan. Union City, CA: Pan Asian Publications, 1998 Cloth 1-57227-054-3. Illustrations by Song Nan Zhang.

Wishinsky, Frieda. *The Man Who Made Parks: The Story of Park-builder Frederick Law Olmsted.* Toronto: Tundra Books, 1999 Cloth 0-88776-435-5. Illustrations by Song Nan Zhang.

Awards

1993 Mr. Christie's Book Award for *A Little Tiger in the Chinese Night*

Selected articles about Song Nan Zhang

"Day Care, Canada, and two views of the Far East." *The Globe and Mail* 13 Sept. 1997

A Word About Us

A national, non-profit organization founded in 1976, The Canadian Children's Book Centre promotes and encourages the reading, writing and illustrating of Canadian children's books.

We are here for anyone who cares about the books that children read. We assist parents, teachers, librarians and students as well as writers, illustrators, publishers and booksellers.

The Canadian Children's Book Centre organizes Canadian Children's Book Week, the single most important celebration of books and reading in this country. Every November, thousands of children and adults meet authors and illustrators in schools, libraries, bookstores and community centres throughout this week-long, national festival.

The Centre also has a reference library of Canadian children's books, as well as extensive information on Canadian children's authors, illustrators and the book trade, both in print and on our Web site. Our collection is accessible to the public in five different sites across the country — at our national office in Toronto and in Halifax, Winnipeg, Edmonton and Vancouver.

If an author you are researching is not included in this book, please contact The Canadian Children's Book Centre. We have information on more than 300 authors and illustrators on file and each year these resources expand.

You, too, can become a member of The Canadian Children's Book Centre. As a member, you'll receive *Our Choice,* our guide to the best of Canadian children's books and media; as well as our magazine, *Children's Book News,* which will keep you up-to-date on what's happening in the Canadian children's book world.

For further information on becoming a member, ordering our publications, or learning more about the Centre's work, please contact us at:

The Canadian Children's Book Centre
35 Spadina Road
Toronto, Ontario M5R 2S9
Tel: (416) 975-0010
Fax: (416) 975-1839
E-mail: ccbc@sympatico.ca
www3.sympatico.ca/ccbc
Please note: After September 2000, we will be at 40 Orchard View Blvd., Toronto M4R 1B9.